The Shady Economics of International Aid

Saeed Ahmed

To my lovely daughter, Ammarah Saeed, whose encouragement inspired me to write this book, allowing me to give back to the nation that shaped me. This book is dedicated to you, a testament to your unwavering support and belief in me.

Published by Upriver Press
P.O. Box 51455
Colorado Springs, CO 80949
upriverpress.com

ISBN Print Version: 9798990623668
ISBN Ebook: 9798990623675

Library of Congress Registration: 2025932238

Cover Design: James Clarke (jclarke.net)

Printed in the United States of America

Upriver Press publishes books by leading scholars and industry experts who bring well-researched, evidence-based ideas to public discourse. The views of our authors do not necessarily represent the opinions of Upriver Press.

The Shady Economics of International Aid

Saeed Ahmed

upriver
PRESS

Foreword

When I started writing this book in the summer of 2023 (winter in Australia), I never anticipated that some of the issues I explored would surface so powerfully even before its release.

On his first day in office in January 2025, President Trump signed an executive order freezing all USAID and State Department programs for ninety days. During this period, a thorough review of all USAID programs would be conducted to determine whether they should be cancelled, continued, or changed to better align with President Trump's priorities.

The decision impacted activities worldwide totalling about $42 billion in 157 countries for over 6100 projects covering all sectors. Those directly impacted, particularly more than ten thousand USAID staff working all over the world, strongly criticized the decision.

On March 18, 2025, following a sweeping six-week purge of USAID programs, Secretary of State Marco Rubio, announced massive cuts eliminating 83 percent of programs run by the agency, posting that roughly 5200 of USAID's 6200 global programs had been terminated. According to Rubio, those programs spent tens of billions of dollars in ways that did not serve, and in some cases even harmed, the core national interests of the United States. He added that the surviving initiatives would be absorbed by the State Department.

Legal battles are currently underway in US courts. A federal judge said President Trump had overstepped his constitutional authority in shutting down most foreign assistance, and that the administration could no longer simply sit on the billions of dollars that Congress had provided for foreign aid. Another federal judge has ruled that the so-called "Department of Government Efficiency" (DOGE) likely violated the US Constitution by shutting down USAID, ordering the Trump Administration to reverse some of the actions it implemented to dismantle the agency. Whatever the outcome of these battles, it is probable that US aid to developing countries will decrease drastically.

So, what are the implications of these actions? What will happen to the international aid system? Can another international aid organization step in to fill the gap? Should USAID programs have been abruptly and massively terminated? And, based on the arguments and findings in my book, do I, as a scholar, support or oppose the dismantling of USAID? Let me briefly address these questions.

Clearly, the shutdown of USAID will have a significant and immediate impact on the direct and indirect beneficiaries of its projects, including many people who are poor and vulnerable, as well as the staff employed in USAID offices and projects, consultants, and local officials involved in these activities. These disruptions, however, are unlikely to have any major social, political, or economic consequences within recipient countries. For instance, Pakistan will not experience a major financial squeeze. In fiscal year 2023, USAID only committed $132.6 million across various sectors, including humanitarian aid, health and population, governance, education, infrastructure, and agriculture. This funding was reduced to $116 million in 2024, primarily due to a decline in humanitarian assistance, from $43 million in 2023 (due to the 2022 devastating floods) to $18 million in 2024. For a country like Pakistan, USAID funding levels are negligible relative to the size of its $375 billion economy. Therefore, cancellation of this funding will not make any difference to Pakistan's overall economic performance. It will only affect the indirect beneficiaries: USAID employees, consultants, and their local counterparts. The same holds true for most African countries, where USAID's spending is minimal. The aid that actually reaches intended beneficiaries is only a small fraction of the overall aid disbursement figures.

Another issue is whether the reduction of US aid will have any significant impact on developing countries' overall *economic growth*. This book explores this topic at length. Several cross-country studies do not show any robust positive relationship between growth and the amount of aid received. The situation may change if the US also withdraws from the International Monetary Fund, the World Bank, and other multilateral development banks, or if the US withdraws from UN agencies, such as the Food and Agriculture Organization. Such decisions seem unlikely to me; however, if I am wrong, these decisions would be bad for the United States. By abandoning the IMF and the World Bank, the US would surrender a key source of global influence and economic leverage.

The US has long maintained tight control over these institutions, shaping their policies and leadership to align with its national interests. It has consistently appointed the World Bank's president, approved Europe's choice to lead the IMF, and selected the fund's first deputy managing director. Moreover, the US remains the only country with the power to unilaterally block major decisions, as both institutions require an 85 percent majority for approval.

The US uses the IMF as a "first responder" to safeguard its economy, and it uses the World Bank to strengthen security and economic alliances, counter terrorism threats, and support postwar reconstruction in countries like Iraq and Afghanistan following US-led invasions. Thus, if the US withdraws from the multilateral system, it will forfeit vital tools for supporting its allies and for withholding financing from its adversaries. And even if the US withdraws from the multilateral system, other countries will save it anyway.

If USAID is eliminated, the agency's former beneficiaries will desperately search for alternative sources of funding, including from international NGOs and foundations. No single entity in the world can plug the gap that would emerge from USAID's demise, so the search will be arduous.

That said, some leaders and policymakers in developing countries see a silver lining in the possible loss of USAID. For example, Ambassador Arikana Chihombori-Quao, president and CEO of the African Diaspora Development Institute, and former Ambassador of the African Union to the United States, described this decision as a blessing in disguise that would lead to self-sufficiency in Africa and reduce dependency on foreign aid. "Far from being a tragedy for Africa, the demise of the USAID at the hands of President Donald Trump's administration should be cause for celebration," she argued in a televised interview with Al Jazeera on March 17, 2025. She told host Steve Clemons that USAID doesn't have much to show for its decades of education and healthcare projects in Africa, adding that foreign aid often destabilized countries under the guise of environmental, human rights, or social justice agendas. She went on to say that "USAID was a wolf in sheep's clothing."

In principle, I share the view that a possible elimination of USAID, while difficult for many people, could present developing nations with an opportunity to gain increased self-reliance and sustainable economic growth. Sometimes good things can come from adversity. Over time, as the system stabilizes, aid agencies may become more accountable to the taxpayers who fund them.

However, I disagree with the "chainsaw" approach to closing USAID. It should be reformed rather than shut down entirely. It would be more logical to allow ongoing USAID projects—where commitments have already been made—to continue in order to avoid mass disruption, legal challenges, and the violation of contractual obligations. I believe the current administration should use a more precise, surgical approach.

Up to now (April 2025), the Trump administration has done away with entire categories of humanitarian and development aid. Politicians and the media often lump all forms of aid together, which is incorrect. There are different types of aid—humanitarian relief, refugee assistance, and economic development aid. This distinction is a central focus of my book. My critique in the pages that follow does not extend to the much-needed humanitarian and emergency assistance in response to natural disasters or geopolitical conflicts that displace innocent people. Again, we need a thoughtful, nuanced view of international aid. That is why I believe this book is more important than ever. The USAID fiasco has vindicated several evidence-based arguments presented in my book.

First, aid is political. Donor countries put their national interests over and above the stated objectives of aid programs. The poverty alleviation narratives glorified by donors run contrary to the on-the-ground realities.

Second, as I reveal in my book, the international aid and development industry, worth $224 billion, is fraught with issues ranging from misallocation of funds to a glaring lack of accountability for the failed outcomes of donor projects. Bureaucrats in donor agencies act recklessly, allocating taxpayer dollars to projects that contradict sound economic policy or local priorities. This happens largely due to a glaring lack of accountability. It is, therefore, critical to review the operations of donor agencies worldwide and implement major reforms in international aid.

Third, what has happened in the US should be a wake-up call for developing countries. Instead of relying heavily on external assistance, they must address gaps in human development by pursuing proven economic policies, putting in place systems to create economic growth while integrating with the global economy, and exploiting their own abundant resources. Developing nations need to prioritize their own national interests.

This is a time of tremendous change and uncertainty. However, the core principles advocated in my book are lasting and overarching. The book provides a deep analysis of the underlying complexities of international aid. I present evidence-based arguments pertaining to the fundamental, systemic problems in international aid—issues that run far deeper than the political battles currently taking place. While the USAID shutdown has brought some of these issues into the spotlight, the insights and recommendations in my book remain relevant and enduring. The structural problems—what I term the "shady economics" of international aid—will persist unless the entire aid architecture undergoes a significant overhaul.

This book is designed to provide timeless principles for significant long-term change. The media will report sporadic, temporary events, and politicians will come and go. In this context, my book is designed to help people *think*, not *react*! And with the economic conditions for millions of people being at stake, one hopes that people will do more thinking than reacting.

Saeed Ahmed, April 2025

Contents

Preface

One may wonder why a man who grew up in an underprivileged milieu of rural Pakistan, who has a PhD in economics from Cambridge University, and who served on the executive board of the International Monetary Fund would write a book that questions the efficacy of international aid agencies.

During my long career, I have heard many hyperbolic narratives about poverty alleviation proffered by international development agencies (donor agencies). I have seen that these narratives often do not fit on-the-ground realities. In fact, the system of borrowing and lending between donor agencies and developing countries has turned poverty alleviation into a lucrative business for development professionals, but it has not done much to help people in need. The system often makes the economic and political situations in recipient countries worse. Taxpayers in wealthy nations, the people who have funded the system for decades, have not received a meaningful return on their investment. There are better ways to help developing countries grow and prosper, but many policymakers resist change.

While working at the State Bank of Pakistan and at the IMF, I realized that, despite all the strategy, planning, and coordination with international organizations, we only made miniscule progress toward improving the lives of the most vulnerable people. It was not for lack of hard work or passionate commitment, but eventually I had to conclude—based on the economic evidence—that these programs had produced very few positive outcomes.

I am not the first person to write about the problems between donor agencies and recipient nations. In 2004, John Perkins published *Confessions of an Economic Hit Man* in which he told his story of working for a private US consulting group that, he claimed, deliberately raised the debt of developing countries. Perkins explained how he had been indoctrinated into a system in which wealthy nations used donor agencies to cheat poor countries out of billions of dollars, bury them in insurmountable debt, and then use that debt as leverage for demanding the poor nations' natural resources, military assistance, and political support.

However, many of Perkins's critics considered him to be a conspiracy theorist who failed to provide sufficient evidence to support his claims. In the view of those critics, the book was merely "autobiographical fiction." *Confessions* certainly lacks solid economic evidence, but was Perkins on to something important?

To evaluate the workings of international donor agencies, which is a complex global system, we need rigorous economic analysis, not personal anecdotes and autobiographies. So, in *The Shady Economics of International Aid*, I provide evidence that shows how donor agencies undermine the economies of developing countries. The data and analysis presented in the book support the view that donor agencies invariably put their own political agendas first.

This book also shows that local counterparts—the countries that receive billions of dollars in international aid—play a role in this broken system. They frequently relinquish their responsibility for independent policy formulation, allowing foreign entities with no genuine commitment to their countries' development to take charge. Together, donors and national policymakers forge formidable partnerships and networks that prove resistant to change. Thus, both groups share responsibility for the deplorable conditions, misgovernance, and state of paralysis in each country.

Due to my extensive experience within Pakistan's government and central bank, I decided to present Pakistan as a case study that illustrates how international aid affects life for people in other parts of the world. By focusing part of the book on Pakistan, readers will gain a deep understanding of what happens in most other developing countries. The broader analysis of data from other nations is largely based on my tenure on the executive board of the International Monetary Fund (IMF) where I represented the interests of eight emerging markets across South Asia, North Africa, and Sub-Saharan Africa.

Despite the hard truths in the book, my intention is to identify problems so that we can design solutions for positive change. The book offers a roadmap for effective reforms of this broken international system. I provide ideas for how recipient countries can restructure their national tax policies, governance systems, and financial and energy sectors. Such changes within developing countries can help them become less reliant on foreign loans. I also provide ideas for improving IMF programs and the overall international aid architecture. We need to hold the donor agencies accountable for producing real and measurable benefits.

The revelations in this book might seem distasteful—even bitter—to many of my friends and colleagues with whom I have worked around the world. Nothing in the book is intended to express disdain toward any person; instead, the book is about the failures of the international aid system in which we have all worked, including myself.

Before proceeding further, it is essential to clarify that "aid" in the context of this book refers specifically to grants and concessional loans extended directly to governments by other governments or institutions such as the International Monetary Fund and World Bank. My discussion excludes humanitarian or emergency aid provided, for example, in response to conflicts (e.g., in Ukraine, Middle East), natural disasters (floods, earthquakes), or public health crises (e.g., the Covid-19 pandemic). Moreover, the following critique is not aimed at discrediting the concept of international aid, but rather at exposing the system's shortcomings in its current form—shortcomings that are numerous and significant.

My hope is that this book will inspire all involved to make changes that truly benefit the millions of people around the world who are burdened by a shady international economic system.

SECTION I

Maybe John Perkins Was Right

CHAPTER 1

That Inspiring (but False) Narrative

Thanks to the generosity of taxpayers in advanced countries, international aid organizations can allocate huge sums of money designed to uplift poor people in developing countries. These funds are routed through bilateral donor agencies, such as USAID, UK Aid, Deutsche Gesellschaft für Internationale Zusammenarbeit (GIZ), and the Japan International Cooperation Agency (JICA). The money also flows through multilateral development institutions such as the International Monetary Fund (IMF), the World Bank, the International Finance Corporation (IFC), and the Asian Development Bank (ADB).

Nearly all these donors set poverty alleviation as their primary objective, but some also focus on broader economic development agendas. To procure the support of taxpayers in developed countries, donor agencies present themselves as torchbearers for a better world, as organizations that work to end extreme poverty and tackle the global challenges of our times: inequality, hunger, disease, mass migration, insecurity, conflict, and injustice. However, as this book will demonstrate, this narrative does not match reality.

Wealthy nations contribute remarkable amounts of money to these noble efforts. According to data published by the Organization for Economic Cooperation and Development (OECD), international aid from official donors rose in 2023 to a new all-time high of $223.7 billion, up from $211 billion in 2022.[1] Some of this increase reflected the uptick in aid to war-torn Ukraine, but large funding increases also went to humanitarian assistance efforts within many developing countries.

The Major Players

Within the OECD, there is a "forum" of thirty-two countries who are the major players in the international aid system. This group is called the Development Assistance Committee (DAC).

Beyond the donors that comprise the DAC, many other public and private entities provide economic aid to developing countries. The UN, established in 1945, has remained one of the most vital institutions in the development sector, delivering diverse projects related to climate change, education, health, and social infrastructure. The UN is composed of specialized agencies, programs, and funds, each with its own mandate. The UN's income grew from $58.5 billion in 2017 to more than $74 billion in 2022. The data shows where this money came from and where it was spent.

The UN's income primarily comes from the assessed contributions of its 193 member states, and from the voluntary contributions of government and nongovernment donors. The US was the biggest bilateral donor in the five-year period 2017-2022, accounting for about 24 percent ($18.095 billion) of the UN total income in 2022. The US was followed by Germany ($6.836 billion), Japan ($ 2.717 billion), the UK ($2.14 billion), China ($2.118 billion), Canada ($2.035 billion), Netherlands ($1.715 billion),

France ($1.452 billion), Norway ($1.343 billion), and Sweden ($1.129 billion).

Additionally, the UN receives revenue from other public contributors, such as the European Commission, the UN interagency pooled funds, the global vertical funds, and various international financial institutions. The UN also receives funding from nongovernmental organizations, public-private partnerships, foundations, and academic and research institutions.

The UN agencies' expenses are classified into four main functions: humanitarian assistance, development assistance, peace operations, and global agenda and specialized assistance. The UN's total spending in 2022 was $67.45 billion. Of this amount, about 46 percent, or just over $31 billion, went to humanitarian assistance, of which most ($12 billion), went to the World Food Programme. Development assistance ranked second with $20.14 billion in 2022, or 29.9 percent of the total. Spending on peace operations amounted to $8.68 billion, or 12.87 percent of the total. Lastly, $7.52 billion (or 11.15 percent) was spent on the global agenda and specialized assistance.

The UN agencies also have expenses classified according to their target "sustainable development goals" (SDGs). These goals are focused on reducing hunger, promoting peace, justice, and strong institutions; and improving health and well-being.

Beyond the UN, there are many private entities that fund international development efforts. The OECD publishes a list of the largest foundations that operate in this sector. These foundations have a track record of funding issues such as climate change, gender equality, health, hunger, and poverty alleviation. Approximately forty private philanthropies report to the OECD. They spent $11 billion on development in 2022. Although this paled in comparison with the $211 billion in aid spending by DAC countries, some of these private funders have become household names in global development.

Based on OECD data, the ten largest foundations and their total spending to developing countries in 2022 are as follows.

1. The Bill and Melinda Gates Foundation $4.977 billion
2. Mastercard Foundation $1.159 billion
3. Open Society Foundations $431.2 million
4. Children's Investment Fund Foundation $399.2 million
5. Wellcome Trust $396.4 million
6. Bloomberg Family Foundation $387.9 million
7. Ford Foundation $310.5 million
8. IKEA Foundation $260.7 million
9. LEGO Foundation $258.4 million
10. Oak Foundation $250 million

The Gates Foundation started by giving a $1 million grant to the Seattle Art Museum in 1994. Since then, it has become the largest philanthropic organization in the world. The foundation works with grantees and partner organizations across the globe to address critical health and development priorities, such as infectious diseases, agricultural development, and financial services. Overall, the goal is to benefit the world's poorest people. The Gates Foundation has awarded thirty thousand grants in a span of two decades to more than eleven thousand organizations.

The Gates Foundation increased the amount of its total grants by 41.4 percent between 2017 and 2021. In 2022, it provided $37.4

million to support developing countries' Covid-19 response. Of this, 68.2 percent targeted medical intervention efforts to control the spread of the coronavirus.

To be clear, my critique of the international aid system in this book does not extend to private philanthropic organizations like The Gates Foundation. But these private groups play a meaningful role in the overall landscape.

Understanding the Categories of Aid

The OECD attempts to track all "official" development aid, which it calls "Official Development Assistance" (ODA).[2] The OECD defines ODA as government aid that promotes the economic development and welfare of developing countries. It includes both humanitarian and reconstruction aid, but it excludes military, counter-narcotics, and other transfers. Loans and credits for military purposes are excluded from ODA classification. Aid may be provided bilaterally, from donor to recipient, or channeled through a multilateral development agency such as the United Nations or the World Bank. Aid includes grants, "soft" loans, and the provision of technical assistance.

The nearly $224 billion of ODA in 2023 (mentioned above) amounted to 0.37 percent of the combined gross national income of DAC countries. This money went to the following subcategories: bilateral development projects, programs, and technical cooperation ($106.43 billion); multilateral ODA ($52.32 billion); humanitarian aid ($25.05 billion); refugee costs ($29.07 billion); and net debt relief grants ($0.04 billion). About 82 percent of all ODA was contributed by six countries: the US, Germany, the EU, Japan, the UK, and France, for a total of about $184 billion.

The total ODA in 2023 rose by a modest 1.8 percent over 2022 in real terms (i.e., adjusted for inflation and for exchange rate fluctuations), but aid *as a share of gross national income* increased from 0.31 percent in 2010 to 0.37 percent in 2023. Nevertheless, *collectively* nations have been giving more and more. The 2023 amount represented the fifth consecutive year that ODA surpassed record levels. Most of the increase in 2022 and 2023 was used to support refugees.

Where has all this money been going? In 2022, Ukraine had received the most ODA funding of any nation. As stated earlier, ODA excludes military funding (weapons, etc.); however, there is no question that the large ODA amounts for Ukraine were attributable to Russia's war there. After Ukraine, Syria received the second largest amount, likely due to the country's internal political turmoil. (In late 2024, rebel groups overthrew the Syrian government.)

Due to the duration of Russia's war in Ukraine, DAC members increased their ODA (nonmilitary) funding to Ukraine in 2023 to $40.5 billion, of which about half came from the EU. At the time of this writing, that was the largest amount of ODA funding ever received by one country in a single year. By comparison, Ukraine only received $2 billion in 2021.

Some other trends in ODA are noteworthy. In 2022, ODA transfers to "least developed countries" (LDCs) and other low-income countries (LICs), *decreased* by 3 percent compared to 2021 levels. Excluding pandemic-related support, cross-border aid to least developed countries has remained stagnant for about six years, with 2022 disbursements reaching $57 billion, roughly the same as in 2017.

ODA takes many forms: loans, grants, etc. In recent years, least developed countries have increasingly received aid in the form of loans rather than grants. Between 2021 and 2022, grants to these countries dropped by 5 percent. If we exclude pandemic support, grants to least developed countries fell by 11 percent between 2017 and 2022, a loss of about $5 billion (in constant prices).

Obviously, this trend—offering loans rather than grants—puts greater debt burdens on the recipient countries. The external debt owed by these governments has risen by $200 billion since 2011. A significant portion of this increased debt, which is now at $344 billion, stems from loans provided by multilateral organizations and DAC members. As a result, ten of the least developed countries are in debt "distress" and another twenty-six are at high risk of falling into a distress situation.

Debtor nations are also paying higher interest rates on these loans. The average interest rate on new loans from DAC members rose substantially from 0.9 percent to 2 percent in 2022, reflecting broader interest rate hikes designed to reduce post-pandemic inflation in creditor countries. This has translated into higher borrowing costs for developing countries, exacerbating their debt burdens.

The immediate impact of these developments may be moderate because loans are dispersed gradually, but the trend toward offering loans instead of grants poses significant concerns for long-term development efforts. The least developed countries risk falling further behind.

Donor Agencies: Torchbearers for a Better World?

The previous paragraphs provide an overview of the massive scale and costs of the international aid system. Most of this funding originates from taxpayers in the world's wealthiest nations. The question is whether the system is really helping people in need.

As stated earlier, donor agencies present themselves as torchbearers for a better world. They claim that their work is building a safer, healthier, more prosperous world for people in developing countries. They claim to be improving the lives of girls and women by giving them more access to education and improved family planning, and by reducing violence against them. They claim to be mitigating the effects of climate change by encouraging low-carbon economic growth. Donor agencies go to great lengths to portray their international work in a positive light. Some examples follow.

As the world's largest provider of official development assistance (ODA), the United States has substantial development programs in all sectors and regions. The US Agency for International Development (USAID) is a prominent player. (At the time of this writing, the agency has been shut down by the Trump administration, so its future is in doubt.) Its mission is stated below.

On behalf of the American people, we promote and demonstrate democratic values abroad, and advance a free, peaceful, and prosperous world. In support of America's foreign policy, the US Agency for International Development leads the US government's international development and disaster assistance through partnerships and investments that save lives, reduce poverty, strengthen democratic governance, and help people emerge from humanitarian crises and progress beyond assistance. . . . [The objective is] to support partners to become self-reliant and capable of leading their own development journeys.

In November 2023, the United Kingdom published a white paper about its international cooperation. The paper, titled "International Development in a Contested World," was published after the government made significant changes to its development cooperation architecture and policy in 2020. This overhaul coincided with the creation of the Foreign, Commonwealth and Development Office (FCDO) and the United Kingdom's exit from the European Union. The white paper stated the United Kingdom's strategic goals of eliminating extreme poverty and tackling problems like climate change and the loss of biodiversity. Focusing on the world's poorest people, the paper stipulates that the UK aimed to spend 50 percent of its bilateral ODA in least developed countries, and that it would support the global goal of providing at least 0.2 percent of its gross national income to those countries. "We safeguard the UK's security, defend our values, reduce poverty, and tackle global challenges with our international partners," said the FCDO.[3]

Most UK donor-funded project narratives have, for many years, boasted about changing lives. UK Aid reported in 2010 that it had empowered communities in Afghanistan to "build facilities like roads, schools, health clinics, and water systems."[4] In 2011, the same UK agency stated that it had been "helping to build 13,400 flood resistant houses across Pakistan."[5] The UK's Department for International Development reported that it had provided, in 2015, a grant of £724,500 so that the nation's doctors could "deliver trauma support and plastic reconstructive surgery for many of those injured in the recent Gaza conflict."[6] UK Aid also announced, in 2015, that it had helped more than two hundred thousand Syrian refugee children living in Lebanon to enroll in school, "thanks to a Lebanese government enrollment program, backed by UK Aid and UNICEF."[7] And USAID, in 2017, stated that it had provided merit-based scholarships to Pakistani women, helping them to learn how to run businesses. "With USAID's help, young Pakistani women are reaching for a brighter future—for their families, communities, and country."

These outcomes are certainly important for those living in developing countries, and for development finance institutions. There is no question that these efforts have some positive effects, especially for the individuals who directly receive humanitarian assistance and disaster relief. We should not diminish the hard work and sacrifices of the on-the-ground workers who help people and who are enduring extreme hardships.

But there is a bigger picture to consider. Scholars, in peer-reviewed academic articles, have documented the ulterior motives of bilateral donors, showing that they are not only interested in the welfare of recipient countries.[8] Researchers have found that many donors use foreign aid as a lever of "soft power."[9] They use aid to advance their own geostrategic goals, such as buying votes in international organizations, supporting friendly governments before elections, securing market access for exporters, deterring asylum seekers, and fighting terrorism.[10]

Soft power involves using bilateral aid to influence international public opinion about the donors' governments.[11] To this end, governments spend a considerable amount of time and money disseminating positive messages about their generosity to members of the public in developing countries. They attach their logos to aid shipments. They place signage at project sites and airports to inform the public of their activities. They organize public ceremonies to mark the launch of new projects and the completion of existing ones. Some broadcast their messages through social media platforms, and they cultivate journalists to encourage media coverage of their accomplishments. Others are more aggressive, forging content-sharing partnerships with a recipient nation's radio stations, television channels, and newspapers, or by building telecommunications systems that make it easier to transmit information to the public. In short, aid is used to shape public perceptions in developing countries. This type of "brand management" is one of the most important reasons why donor governments extend foreign aid bilaterally rather than multilaterally.

Moreover, half of all international development aid is "tied," meaning that recipient countries must use it to buy goods and services *from the donor nation*. I will present the implications of this fact later in the book. For now, consider a statement once posted on the USAID website. (It was deleted in 2006, perhaps because it was too embarrassing for the agency.) "The principal beneficiary of America's foreign assistance programs has always been the United States. Close to 80 percent of the US Agency for International Development's contracts and grants go directly to American firms." The post went on to say that USAID funding had "created new markets for American industrial exports and meant hundreds of thousands of jobs for Americans." Long before Trump became the US president, USAID was already "putting America first."[12]

The US is not alone in its use of soft power. Former British Prime Minister Theresa May had proclaimed in Cape Town in August 2018 that, in the post-Brexit world, Britain's aid budget would be used to promote British trade and political interests. "I am unashamed about the need to ensure that our aid program works for the UK. So today I am committing that our development spending will not only combat extreme poverty, but at the same time tackle global challenges and support our own national interest." She added that, "This will ensure that our investment in aid benefits us all and is fully aligned with our wider national security priorities."[13]

In contrast to the noble narratives advanced by donor agencies, the on-the-ground realities are manifestly different. The lifestyles of those working within the donor community defies the poverty alleviation objective. Foreign donors and their local snobby staff have contributed to various forms of financial, intellectual, or moral corruption that undermine the recipient countries' institutions. Many donors support capacity development initiatives that allow CEOs and top executives to travel in business class and stay in five-star hotels while attending events at exotic locations around the globe. For instance, a global microcredit summit campaign was held in a beautiful location in Spain. A micro-savings conference took place in France. Global policy forums on financial inclusion have been held in picturesque resorts in Bali, Cape Town, and Cancun. In Pakistan every year, a donor-supported microfinance conference is held in Islamabad's grandiose Serena Hotel where nicely attired executives of the microfinance sector, who look more like investment bankers, discuss inclusion and poverty in lavish environments. The event is followed by dinners and musical programs—dedicated to helping the poor.

Donors often pursue self-serving agendas that undermine the sovereignty of developing nations, erode the autonomy of state institutions, and interfere in the decisions of government ministries. The extensive funding "safeguards" required by donors often threaten the independence of national institutions. To receive funding, recipient countries usually must disclose confidential information, which interferes in policy formulation and execution.

The staff of donor agencies typically have little or no technical expertise in the areas to which they are assigned. The same people who work on financial inclusion, for example, will later shift to tax policy and administration reforms. Then they might move to the education sector, and then to work on justice initiatives. They learn on the job. Invariably, they rely on development consultants to prepare reports, design programs, and develop implementation frameworks. They act like viceroys and vicereines.

Despite all this activity, it is difficult to find positive outcomes. The tax-to-GDP ratios in many least developed countries have stagnated or worsened. Government corruption has surged. Financing for small and medium enterprises (SMEs) has not, as a general rule, increased even though donors have contributed millions of dollars over the past two decades. There is little evidence that donor-funded programs designed to help vulnerable women in Pakistan have helped. Access-to-justice programs have done little to enhance the efficiency of the judicial system for the common person. The sectors that receive donor support often remain inefficient. Donor agencies, instead of collaborating, frequently compete to fund projects, which can lead to the inefficient allocation of resources and moral hazard.

Perhaps it should not be a surprise that British writer and

broadcaster Kenan Malik described foreign aid as a "fraud" perpetuated by rich countries to bribe or blackmail weaker economies.[14]

CHAPTER 2

A "Noble Cause" or Self-Interest?

Every year, the US allocates billions in foreign aid to promote global stability, national security, and its own economic interests. The US provides funding for many programs around the world, including the UN's World Food Programme, operas in Peru, and education to help women escape sex work in Ethiopia—to name a few efforts. Over the past decade, US aid spending has steadily increased, rising from $36.4 billion in 2012 to $47.8 billion in 2021. According to OECD data, the United States was the biggest cash donor among all nations in 2022, spending $55.3 billion that year. This marked an 8.2 percent increase in real terms from 2021, primarily due to additional support for the conflict in Ukraine and its domestic refugee costs. All of this was paid by American taxpayers, some of whom are increasingly unhappy about the way their dollars are being spent.

In 2022, the US gave the most aid to Ukraine ($11.2 billion). Israel received the next largest amount ($3 billion) from the US, followed by Afghanistan, which received $1.9 billion. The other top recipients of US aid in 2022 included Ethiopia, Egypt, Yemen, Jordan, South Sudan, Nigeria, and Syria.

If poverty alleviation or stimulating economic growth in the world's poorest countries were the primary objectives of US foreign aid, then one might assume that most aid would go to places with the lowest GDPs, such as South Sudan, Burundi, the Democratic Republic of Congo, and Mozambique. The reality, however, reflects a different priority: serving US geopolitical interests. This is not new or limited to just the US. During the Cold War, Western countries used aid to buttress anticommunist governments, and since 9/11, aid has been a vital instrument in the war on terror.

More recently, aid has been offered as a means of reducing migration. The EU has increasingly made aid to African nations conditional on curbing migration to Europe. An EU official stated in 2016 that, "Those countries who . . . work with us will get certain treatment. Those who don't want to or are incapable will get different treatment, and that will be translated via our development and trade policies." For the EU, aid can be seen as either a bribe (at best) or a form of blackmail (at worst).[15]

Similarly, the US channels aid to countries like Ukraine, Israel, Egypt, and Jordan as a means of prioritizing American geopolitical interests more than poverty alleviation. These aid packages often come with stringent conditions, including requirements to spend aid on goods manufactured by the donor country. Recently, the EU has also tied aid to conditions such as the recipient country's ability to control emigration, effectively outsourcing border controls to nations with controversial human rights records. In 2023, ODA to Ukraine broke all records. Since Russia's invasion in February 2022, Ukraine has become far and away the top recipient of nonmilitary US foreign aid. This marks the first time that a European country has held the top spot since the Harry Truman administration used the Marshall Plan to direct vast sums toward rebuilding the continent after World War II. This further demonstrates that, when it comes to international aid, the donors' political agendas come first. The fact that aid aligns more with strategic interests than genuine poverty reduction underscores the dual nature of aid as both a diplomatic tool and as a development resource. And that raises questions about the aid's effectiveness in achieving humanitarian goals.

In an insightful 2024 article published by the Council on Foreign Affairs, Jonathan Masters and Will Merrow provide useful information about how much US aid is going to Ukraine.[16] Since the war began, the US has provided Ukraine with $175 billion in aid, an amount that includes military assistance. Out of this, $57.4 billion was nondefense assistance for Europe, Eurasia, and Central Asia (e.g., economic support fund, assistance for refugees, and funding for democracy and diplomacy). As an aside (our focus is on nonmilitary aid), it is important to know that a large share of US military aid for Ukraine is spent in the United States, paying for American factories and workers to produce weapons for Ukraine or to replenish US weapons stocks. One analysis by the American Enterprise Institute found that Ukraine aid is funding defense manufacturing in more than seventy US cities.[17] Twenty-nine other countries have also made major arms transfers to Ukraine since the war began.

Historically, many evaluations of foreign aid programs have cited the ineffectiveness of using aid for the dual purpose of promoting economic development and advancing the donor nations' geopolitical interests. In 1989, a House Foreign Affairs Committee report stated that US foreign aid programs "no longer either advance US interests abroad or promote economic development."[18] Similarly, a Clinton administration task force concluded that, "Despite decades of foreign assistance, most of Africa, and parts of Latin America, Asia, and the Middle East are economically worse off today than they were twenty years ago."[19]

There is also ample real-world evidence showing the ineffectiveness of dual-purpose aid efforts. For example, the US has persisted in its aid efforts in Afghanistan, a country plagued by waste, fraud, and abuse. In a recent commentary published by the Cato Institute, Johns Hopkins University Professor Steve Hanke presented an eye-opening story of how US aid funding has fueled corruption in Afghanistan, which is a poster child for foreign aid failure.[20] Nevertheless, in an August 2021 address to the nation about Afghanistan, President Biden sought to justify America's withdrawal by asserting that, among other things, "Our mission in Afghanistan was never supposed to have been nation building." He went on to say that our mission "was never supposed to be creating a unified, centralized democracy."[21]

These assertions, according to Hanke, seemed to overlook the Bonn Agreement signed in December 2001 after the ouster of the Taliban, and subsequent events that clearly showed that the United States and its allies were engaged in a nation-building exercise, one that was focused on constructing a centralized government. Few are willing to discuss the failures of foreign aid and nation building efforts in Afghanistan, a fact that Hanke attributes to a tightly knit epistemic community of professional elites who are heavily reliant on foreign aid delivery and who are determined to maintain the status quo. To highlight the magnitude of waste, fraud, and abuse in Afghanistan, Hanke points to ODA numbers, which totaled $76.6 billion between 2002 and 2019, making Afghanistan one of the largest recipients of such aid, second only to Iraq ($79.4 billion) during the same period. Notably, ODA accounted for a substantial portion of Afghanistan's GDP, reaching 22.2 percent in

2019. The portion of Afghanistan's GDP provided by ODA, and the fact that it has remained relatively large for the better part of twenty years, means that the formal economy of Afghanistan remains heavily aid-dependent. The training wheels have never been taken off. Interestingly, the surge in aid coincided with the Obama administration's escalation of operations in Afghanistan, including troop deployments, which peaked at 110,000 in 2011. However, despite the withdrawal, the legacy of this aid remains.

Hanke argues that this massive influx of aid led to rampant corruption, with bribery reaching shocking figures, surpassing the taxes collected from Afghan citizens. In 2010, bribery amounted to a staggering $2.5 billion in Afghanistan. It then shot up to $2.88 billion in 2016 and settled down to $1.6 billion in 2018. To put these sums into perspective, the amount of taxes collected from Afghans was only $1.12 billion in 2018 and $889 million in 2019. Just what has this gravy train of aid delivered? One thing is a cornucopia of corruption.

We also need to consider what foreign aid has *failed* to deliver. In Afghanistan, for example, sustainable economic development never occurred. Instead of fostering traditional agriculture and markets in the rural areas where most Afghans live, misguided policies inadvertently fueled opium production, with over 40 percent of Afghanistan's agricultural land dedicated to opium poppies. The country produces 85 percent of the world's opium.

Despite two decades of foreign aid, Afghanistan ranks a miserable 169 out of the 189 countries covered in the UN's 2020 Human Development Report, which reports countries' standards of living, health, and education. Afghanistan's position is only one notch above Haiti, another failed state that has been lavished with foreign aid. In the past five years, Afghanistan's ranking has been sinking. In fact, Afghanistan's rank has not significantly improved since 1993, raising serious questions about the efficacy of foreign aid in improving the country's human development. As Hanke rightly suggests, the foreign-aid community seems afflicted by what Moisés Naím terms "ideological necrophilia," a persistent attachment to ideas that have repeatedly failed. As many regional experts predicted twenty years ago, the US effort to transform Afghanistan with foreign aid has been a resounding failure. As occurred in Iraq, the hundreds of millions thrown at NGOs, projects, workshops, and schools simply did not do what the money was intended to do.

To promote the idea of liberal democracy as a model for all nations, regardless of their histories or cultural beliefs, the US has funded projects that would appeal to those who already lived in liberal democracies. The fact that these projects were all donor-driven geared them toward making America's nation-building plans look good, at least on paper. Whether they would result in any real change seemed at best an afterthought to the donors. In fact, foreign aid distributed all over the world is often provided without any serious intention to bring about significant long-lasting changes. It is often used by the US and other wealthy nations as leverage over the corrupt governments that receive aid. The road to becoming a superpower, it appears, is lined with a lot of aid money. As a 2014 report by the US Congressional Research Service put it, aid "can act as both carrot and stick and is a means of influencing events, solving specific problems and projecting US values."[22]

There is another potential reason why rich countries choose to disburse aid to broken governments: It creates the impression that they are in a superior moral and intellectual position over the aid recipients. This is a form of intellectual condescension. By giving large amounts of aid to poorer countries, wealthy countries can be seen as altruistic global thought leaders and thus amplify their positions in the world.

In recent years, as Pakistanis know well, the Chinese have been developing a presence in various parts of the world. China is not motivated by altruism. The Chinese Belt and Road Initiative (BRI), for instance, is openly designed to serve China's interests. Instead of *giving* money to the governments involved in the BRI, the Chinese have created schemes of structured debts that recipient governments must pay back once the BRI projects begin to generate revenue.

This is a novel approach to international aid, but it is not guaranteed to avert tragedy. As we know, aid projects do not always work, especially when they are implemented on a large scale. If a particular Chinese-funded project fails to be sufficiently profitable for the recipient nation to repay the aid, that government will end up poor and severely indebted. In this situation, the trade benefits that everyone hoped would accrue may never materialize.

So, the only guaranteed winners are the donor countries. They gain geopolitical influence as a means of achieving their broader goals, and they come to be seen as the noblest, smartest, and most helpful. However, the publicly stated humanitarian goals—funding enormous infrastructure projects or building thousands of schools—are seldom achieved. Aid has not lifted the truly vulnerable out of poverty or delivered the better lives that donor governments promise and that recipients tragically continue to hope for.

This pattern also appears in Pakistan, which has been heavily dependent on foreign aid ever since its independence. The United States has been Pakistan's largest single bilateral donor. Since

1947, the United States has allocated over $70 billion to Pakistan for a multitude of purposes, including counterterrorism efforts, healthcare, and education. These aid disbursements have fluctuated in ways that have been closely tied to shifting American geopolitical interests in the region. The US supported Pakistan unconditionally in the 1980s, which is when the Soviet Union invaded Afghanistan. Pakistan was also a US ally during the war on terror. However, depending on the US political agenda, Pakistan has been left to face its own economic, political, and humanitarian problems without much US support. Generally, the United States has provided aid to Pakistan to propel its own strategic interests, fulfill some humanitarian obligations, and help the country avert an economic crisis.

In September 2013, a report submitted to the US Congress disclosed that Pakistan had received $25.91 billion in military and economic assistance from the United States since the 9/11 attacks. A May 2019 report from USAID, which highlights historical trends, noted that US *economic* assistance to Pakistan peaked in 1962 (more than $2.3 billion) and that *military* assistance amounted to $2.5 billion in 2010. Conversely, US aid levels hit bottom in the 1990s when President George H. W. Bush suspended aid due to Pakistan's burgeoning nuclear program. There were also substantial reductions in US military assistance following the Indo-Pakistani conflicts of 1965 and 1971.

The USAID report added that during the 1970s, President Jimmy Carter suspended all aid (except food) to Pakistan in response to Pakistan's decision to construct a uranium enrichment facility. In 2018, the Trump administration cut aid to Pakistan by approximately $300 million, which marked the cancellation of all

US military aid to Pakistan. The Biden administration continued to cut aid, with total civilian assistance dropping to less than $200 million in 2022.

The ups and downs of US economic aid, driven by geopolitical self-interest, can also be seen in the way it has handled military aid. In the early 1980s, the United States agreed to sell sophisticated F-16 fighter jets to Pakistan. At that time, the United States was working closely with Pakistan to repel the Soviets from Afghanistan. The F-16 was the most important element in Pakistan's air force. However, when the US slapped sanctions on Pakistan in 1990 (under the Pressler Amendment) to stymie nuclear proliferation, the US canceled the delivery of several F-16s that had already been purchased. Pakistanis routinely cite this as evidence of American perfidy and to claim that the US is not a trustworthy ally. Many American and Pakistani interlocutors recount redacted variants of this sordid affair for various purposes, but it remains a fact that the US unfairly deprived Pakistan of the F-16s it had purchased. The US demurred from reimbursing Pakistan when sanctions precluded delivery, and the US even charged Pakistan for the storage fees while American officials sought a third-party buyer for the planes.

The US's military and economic relations with Pakistan have been marred by a lack of transparency, and the aid relationship between both countries is badly out of balance. Heavily weighted toward military aid rather than economic assistance, the aid has strengthened the hand of Pakistan's powerful security establishment at the expense of the civilian government. Both countries have reasons to be disappointed that so much US aid has achieved so little. Washington and Islamabad would both be better served if they focused on civilian and development assistance. Traditionally,

Pakistani civilians have had little control over the military. This tendency is further reinforced by the heavy flow of American aid to the country's security establishment. To help build a more stable Pakistan with stronger democratic institutions, the US must shift its focus to civilian and development assistance.

The US is not alone in providing aid with self-interested objectives. In 1970, Britain pledged to spend at least 0.7 percent of Gross National Income (GNI) on foreign aid as part of a UN pact.[23] It is among thirty wealthy countries that have vowed to meet this minimum commitment each year. However, in 2020, Britain's conservative government reduced overseas aid from 0.7 percent to 0.5 percent of GNI to free up cash for domestic spending during the Covid-19 pandemic, slashing billions from programs that supported the world's poorest people.

The OECD data shows that Britain spent $15.7 billion in aid in 2022—including domestic spending, such as refugee programs— slightly down from $15.8 billion in 2021. The top five countries to receive UK aid in 2022 were Afghanistan, Ukraine, Nigeria, Somalia, and Ethiopia. Almost all funds went to countries in Africa and Asia, according to government data.

The UK has a strong track record of delivering development assistance to Pakistan. From 2015 to 2019, Pakistan was the largest single recipient of bilateral ODA from the UK. However, in 2020, Pakistan's ranking dropped six places, receiving £200 million. This downward trend continued, with Pakistan slipping to ninth position in 2022, with an allocation of £58 million. According to the UK government, the current level of ODA funding reflects Pakistan's evolving status as a lower middle-income country, undergoing a transition toward self-financing its development efforts.

UK Aid has sought to advance Pakistan's development while also pursuing its own objectives on shared values, including the needs of girls and women, inclusion, religious and media freedom, and gender inequality. It has also focused on promoting jobs, growth and trade, and climate resilience. However, as shown above, the UK has dramatically cut its aid to Pakistan, even though Pakistan is a country with huge development potential. Due to its smaller aid budget (compared to the US budget), the UK needs to be highly strategic with its aid spending. Is should focus intently on opportunities for Pakistan's economic development rather than other objectives.

Aid programs are most effective when donors work to ensure that their efforts complement each other. However, the UK House of Commons' International Development Committee (IDC) stated in its "UK Aid to Pakistan" report that coordination among donors is lacking. The committee recommended a more cohesive strategy that amplifies the impact of aid programs. In addition, the IDC report acknowledged a disparity between UK aid programs that are focused on fostering an open society and the policy objectives of the Pakistani government. For example, the IDC reported that the UK missed opportunities to reduce food insecurity, which remains a significant hurdle for development in Pakistan. Specifically, the report noted (paragraph 37) that "despite the FCDO having recorded 62 percent food insecurity in one district, it did not support food assistance despite a recommendation to do so." Ironically, while the FCDO invests in Pakistan's profitable financial sector, crucial development challenges remain unaddressed, suggesting that the FCDO currently prioritizes investments vis-à-vis the country's fundamental development needs.

In another instance, the UK government has faced strong criticism for the way its aid is being used for superfluous programs, such as training soccer referees and coaches across China, even when spending cuts were predicted to lead to thousands of deaths across Africa and Yemen. An official watchdog and various other aid organizations demanded to know why the Premier Skills Programme, run by England's Premier League for the purpose of inspiring young people in China, was partly funded by ODA. The program planned to spend nearly $230,000 on the grassroots project from 2021 to 2024.[24] Paradoxically, the UK government admitted that thousands of people in "acute humanitarian need" would die unnecessarily from hunger, poor health care, and during childbirth because of its ongoing aid cuts in low-income countries. It is not as though the Premier League needs government money; it is the world's richest soccer league, generating revenue of £5.5 billion in 2021-2022.

Sir Hugh Bayley, a commissioner at the UK's Independent Commission for Aid Impact, which has highlighted the lack of a government strategy to rein in UK aid to China, also criticized UK funding for soccer. Commissioner Bayley, who led the review, said this: "While UK aid to China has fallen rapidly in recent years, taxpayers are still not being told clearly how much aid will continue and what it will be spent on."[25]

The UK has traditionally given more of its aid in the form of grants rather than as loans. But in 2014, the International Development Committee called for a shift in emphasis to loans. And Theresa May's Cape Town speech clearly suggested that she saw aid as leverage for trade.

Beyond the UK, a high proportion of foreign aid is allocated in the form of loans, which burdens countries with debt. Many rich nations receive more in interest payments from recipient countries than they give in aid. Since the 2008 financial crisis, Western governments have increasingly exploited their ability to borrow money at low rates. Then they set up aid programs that lend money to poor countries at much higher rates, minting money on the backs of the poor. Consequently, African debt currently stands at around $350 billion. This is not aid; it is a scandal.

Some development programs are crucial to countries in the global South, and certain forms of aid, particularly disaster relief, are essential and necessary. But as a global system, foreign aid is a fraud.[26] It has become a means of entrenching inequality, not of ameliorating it.

How Donors Measure "Success"

Donors keep moving the goal posts during the game. They establish one set of goals only to adopt a new set of goals later. For example, twenty-five years ago the issue of financial access for the poor was a low priority. Few international aid efforts sought to address that need. Today, providing financial access to people in the developing world has become an important item on the agenda of global leaders who are concerned about inequality and inclusive growth.[27]

Donor agencies have redefined goals pertaining to helping people improve their financial well-being. In the mid-1990s, international aid donors focused primarily on addressing the *microcredit* needs of poor families in the informal economy. The innovation of social collateral made it possible to serve low-income segments that previously had been considered "unbankable."

Then, by the mid-2000s, donors shifted their focus to *microfinance*. Donor agencies realized that poor families in the informal economy are simultaneously producers and consumers. Their microbusiness activities and household needs are often intermingled. As producers, they need access to financial services to invest, generate income, and build assets. As consumers, they need to smooth consumption in the face of irregular income and expense streams, and to manage risks. Providing financial services, such as savings and insurance, emerged as the new goal.

The goalposts shifted again in the late 2000s when donor agencies realized that it was too expensive to provide financial services for the poor, especially in remote areas. So, the donors started to focus on driving down costs and, more broadly, on providing *access to finance*. In many ways, the donor agencies were merely responding to technological advances outside their purview. In particular, the advent of the mobile phone and other technology-based solutions during those years significantly increased the reach of financial access and lowered the delivery costs of financial services—without much need for donor agencies.

More recently, market saturation and over-indebtedness have forced donor agencies to refocus on promoting consumer protection and financial literacy measures. Donors have also been lining up behind government efforts to improve *financial inclusion;* that is, to help more people participate within their country's mainstream financial system. As a result, there is now a chance to reach far more of today's excluded poor with the broader range of financial services.

If we look only at these efforts to improve financial well-being, we can see that donor agencies have frequently redefined measures of success. They tack in different directions depending on the winds. They try to stay relevant, regardless of the original goals.

Here is another example. In September 2000, the United Nations General Assembly adopted its Millennium Declaration, which called for a global partnership to reduce extreme poverty and provided a global strategy for all UN member nations and leading development institutions to reach quantifiable targets. To support the declaration, former UN Secretary General Kofi Annan established eight accompanying objectives. These objectives were set with a deadline of 2015 and became known as the Millennium Development Goals (MDGs).

Were the MDGs successful? This question has been the subject of considerable debate. Some people argue that the development agenda promoted by the MDGs has spearheaded an unprecedented international movement against extreme poverty, reducing it by more than 50 percent globally. However, critics say that progress toward the specific targets set out in the MDGs has been regionally and thematically unbalanced. For example, many countries adopted a piecemeal approach, choosing to pursue some but not all goals. In addition, the MDGs only applied to countries of the global South, and those countries did not play a significant role in their design. Critics have also argued that developed countries had *imposed* the MDGs on developing countries.

Despite these disputes, the goalposts changed again. In January 2016, we saw the emergence of seventeen new benchmarks collectively called the Sustainable Development Goals (SDGs) for 2030. With these targets, countries were encouraged to end all forms of poverty, fight inequalities, and tackle climate change while ensuring that no one was left behind.

What makes the SDGs different than the MDGs? The SDGs are uniformly applicable to all countries of the world, removing the "developing" versus "developed" dichotomy that left the MDGs open to criticism. There are similarities between the two sets of goals, but the SDGs have significantly expanded the scale and content of the MDGs. The SDGs are more focused on the environmental sustainability of global development, whereas the MDGs maintained a narrow focus on poverty reduction.

These frequent changes to long-term goals demonstrate that donors measure success in relative terms. Donor agencies often opt to use their own benchmarks for progress, which makes it hard to assess actual on-the-ground success. Sometimes the goals are lofty and noble, as in the case of the SDGs, which are "universally applicable" to all countries.[28] However, the cost of achieving the SDGs has stifled progress toward meeting them. For example, a 2021 International Monetary Fund working paper assessed the additional spending required to make substantial progress toward reaching the SDGs in Pakistan. The paper focused on critical areas of education, health, electricity, roads, water, and sanitation. For each sector, the IMF documented the progress to date, assessed where Pakistan stood relative to its peers, highlighted key challenges, and estimated the additional spending required to make substantial progress. The IMF found that Pakistan would need to spend 16 percent more of its GDP by 2030 to achieve the SDGs. In the context of a cash-strapped economy burdened by unsustainable debt, where a mere 5 percent of the GDP is currently allocated to social sectors, how can Pakistan possibly achieve the SDGs by the 2030s?

In this context, the UN acknowledged in 2024 that only

16 percent of the SDGs are on track to be fully implemented by 2030.[29] The report further warned that none of the seventeen SDGs will be met by the target date. Progress has stagnated in critical areas of development, including reducing poverty, eliminating hunger, improving quality education, expanding peace and justice, and providing clean water.

The overall outlook is grim, but there are some bright spots, at least in advanced countries or fast-growing emerging markets that are not aid-dependent. For example, the Nordic countries, particularly Finland, Sweden, and Denmark, are global leaders in making progress toward achieving their SDG goals. Likewise, members of the BRICS alliance (Brazil, Russia, India, China, and South Africa), as well as BRICS+ nations (Egypt, Ethiopia, Iran, Saudi Arabia, and the UAE), are outpacing the world average in terms of implementing the SDGs.

Unfortunately, the world's poorest countries are drowning in debt. As a result, they are unable to access affordable long-term funding needed to invest in their SDGs. Sadly, low-income countries have moved slightly backward in relation to these goals since 2022. If we measure progress as a percentage, with 100 percent being the attainment of all SDGs, the ten countries with the lowest scores are poverty-ridden, aid-dependent countries: South Sudan (40.1); Central African Republic (44.2); Chad (45.1); Somalia (45.4); Yemen (46.9); Afghanistan (48.2); Democratic Republic of Congo (48.7); Niger (49.9); Sudan (49.9); Madagascar (51.2). This underscores that the biggest obstacle to implementing the SDGs is the lack of long-term investments, which will require a complete overhaul of the global financial architecture. The current system, in which individual nations lead the implementation of the SDGs, has locked at least one billion people in deep poverty. Billions more face severe material deprivation, large-scale environmental crises, and deepening divisions among major powers.

The UN's admission of failure demonstrates that management and investment challenges cannot be addressed within the existing global financial architecture. Without *systemic change*, aid organizations cannot be effective in delivering meaningful long-term assistance to the neediest countries. That's why the donors keep changing goal posts.

Competition vs. Collaboration

As shown in the next chapter, donors often implement overlapping projects with similar objectives across all sectors. For the past two decades, the World Bank, the ADB, and the UK's FCDO have all launched tax reform projects in Pakistan with the same objective: to increase the tax-to-GDP ratio by improving Pakistan's tax policy and administration. The ADB has also initiated more than a hundred energy sector reform programs in Pakistan even though the World Bank has also been working to improve the nation's energy sector. Additionally, the most important donors, including the World Bank, the ADB, the IFC, and The Gates Foundation have all worked on overlapping efforts to support banks and financial institutions—to increase the access of small and medium enterprises to finance and to advance digital financial inclusion. Many other major donors run similar programs to improve agriculture, food security, education, health, climate change, and to empower women. In most cases, these donors compete rather than collaborate.

The similarities between these programs can be seen in program design documents and presentations used by donors to sell their projects to national authorities. The designs reflect cookie-cutter approaches that hardly fit the local context or address on-the-ground realities. The so-called "best practices" fail to address the root causes of the problems. They avoid proposing solutions that might fall outside status quo policymaking. As resources go down the drain, the underlying problems become more complex and more difficult to solve.

CHAPTER 3

The Kingdom of Consultants and Contractors

Decades of growing global cooperation and increased funding have changed the development industry from what used to be a relatively small sector into a juggernaut that provides jobs for hundreds of thousands of consultants around the world. Today there is a $224 billion aid and development industry—a kingdom of sorts. Workers in these fields have formed a heady culture of forward-thinking philanthropists, social entrepreneurs, and government officials.

According to the UN, development consultants are individuals engaged in an advisory or consultative capacity. They act as an "authority or specialist in a specific field." Such work is typically short-term and supposedly results oriented. In the context of the UN system, roles usually involve "analyzing problems, directing seminars or training courses, preparing documents for conferences and meetings, or writing reports on matters within their area of expertise."[30] The UN has pushed the growth of consultancy work by defining the term to include a wide range of job descriptions.

The global development industry hires vast numbers of people every year. According to an October 2023 article published by Devex, the media platform for the global development community, more than thirty-five thousand short-term roles had been advertised on its site since the start of that year. The top employers have been UN agencies or other multilateral agencies, such as development banks.[31] The increased hiring of consultants can also be measured by looking at "projectized" funding, organizational reticence to provide staff with long-term contracts, and changes in workplace trends brought about by post-pandemic digital technology.

In the past, NGOs and aid agencies received grant funding that would allow for larger numbers of long-term staff. More recently, donor funding has been increasingly granted on a project-by-project model. As a result, the agencies maintain a skeleton staff. They apply for funding, and then, if the funding is awarded, recruit short-term consultants to implement the programs. People with only a few years of experience can be consultants. These development contractors and consultants benefit heavily from donor funding, but they rarely have a measurable impact on reaching the agencies' objectives. In fact, considerable sums of money received by donor agencies from donor countries go back to the advanced countries through the consultants' bank accounts.

The United Nations worldwide work has increasingly relied on consultants with short-term contracts, which seriously hampers the organization's overall professionalism. According to an internal document procured by the Swiss newspaper *Le Temps*, nearly 40 percent of those working with the UN and its agencies are hired as short-term or "non-staff" contractors. This creates a two-tier system comprising full-time or tenured employees who have complete social benefits and another group of independent consultants who have few if any benefits.[32] The report maintains that this two-tier arrangement has emerged largely because UN agencies want greater "flexibility" and to reduce costs. However, this approach is not aligned with international principles for labor rights, and it does not represent the UN's *own values.* The Joint Inspection Unit (JIU), the only independent oversight body mandated to inspect and evaluate the UN, considers the consequences of the current system "problematic and counterproductive." The JIU adds that the UN could engender an increasingly poor image while threatening employee stability and motivation. Furthermore, such practices could lead to an enormous number of lawsuits.

These types of lackluster labor policies diminish the cohesion and motivation of people sent on missions, and they increase employee turnover. JIU investigations in 2013 looked at UN operations in six different countries—the Democratic Republic of Congo, Ethiopia, Haiti, India, Thailand, and Vietnam. The study revealed that the reliance on temporary contractors weakened the UN's humanitarian missions. As reported by *Le Temps,* "the current situation is that the United Nations is working with a dual labor force: the first is granted all the rights and privileges attached to the job; the other enjoys few if any rights."

According to the same report, at least 50 percent of the workforces at the Rome-based UN Food and Agricultural Organization and at UN Operations headquartered in Copenhagen are consultants. The World Health Organization also has a high number of temporary and contract workers, which, as stated above, can lead to enormous frustration and low morale among those workers. They are often uncertain whether they should renew leases on their flats, or whether they will be able to afford to send their children to international schools. Even the International Labor Organization has been criticized for failing to uphold some of the labor rights of its workers—the same rights it promotes among governments, companies, and trade unions worldwide.

The JIU found a severe lack of information regarding the situation of consultants, but it concluded that the UN's two-tier approach to labor relations produces inequalities among personnel and encourages fraud and nepotism. "All this is in violation of international labor principles and the values on which the United Nations is founded," the report points out.

The salaries of full-time staffers and professional consultants can vary enormously. Some agencies pay consultants well, taking into consideration possible time lapses between contracts, but many consultants do not receive contributions for social security, pensions, or taxes, despite working many years for the UN.

The JIU, which has produced thirteen recommendations to improve the situation of workers, maintains that the UN should not use short-term consultants on a long-term basis simply to save money. As noted by one senior UN source, "It is very much in the UN's interest to maintain high professional standards. We need to have the best people, and it makes sense to be consistent and transparent on all fronts."[33]

"When I started working in development, I idolized development consultants," wrote one conscientious consultant. "They seemed such awe-inspiring figures: wise, glamorous, and with experience seeping from every pore. Now I work as a development consultant myself. The awe has faded and been replaced with an increasing concern that the growth of consultancy is a serious threat to the effectiveness of the aid sector."[34]

There is a deeper problem. Many consultants are fantastic, dedicated, and intelligent people, but in my experience, most of those workers do not add much value. This is for two reasons. First, consultants are much less able than full-time staff to genuinely help an organization make changes. Full-time staff develop deep experience and knowledge about on-the-ground situations, and they learn how to roll out changes over time. By contrast, consultants are expected to quickly implement initiatives, often with less knowledge about the local situation. It is easy for a consultant to produce deliverables, such as reports, frameworks, or workshops, but it is much harder for them to ensure that all the work leads to meaningful improvements.

Second, consultants typically do not receive feedback about their work, nor do they find opportunities for training and professional development. The problem is analogous to *locum tenens* doctors who work short-term contracts in different hospitals. Without the training and support of the normal medical system, they have a harder time moving into more advanced jobs. In short, development consultants are overpaid, overrated, and overused.

Development organizations should stop relying on consultants and invest in long-term staff. Donors need to stop considering trained, motivated staff as an overhead cost and think of them as a foundation for effective development work. Both donors and recipient organizations need to provide training and support. Doing so will increase the quality of their staff and build a rewarding work environment that improves on-the-ground outcomes.

The Circular Flow of Money

In most circumstances, labor costs for contractors and consultants are embedded in each program's total costs. This means that a portion of the total amount given by donor countries does not reach the recipient country. There is nothing wrong with that *per se*, if the percentage of funding for administrative costs is reasonable. However, if we look at where the money goes, we see that large amounts have been awarded primarily to people who work for the donor country rather than to recipient countries. This means that taxpayers fund programs and then a large portion of that money flows back to the workers who are from the donor countries.

Devex analyzed data from fiscal year 2013 to fiscal year 2022 to see which development organizations won the most money in each year, for grants, cooperative agreements, and contracts. What follows is a summary of the findings.

The US's total budget for international cooperation is set in accordance with the State, Foreign Operations, and Related Programs Appropriations law, which also provides details on how funds should be used. The law covers contributions to multilateral organizations and budgets for the USAID and the Department of State. The USAID is the primary agency for development and humanitarian activities. The US mainly awards grants and contracts to different organizations across the globe through USAID's acquisition and assistance mechanisms. In 2021, the USAID accounted for around 59 percent of ODA, while another 17.4 percent was managed by the Department of State. The rest of the ODA went through other agencies, including the Department of

Health and Human Services, the US Department of Treasury, and the Millennium Challenge Corporation.[35]

In this context, it is also important to look at where these procurements were initiated—either at the USAID headquarters in Washington, DC or at the agency's missions across the globe. During the eight-year period leading up to 2022, more than 60 percent of the assistance and interagency agreements were procured in Washington, DC. Then, in 2022, that rate jumped to 86.1 percent of assistance, worth $24.1 billion.[36]

Overall, between 2013 and 2022, USAID obligated a total of $137.5 billion through grants and cooperative agreements. The top ten grantees were a mixture of multilateral agencies and large international NGOs, among which the World Food Programme was the overall top beneficiary, receiving a total of $21 billion, or 15.3 percent of the total obligation made in the ten-year period.[37]

However, the top ten grantees—the organizations that implement development programs—during that period were based in three countries: the US, Switzerland, and Italy. That fact alone demonstrates how money cycles back to the countries where the grants originated. There is more. The USAID also lists the "place of performance," which is where the grant was implemented. The US, Switzerland, and Italy remained among the top places of performance. In those cases, the grants were awarded to multilateral donors and international NGOs.

If we look at the overall situation, one number stands out: US-based contractors won around 87.6 percent of the total contract obligation.

A similar pattern occurs in the United Kingdom. In 2019, the UK's Department for International Development (DFID) disbursed

£11.1 billion in official development assistance (ODA), which was 73 percent of the total distribution from the UK that year. Devex investigated data to identify the top ten development-related contractors in 2019.[38] The major contractors, ranked by funding awarded in 2019, were: PricewaterhouseCoopers; Mott MacDonald; McKinsey & Company; DAI Europe; Coffey International Development; Ecorys UK; Ernst & Young; WYG; The Halo Trust; and Global Partners Governance. This research by Devex shows that nearly three-quarters of total ODA from UK contracts were awarded to UK-based development organizations.

The DFID's use of consultants and independent contractors came under scrutiny in 2012 through two separate government inquiries.[39] These inquiries followed an investigation by *The Sunday Telegraph*, which found DFID was paying hundreds of millions of pounds to a group of primarily UK-based consultants, some of whom earned six- or seven-figure incomes and who had previously worked in government.[40]

Several of the best-paid consultants were former DFID officials who appeared to have gained substantial increases in their personal wealth since leaving the department, even though they were still doing essentially the same work. Despite spending over £1 billion a year on consultants and interim staff, UK government departments are largely in the dark about whether the money spent is worthwhile.[41]

In the UK, an investigation of foreign aid by *The Times* revealed that millions of pounds are spent on salaries for writing pointless briefs. In 2012, aid officials agreed to give a grant worth £17.7 million to a London-based think tank. The International Institute for Environment and Development, a registered charity focusing on climate change research, promised to provide the British government with advice for four years on areas including promoting "green growth" and "low carbon development." It quoted £10,319 to write a single blog post, £10,283 to host a webcast, £26,530 to put on a conference, and £26,223 to write a policy brief, according to government documents reviewed by *The Times*.[42]

Following a series of investigations by the British media, particularly the *Daily Mail* and *The Times,* the UK House of Common's International Development Committee (IDC) conducted an inquiry into UK aid and published in its findings and recommendations in the eighth report of Session 2016-2017. Titled "DFID's Use of Private Sector Contractors," the report found that the amount of aid spent through contractors in cash terms and as a share of total bilateral expenditures had increased. In November 2010, contracts represented 12 percent (£540 million) of bilateral spending. Five years later that amount increased to 22 percent (£1.34 billion). This substantial increase demonstrates the growing use of contractors as a channel for aid delivery.[43]

The report emphasized the lack of accountability in contractor performance. It found that even when contractors underperformed, contracts were often cancelled "for convenience" rather than some type of failure. This approach, the IDC argued, might have saved money in the short term, but it undermined long-term value for money. The report added that by failing to hold contractors accountable, donor agencies missed opportunities for learning and improvement. The IDC also expressed concerns about using contractors to exploit the DFID's limited oversight of cost breakdowns, potentially compromising value for money.

Wasted funding is a critical problem, but how much

development aid goes to recipients in low- and middle-income countries?[44] This question pertains to debates over localization; that is, the amount of money donor agencies give to *local* partners. The United States has become a leading figure in this debate after Samantha Power, appointed as USAID administrator by President Joe Biden in 2021, vowed that a quarter of all eligible money would be allocated to local partners. At the time of this writing, USAID was far from that goal, and now the Trump administration has put the agency's future in limbo. Nevertheless, what are the big players in the world of development doing in relation to localization?

Based on preliminary data from the OECD, the four biggest bilateral donors after the US are Germany, Japan, France, and the UK. These four countries spent $84.1 billion on aid in 2022, or 41.2 percent of the total ODA from the DAC member countries. Usable grant data for the development agencies is not publicly available, but the data about contracts shows that only a small portion of the money goes to organizations in low- and middle-income countries.

In the case of USAID, between 5 percent and 6 percent of its assistance ($1.2 billion) went to local organizations in fiscal year 2021-2022. In addition, approximately 4.7 percent of the total ($276.9 million) was awarded to local organizations through contracts. For Germany, just 6.4 percent of its assistance (€25.7 million) went to local contractors, all of which was disbursed by Deutsche Gesellschaft für Internationale Zusammenarbeit (GIZ).

Japan has been the largest donor in Asia for years, spending around $17.5 billion in 2022. Overall, the Japan International Cooperation Agency (JICA) spent ¥29.5 billion on international contracts in fiscal year 2020-2021. Of this amount, 87.9 percent of the total international contracts went to contractors in lower-

and middle-income countries. However, this proportion goes down to about 13 percent if we compare it with Japan's total contract spending.

France spent $15.9 billion on aid in 2022. More than 40 percent of the country's ODA in 2021 ($7.9 billion) was disbursed by Agence Française de Développement (AFD), which published data on procurement activities and project financing. However, it only included a list of awards co-funded by the EU. Of this, just 2.8 percent (€551.7 million) went to low- and middle-income countries. The largest chunk, 88.8 percent (€20.7 billion) went to French contractors.

The UK disbursed nearly three-quarters (£8.2 billion) of its ODA in 2021 through the Foreign, Commonwealth and Development Office. Of the amount spent on contracts, only 17.3 percent went to low- and middle-income countries. Most of this went to a single contract for the Democratic Republic of Congo, which received £174 million.

As we can see, large sums of taxpayer money for international aid circles back to the donor countries. A much smaller percentage is going to recipient countries, and much of that is poorly used.

SECTION II

The Dark Narrative of Pakistan's
Development Agenda

CHAPTER 4

An Overview of International Aid in Pakistan

The purpose of this section—a case study about Pakistan—is to help readers learn about the country's experience with international aid. Pakistan's story reflects what occurs in developing countries around the world. Although there are many differences from country to country and region to region, Pakistan's struggle is illustrative of global trends and problems. I will first provide an overall picture of Pakistan's aid programs.

Some donor agencies in Pakistan work through the government, but many sponsor their own projects. These groups typically channel funds through the country's Economic Affairs Division. International NGOs operate either with their own funding or they execute projects on behalf of their donors. There are about twenty major donor agencies in the country and approximately the same number of significant international NGOs, each managing multiple projects, some of which involve numerous national and local NGOs.

Consequently, hundreds of projects and local partners concurrently operate across diverse sectors under the direction of foreign agencies and international NGOs. Despite all this work, there has never been a fully integrated development strategy or program for the country. The outsourcing of the country's priorities for development strategy and implementation has resulted in poor outcomes and wasted resources, including borrowed foreign exchange.

Foreign economic assistance in Pakistan is broadly categorized as either *project* financing, *program* financing, or *commodity* financing. Project financing is obtained to fund socioeconomic and infrastructure development projects. Program financing is secured to support wide-ranging economic reforms and to balance payments. It is generally obtained from multilateral development partners, usually on concessional terms with longer maturity. Commodity financing is arranged for the procurement of crude oil, mainly from the Islamic Development Bank. In addition, Pakistan's government raises funds from international financial institutions and capital markets to meet its immediate fiscal and liquidity requirements. Among the multilateral and bilateral development partners, the World Bank and the ADB have the largest portfolio followed by ISDB, China, and AIIB.

The composition of Pakistan's foreign debt is extremely complex, with each funding source imposing its own aid diversification agenda. According to the OECD, Pakistan's foreign debt comes from the following sources: 53 percent multilateral, 31 percent bilateral, and 16 percent commercial. However, these statistics belie important facts. First, the biggest category of aid utilization is the 33 percent of ODA devoted to structural support for the Pakistani economy, which includes interest payments on sovereign debt. Second, despite the official disaggregation between bilateral and multilateral sources, most of this debt is either Western or Western-backed. This means that debt from non-Paris Club members accounts for a very small percentage of Pakistan's overseas borrowing. The country has a long history of borrowing from the IMF, which includes the ongoing $7 billion EFF arrangement.

Over the past decade, China has become Pakistan's most important economic partner, largely due to the $62 billion China-Pakistan Economic Corridor (CPEC). Framed as a win-win for both nations, because it is seen to be a less-conditional and de-securitized alternative to Western aid, the project aims to allow Pakistan to reconfigure regional supply chains to its advantage. China's interests in Pakistan appear less transactional and less donor-driven than Western aid, at least on the surface. For this reason, the narratives about Sino-Pak ties seem to be more "independent," "equitable," and "all weather," as opposed to Pakistan's on-off, ad hoc, and troubled relationship with the US.

In addition to China, the Gulf Cooperation Council (GCC) region has emerged as a smaller, if no-less-important node in Pakistan's donor diversification agenda. The Pak–UAE relationship is strategically important to both states. In the aid sphere, the UAE has undertaken bilateral loans, to shore up liquidity resources, and the UAE-PAP program, which funds public health and infrastructure projects. The Pak–Saudi bilateral relationship also includes aid mechanisms. Recently, Saudi Arabia has provided a $3 billion liquidity support loan to Pakistan.

Analysis of bilateral ODA (the 2020-2021 average) by sectors reveals that 17 percent went to education, 15 percent to health, 25 percent to other social infrastructure and services, another 15 percent to economic infrastructure, 11 percent to humanitarian aid, and only 6 percent to production sectors. Donor agencies compete to get their hands on projects in these strategically important sectors. Instead of pursuing donor harmonization and a uniform development strategy for the country, the donors throw away money on every conceivable project using beautiful jargon and buzz words.

What follows is an overview of the main aid organizations in Pakistan. The list shows that the work of these agencies overlaps across all sectors, including education, energy, finance, agriculture, water, urban management, housing, and social protection.

The World Bank

The World Bank Group works in every major area of development, including agriculture, education, energy, finance, health, industry, trade and services, ICT, public administration, social protection, transportation (aviation and railways), water supply, sanitation, and waste management. The bank provides a wide array of financial products and technical assistance. It offers support to developing countries through policy advice, research and analysis, and technical assistance. Its analytical work often underpins World Bank financing and helps to inform developing countries' own investments.

The World Bank comprises the International Bank for Reconstruction and Development (IBRD) and the International Development Association (IDA). The IDA focuses on the world's poorest countries, while IBRD assists middle-income and creditworthy poorer countries. Established in 1960, IDA aims to reduce poverty by providing zero- to low-interest loans (called "credits") and grants for programs that boost economic growth, reduce inequalities, and improve people's living conditions.

The IDA complements the World Bank's original lending

arm—IBRD. The IDA is one of the largest sources of assistance for the world's seventy-five poorest countries, and it is the single largest source of donor funds for basic social services in these countries. Eligibility for IDA support depends first and foremost on a country's relative poverty, defined as per capita GNI below an established threshold, which is updated annually. In fiscal year 2024, that threshold was $1,315. Some countries, such as Pakistan and Nigeria, are IDA-eligible based on per capita income levels and they are also creditworthy for some IBRD borrowing. These types of countries are referred to as "blend" countries.

Historically, the IDA has been funded largely by contributions from its member countries. Donors meet every three years to replenish IDA resources and review its policy framework. The most recent replenishment of IDA's resources, IDA20, was finalized in December 2021, resulting in a historic $93 billion financing package for IDA countries for fiscal years 2022-2025.

IDA lends money on concessional terms, which means that its credits have zero or very low interest rates, and repayments can be stretched over thirty to forty years. Most IDA countries receive all or half of their IDA resources on grant terms, which carry no repayments at all. Grants are targeted at the low-income countries that have a higher risk of debt distress.

Between 2001 and 2023, Pakistan contracted IBRD loans totaling $4.866 billion. The original principal value of IDA credit was $14.313 billion. By comparison, IDA *grants* to Pakistan totaled $113 million. The World Bank proudly positions itself as Pakistan's development partner, implementing projects across a broad spectrum of sectors, including agriculture, finance, governance, education, health, infrastructure, water, sanitation, and energy. To present a full list of all the bank's projects in Pakistan since 2001 (at least 152 of them), I would need more than fifteen pages. Suffice it to say that the bank's involvement has been pervasive in the country, touching every facet of the country's socioeconomic landscape.

The Asian Development Bank (ADB)

The ADB has for many years supported investments in many important sectors and services in Pakistan, purportedly to help reduce poverty and increase resilience and prosperity. The bank claims its operations are aligned with Pakistan's evolving economic and development priorities. Its country partnership strategy (2021–2025) for Pakistan focuses on three priorities: improving economic management, building resilience, and boosting competitiveness and private sector development.

To date, the ADB has committed 843 public sector loans, grants, and technical assistance efforts to Pakistan for a total value of $41.4 billion. Everything was financed by regular and concessional ordinary capital resources, the Asian Development Fund, and other special funds. Again, if I were to list all the ADB-financed projects in Pakistan since 2000, I would need to add about twenty pages to this book. (I have the full list.) As with the World Bank's influence, the ADB's extensive engagement has reached into virtually every sphere of socioeconomic activity, often intersecting with initiatives by the World Bank and other major donors.

The ADB's ongoing sovereign portfolio in Pakistan includes fifty-three loans and three grants worth $9.59 billion.[45] In 2022, ADB's loan and grant disbursements to Pakistan amounted to

$2.49 billion. This includes $1.8 billion in program lending, $680 million from project lending, and $4.6 million from grants. The ADB provided $1.5 billion to help Pakistan boost social protection, promote food security, and support employment for people.

The ADB has also helped Pakistan mobilize domestic resources, improve financial inclusion, and reform the energy sector, all to support the government in its macroeconomic management. To build resilience, the bank has agreed to support Pakistan's adaptation to climate change and transition to clean energy.

United States Agency for International Development (USAID)

The United States has disbursed a notable $33 billion in aid to Pakistan since fiscal year 2001-2002. That funding has been distributed across many aid categories and for many purposes, including counterterrorism, healthcare, and education. These aid disbursements have fluctuated in ways that are closely tied to shifting American geopolitical interests in the region. In 2018, the Trump administration cut aid to Pakistan by approximately $300 million. Aid cuts continued into the Biden administration, with total civilian aid dropping to less than $200 million in 2022.

The USAID's work advances US national security and economic prosperity, and it demonstrates American generosity. The agency claims to promote a path to each recipient's self-reliance and resilience. In fact, the USAID website states that the purpose of its foreign aid should be to end the need for the USAID's aid. The USAID site goes on to describe a long list of its services, support, and programs in a variety of areas: energy, economic growth, education, health, etc.[46]

The USAID's goal under the 2023-2028 Country Development Cooperation Strategy (CDCS) is to foster "a more resilient, gender-equitable, inclusive, and prosperous Pakistan." The strategy fosters broad-based, climate-resilient economic growth; strengthens inclusive, democratic, and accountable governance; and promotes a healthier, more educated population. It focuses on improving health and education, promoting women's economic empowerment, strengthening democratic systems to be more representative and accountable, and advancing human rights, particularly of women and vulnerable groups. Additionally, the strategy emphasizes an integrated approach to climate resilience and preparedness, flood recovery, and conflict sensitivity. It emphasizes gender and social inclusion, investing in youth, locally led development, and private sector engagement across development objectives.[47]

The USAID deploys extensive media and publicity campaigns in Pakistan, including advertisements at airports. These campaigns create the impression that Pakistan would be doomed without development assistance "from the people of the United States." This portrayal is strikingly disproportionate when considering the context. USAID's total civilian aid to Pakistan was less than $200 million in 2022, which was a small fraction of Pakistan's $375 billion GDP in the same year.

The UK Foreign, Commonwealth and Development Office (formerly DFID)

Historically, Pakistan has been a priority country for the UK's development spending. From 2015 to 2019, Pakistan was the largest single recipient of bilateral ODA from the UK. However, in 2020, Pakistan's ranking dropped six places, making it the seventh largest recipient of bilateral UK aid, receiving £200 million. As stated earlier, this downward trend continued. By 2022, Pakistan slipped to ninth position with an allocation of £58 million.

Nevertheless, the UK's aid targets a wide variety of initiatives related to health, climate change, and education. The top three bilateral aid programs in 2023, according to budgeted expenditures, went to the following efforts: Delivering Accelerated Family Planning in Pakistan (DAFPAK), which aims to increase access to quality family planning information and services, particularly to underserved groups such as rural women; Girls and Out of School Action for Learning (GOAL), a program designed to improve education outcomes for the most marginalized girls; and Revenue Mobilization, Investment, and Trade (REMIT), which aims to support macroeconomic stability and reduce poverty. There are many other UK initiatives related to water resources, humanitarian relief, the reduction of hate speech and disinformation, and taxation. I could go on.

When we look at the whole picture in Pakistan, we can see that these international aid agencies work in a vast array of sectors. However, they only allocate small amounts of funding to each area. This diffuses the impact of each investment. In addition, these large agencies *compete* for projects rather than *coordinating* their efforts. As a result, they end up duplicating their services. They all claim to be moving Pakistan toward greater self-reliance and self-sufficiency, but that claim is contradicted by the scale and number of projects undertaken—for decades—by USAID and other development partners.

The facts and on-the-ground realities do not support the agencies' claims, as I will show in the next chapters.

CHAPTER 5

Pakistan's Professionals Outpace Foreign Consultants

In this chapter, I provide an insider's view of how Pakistan dramatically improved financial inclusion—despite major technological, geographical, and funding barriers—with only minimal help from the UK. It is a story of how a developing country can greatly improve the economic situation of its poorest communities without heavy reliance on foreign donors. This positive story begins in 2007 and extends to 2015. Unfortunately, the story took a darker turn in 2016, which is the focus of chapter 6.

Financial inclusion—providing citizens with access to formal banking, payments, and insurance services—has increasingly become a focus of international aid organizations. When large segments of a country's population do not have bank accounts or secure ways to pay for services and products, they struggle to save money, receive social benefits, or start businesses. Exclusion from the formal economy is, therefore, a leading cause of persistent poverty.

CGAP, a global partnership of development organizations that focuses on improving financial inclusion for people living in poverty, reported in 2023 that approximately $68 billion was contributed to international financial inclusion projects in 2021. Public funders accounted for $45 billion of that amount and the rest came from private funders. Development finance institutions are still the largest funders of financial inclusion efforts, followed by bilateral and multilateral funders.

If we analyze these amounts in relation to the funding's purpose, we discover that 41 percent went to financial service providers, albeit in the form of loans (debt). Approximately 7 percent in 2021 went to a category called "market support actors." This category includes entities like NGOs, foundations, facilitators, digital and market infrastructure actors, and academic institutions— all of which strengthen infrastructure and build the knowledge base to make financial markets more inclusive, efficient, and responsible. Governments received about 3 percent of the 2021 total, usually in the form of grants. About 20 percent of those grants to governments aided with advancing digital finance measures in responsible ways.

In this context, it is important to understand that some public funders, most frequently multilateral ones, employ a mechanism known as "policy-based lending." This is a means of supporting partner governments to achieve medium- to long-term sustainable development outcomes.[48] Such funding is also referred to as "development policy financing" or budget support. Regardless of terminology, policy-based lending is a distinct mechanism that is usually debt-based, non-earmarked budget financing designed to advance government reforms.[49]

CGAP, in the 2023 survey, excluded policy-based lending values because that category represents fungible (albeit conditional) liquidity for the recipient, not defined project activities. Nevertheless, this type of programming plays an important role in advancing financial inclusion. For example, the World Bank noted that policy-based lending activities have helped to narrow gender gaps in access to financial services.[50] The 2021 survey uncovered thirty-seven active projects with some connection to financial inclusion objectives, totaling $6 billion. In short, policy-based lending was a key component of the pandemic crisis response in 2020 and 2021.

I approached CGAP to seek information on *actual disbursements* as opposed to *commitments*. In reply, CGAP said they typically ask funders to provide that information. As a result, CGAP has not, historically at least, obtained good data about actual disbursements. In fact, CGAP could not even provide me with an estimated figure.

That said, the CGAP dataset shows that various entities had at least promised to disburse $983 million for financial inclusion efforts in Pakistan in 2021, an amount that has been fairly consistent since 2017. Understandably, CGAP was unable to provide a cumulative commitment figure or credible disbursement number.

How much of the promised money was disbursed and where did it go? To answer those questions, we need to look more closely at Pakistan's overall financial sector.

Pakistan's Financial Sector

I spent the most fulfilling part of my career at the State Bank of Pakistan (SBP). In the 1990s, Pakistan implemented financial sector reforms that, like many emerging economies, expelled most forms of government repression. This gave the SBP freedom and independence to make the best economic and policy decisions for the country with less political interference, which in turn improved the domestic financial system. However, the challenge was to enhance the broader population's access to financial services.

Pakistan's financial sector is mainly regulated by the SBP and the Securities Exchange Commission of Pakistan (SECP). The SBP supervises banks, development finance institutions, microfinance banks, digital banks, and exchange companies. The SECP supervises the remaining financial institutions, which include insurance companies, asset management companies and mutual funds, leasing companies, modarabas, venture capital firms, and nonbank microfinance institutions. The SBP has a robust supervision regime that has the capability to rapidly identify various risks. However, before the reforms, the SBP struggled to improve the population's access to banking services. Mainstream commercial banks only provided banking services to corporates, businesses, and high-net-worth individuals.

Beginning in the 1990s, the government began to build a foundation for the national microfinance sector. This work included the establishment of Pakistan's first microfinance bank, the Khushhali Bank, which received funding from the Asian Development Bank. The bank also received World Bank credit in the amount of $90 million for an apex-funding body called the Pakistan Poverty Alleviation Fund (PPAF).

Pakistan was the first country in South Asia to issue a microfinance law—the Microfinance Institutions Ordinance of 2001. It paved the way for the creation of second-tier banks with lower capital requirements. These banks catered to low-income segments of society, which previously had been excluded from mainstream commercial banks. The law significantly helped to develop the financial sector. It also provided legislation for NGOs to become SBP-supervised microfinance banks thereby improving protection for depositors while also safeguarding these institutions against political and other interferences. Microfinance banks were allowed to mobilize public deposits as the cheapest way to fund their loan portfolios. By 2007, six had been established, but most were struggling to be financially and operationally sustainable. On the other hand, the unregulated, non-deposit-taking microfinance institutions (MFIs), which were reliant on charity or donor funds, were also unable to achieve scale.

The playing field for microfinance providers was not level. Some institutions, such as the Khushhali Bank and Kashf Foundation, had privileged access to donor and/or government funding, giving them an artificial edge. Subsidies were operational with a low client-retention ratio, which raised questions about whether resources were deployed fairly.

As a whole, the microfinance sector had only nine hundred thousand active borrowers by the end of December 2006. The industry struggled to become a dynamic participant within the financial sector.

The year 2007 heralded a second phase in which the policy and strategy aimed to accelerate growth in a sustainable manner. The governor, a small team in the SBP, and I envisioned the transformation of microfinance into a dynamic industry that was integrated with the overall financial system. We wanted to provide financial services to underserved economic and geographic segments through self-sustaining business models and demand-driven products. We also wanted to maintain high standards of governance and service delivery, all supported by an agile regulatory environment. With this strategic vision, we began the mission of advancing financial inclusion in the country.

We immediately faced many barriers, including limited HR

capacity, out-of-date technology, a lack of diversified funding sources, and high credit risk, to name a few. The Khushhali Bank had widespread district coverage with 290,000 borrowers, but it operated under its own law, which gave it an artificially competitive edge. Although it had access to donor funding, the bank had no incentive to mobilize deposits because financial intermediation was so inefficient. Most importantly, its low client retention ratio raised questions about whether the bank was effectively deploying resources and about its general operational efficiency.

Another issue facing the microfinance sector was the inefficient and ineffective model of the Pakistan Poverty Alleviation Fund (PPAF), which operated as an autonomous, not-for-profit company. Founded in 2000, the PPAF emerged as a wholesale supplier of donor-financed credit lines. It provided subsidized funding and capacity building grants, mainly to unregulated microfinance institutions and rural support programs. As a result, the National Rural Support Program, the largest rural retailer of microfinance (reaching 250,000 clients), did have much impact on poverty reduction. Many questioned the NRSP's sustainability, in part because it appeared to be overly dependent on PPAF funding.

Microfinance institutions and NGOs that operated as societies or companies did not accept deposits. This forced them to rely on charities or donor funds. These institutions enjoyed income tax exemptions whereas all deposit-taking microfinance banks were subject to normal income tax. This arrangement delayed the transformation of the microfinance institutions and NGOs into microfinance *banks,* prolonging their inability to accept public deposits, which is the cheapest and most sustainable source of funding.

Therefore, the key barrier to improving Pakistan's financial inclusion was the financial and operational sustainability of microfinance businesses. Complex geographical conditions in Pakistan hindered the building of brick-and-mortar microfinance bank branches. It would have taken years to reach potential clients, thereby leaving a stubborn gap between the supply of and demand for microfinance services. This reality created an urgency to deploy technology and alternate delivery channels, such as Kenya's successful branchless banking model M-Pesa.

So, what was needed to turn the situation around? We needed to commercialize the industry and that required up-scaling microfinance, both in terms of outreach and segmentation. To enhance sustainability, we had to develop and promote a shared vision of financial inclusion; enact policies and regulations; diversify funding sources; invest in systems and human resources; enhance market information to improve integrity; and foster partnerships with national and international players.

Accordingly, the SBP spearheaded its National Microfinance Strategy in 2007.[51] The SBP played a leading role in reforming key institutions. This work involved the legal conversion and divestiture of shareholding in Khushhali Bank, and the transformation of the NRSP into a microfinance bank. To encourage the transformation of NGOs into microfinance institutions, Pakistan (in June 2007) allowed a five-year income tax holiday to microfinance *banks*. The country also helped two of the world's largest microfinance institutions (i.e., ASA and BRAC) to begin operations in Pakistan in 2008. To provide long-term support to our microfinance strategy, the SBP negotiated funding assistance from the UK's Department for International Development (DFID), which shared our desire to implement a large financial inclusion program in the country.[52]

In 2007, we implemented a country-wide, demand-side Access to Finance survey.[53] The results showed that Pakistan had one of the lowest levels of financial inclusion in the world, with only 12 percent of the adult population having access to formal financial services. Another 32 percent had access to informal financial service, and 56 percent of the population was totally excluded. This was an alarming and overwhelming challenge for the central bank. Despite considerable support from the government, donors, and the SBP, the microfinance sector had only been able to connect with a small fraction of the potential market. As for the commercial banks, they were not too interested in serving Pakistan's poor and low-income communities.

In 2008, Pakistan's financial inclusion program received its first foreign funding support, an amount of £50 million approved under the "Pakistan: Financial Inclusion Program." This was a tripartite agreement among the DFID, the government of Pakistan, and the SBP, which served as the grant recipient and assumed responsibility for implementing the program. To accomplish these measures, the SBP set up the Financial Inclusion Program Office (FIP) where I led a small team.

At this point, the goal was to eliminate market failure by improving access to financial services for poor and marginalized groups, and for small enterprises. We worked in that direction along with the UK's team at DFID, which entrusted the program's design to a UK-based consulting firm called Oxford Policy Management. The program's overarching objective was to systematically address industry bottlenecks while simultaneously fostering market-based funding mechanisms and ensuring the self-sufficiency of microfinance institutions. By doing so, it sought to alleviate the liquidity constraints faced by microfinance providers.

The two inaugural implementation facilities began to operate on December 19, 2008.[54] Both were designed in-house within two months by the small FIP team. Although Oxford Policy Management had originally allocated £144,000 for technical consultants to design these two facilities, the FIP team designed them both with no financial incentives. Had we chosen to procure and engage a consultancy firm (with an allocated budget of £10 million), which is always a protracted process, we would not have been able to launch these facilities for at least a year.

It is not necessary to understand the organizational details of the implementation facilities, but it is helpful to understand their basic functions. Our Pakistani team was better able to design them to meet on-the-ground needs within the local context. What follows is a brief description of both.

The first was called the Microfinance Credit Guarantee Facility (MCGF). Its purpose was to foster market development by incentivizing the flow of funds from commercial banks to the microfinance sector. We did that by mitigating the risk perception associated with the sector thereby encouraging mainstream banks to extend credit to them. This facility worked to familiarize mainstream banks with microfinance clients, ultimately leading to the borrower's "graduation" within the financial system. The SBP, operating through its subsidiary, provided partial guarantees to cover the principal in case of default. The SBP also provided guarantees to cover any initial losses, limited to a specified percentage of the principal amount. By extending these guarantees to banks and development financial institutions, we reduced the perceived risk premium. This mechanism also allowed the guarantee fund to be leveraged multiple times.

Banks were responsible for due diligence analyses of interested microfinance banks and institutions. This approach facilitated credit enhancement, and it empowered banks and development financial institutions to gain a more thorough understanding of the risks associated with microfinance. Furthermore, the MCGF played a crucial role in addressing regulatory concerns that had previously hindered unsecured lending by banks and development financial institutions. The SBP posted detailed guidelines about these principles on its website, improving transparency.[55]

The FIP team constantly engaged with market players, formally and informally, to educate them about the MCGF and its objectives. Having strong rapport as fellow Pakistanis, we presented the business case for supporting viable microfinance providers to achieve outreach targets, and we addressed banks' concerns and apprehensions. During our initial interactions with the corporate and commercial heads of banks, some asked us to suggest a few microfinance banks so that they could fund them under the MCGF. We clarified that our intent was not to strike a few isolated deals for the mere success of the MCGF. Instead, we told them that our objective was to broaden market development while diminishing the banks' risk perception about the microfinance sector. We encouraged banks to conduct *their own* due diligence, thereby establishing a sustainable source of wholesale funding for the sector.

This approach eventually paid off. By 2015, forty-six guarantees had been issued under the MCGF to mobilize Rs16 billion in private funding from commercial banks and retail investors. This funding provided loans to more than eight hundred thousand micro borrowers, many of them poor.

In essence, the FIP managed to leverage £15 million in donor funding to achieve a major objective, all *without spending a penny.* The donor money was invested by the SBP in treasury bills, yielding substantial profits in the process. Our work and successes serve as a classic example of how an in-country staff can often outperform foreign consultants.

The second facility established by the FIP in 2008 was called the Institutional Strengthening Fund (ISF). We knew that microfinance providers needed help to put their own houses in order so that they could meet the banks' due diligence criteria. We also wanted to help microfinance providers develop the capacity to improve their services to clients, in part by investing in their human resources. With these goals in mind, we launched the ISF to provide grants to strengthen the microfinance sector and transform microfinance institutions into licensed microfinance banks. We ensured that grants were provided exclusively for transformational objectives. We did not disburse funds for operational expenses.

The ISF approved grants totaling Rs703 million for twenty-six projects that supported fifteen microfinance institutions and banks—more than 60 percent of the microfinance sector. The only entities left out were the NGOs and microfinance institutions that demonstrated little commitment to growth.

In addition to the two facilities described above, the FIP established in 2010 a Credit Guarantee Scheme (CGS) for small and rural enterprises. The program aimed to encourage lending to new and collateral-deficient borrowers. The CGS covered up to 60 percent of credit-loss risk for institutions that offered financing to small and rural enterprises. The CGS involved sixteen participating financial institutions with allocated credit exposure limits of

Rs8.4 billion. Compared with the MCGF, this guarantee was not incredibly successful in terms of its overall impact on lending to small and medium enterprises. The banks were risk-averse in relation to small and medium enterprises, and if they had offered zero-risk coverage it would have promoted moral hazard.

Finally, to spur innovations in the financial sector, the FIP launched three rounds of the Financial Innovation Challenge Fund (FICF). The first effort promoted digital and branchless banking, which, *inter alia*, helped launch Pakistan's first and now largest branchless banking model, Easypaisa. The second FICF round promoted innovative rural and agricultural financial services. And the third established Centers of Excellence in Islamic Finance at three universities, which trained professionals to improve the Islamic banking industry by addressing faith-based exclusion.

We also set up a steering committee, chaired by the SBP governor, for strategic oversight of the program, and technical committees to make operational decisions for each program component. This was aimed at ensuring the highest governance standards, transparency, and accountability. In addition to the central bank's robust internal controls and IMF-approved accounting and auditing standards, the auditor-general of Pakistan scrutinized the FIP every year. The small team dedicated to program management comprised regular SBP employees, people who did not receive any bonuses and other financial incentives. The SBP also did not charge any program management fees to the UK's aid agency (the DFID).

Alongside the FIP, the State Bank of Pakistan introduced a specialized microfinance policy and regulatory framework based on pioneering global best practices. These regulations and supervisory mechanisms helped microfinance banks develop viable business models to realize sustainable growth. The success of microfinance regulations and market development in Pakistan was widely acknowledged by the international community. *The Economist* ranked Pakistan's regulatory framework as the best in the world in 2010 and 2011, and third best in its Economist Intelligence Unit (EIU) reports for 2012 and 2013. During and after those years, Pakistan's efforts to revolutionize microfinance remained in the international spotlight, including at the Arab Policy Forum in 2012, the SAARC Central Bank Governors Symposium in 2015 in Dhaka, Bangladesh, and the World Bank conferences of 2014 and 2015 in Morocco, and in the Netherlands—to name a few.

Alongside these efforts, Pakistan established a microfinance-specific Credit Information Bureau to address the problem of multiple borrowings and over-indebtedness. The MCGF facility helped commercial banks gain more confidence in the microfinance sector, which in turn mobilized substantial wholesale funding from commercial banks and capital markets. Many of these borrowers also benefited from a national financial literacy program designed to educate low-income citizens about basic financial concepts.

As the sector evolved, the SBP strengthened the regulatory framework with an enhanced focus on financial stability. The central bank did this, in part, by revising its minimum capital requirement for microfinance banks in 2011 while allowing the existing microfinance banks to raise the prescribed minimum paid-up capital in a phased manner over the next three years. This step ensured that only entities with adequate financial resources could establish microfinance banks. Additional policies promoted market-based financial services to meet the diverse needs of low-income households and microenterprises.[56]

The Impact of the FIP Initiatives

In December 2007, Pakistan's microfinance sector comprised only six microfinance banks with a total equity of Rs3.4 billion. These banks had about 150,000 depositors and nearly a million borrowers. The micro banking industry was struggling to achieve scale and sustainability, and it faced a dearth of human resources to foster growth. They all struggled to obtain commercial funding to finance their loan portfolios.

Seven years down the road, there were ten microfinance banks in the country and some nonregulated (credit only) institutions, reflecting a growing private sector participation and improved institutional diversity. The sector was catering to more than 2.8 million borrowers by the end of 2014. The microfinance banks served 42 percent of those borrowers. In December 2014, there were almost 5.7 million depositors. That number grew by an average yearly amount of 69 percent. Most importantly, the microfinance banks reported deposits totaling Rs43 billion in December 2014 with an average annual growth rate of 47 percent. These deposits had exceeded the gross loan portfolio of Rs37 billion as of December 2015, suggesting that the microfinance banks had attained long-term funding sustainability. During this period, these microfinance banks provided loans at an average annual growth rate of 35 percent, capturing a 60 percent share in the sector's gross loan portfolio. The micro banking industry held equity of more than Rs14 billion as of December 2014, compared to just Rs3.4 billion in December 2007. The average loan size more than tripled between 2007 and 2014. This growth led to improved injections of domestic and foreign equity in the industry.

By 2015, Pakistan had eight fully functional models of digital and branchless banking. These included the pioneering Easypaisa by Tameer Microfinance Bank (2009), MobiCash by Waseela Microfinance Bank and Mobilink (2012), and UPaisa by U Microfinance Bank and Ufone (2013). Easypaisa is the third largest branchless banking model in the world. The microfinance market had healthy competition, strong private sector players, diversified financial services, and innovative business models. All microfinance banks are privately owned. Strong market potential and a supportive regulatory framework helped to expand ownership of the microfinance banks. These banks saw an influx of international investors, banks, development agencies, investment funds, mobile network operators, and large domestic microfinance institutions, which diversified their approaches to serving clients.

Benefitting from well-timed, far-sighted, and market-based regulations, the microfinance sector in Pakistan in 2015 was ready to grow into a burgeoning industry. The SBP had catalyzed the growth of Pakistan's private microfinance sector, and the State Bank of Pakistan continued to manage systemic risks. As a result, microfinance in the country moved from a donor-dependent, subsidy-driven sector into a dynamic industry providing a broad range of financial services to financially excluded citizens through self-sustaining business models and demand-driven products.

The FIP's interventions addressed the problem of asymmetric information by developing market infrastructure and promoting institutional and technological innovations, such as digital and branchless banking. Large unregulated microfinance institutions became microfinance banks regulated by the central bank. The program promoted competition, addressed inefficiencies in the microfinance industry and agricultural credit market, and strengthened governance.

We can also assess the outcomes by looking at international third-party reviews of Pakistan's microfinance efforts. One example was provided by the UK's Independent Commission for Aid Effectiveness, which rated the FIP as a well-managed program. Objective internal studies also showed the program's success. In 2015, the SBP repeated the Access to Finance Survey. The results revealed that citizens' access to formal financial services increased from 12 percent in 2008 to 23 percent in 2015. The adult population with a bank account increased from 11 percent in 2008 to 16 percent in 2015. Women's access to financial services expanded from 4 percent in 2008 to 16 percent in 2015. Thus, by 2015, the trajectory of microfinance was set to achieve the long-term vision of "financial inclusion for all."

More recent results provide robust evidence of the sector's growth, long-term sustainability, increased financial inclusion, and improved digitalization. Specifically, by the end of June 2024, deposits at microfinance banks have surpassed Rs640 billion, which is much higher than the loan portfolio of Rs376 billion. This was accomplished despite the setbacks caused by the Covid-19 pandemic, which were further compounded by the catastrophic floods in fiscal year 2023 and the ensuing macroeconomic challenges. Moreover, digital and mobile phone banking has increased the number of small borrowers to more than seven million in fiscal year 2024.[57]

Since 2015, Pakistan's digital payments landscape has continued to see remarkable growth. In a bid to foster innovation, financial inclusion, and affordable digital financial services, the

SBP approved in principle to establish five digital retail banks in September 2023.

The private sector in recent years has launched many innovative digital products and services. These new services have made digital payments more convenient, secure, and efficient for customers. During fiscal year 2024, there was a 40 percent increase (compared to the previous year) of digital transactions processed by banks, microfinance banks, and electronic money institutions—a total of nearly 2.7 million transactions. The share of digital payments in relation to all payments grew by 82 percent in fiscal year 2024. This dramatic increase occurred as more people adopted mobile banking apps and internet banking to transfer funds and pay bills. In fiscal year 2024, the number of digital banking transactions reached approximately 1.3 billion transactions, with a monetary value of Rs69.8 trillion.[58]

The FIP was originally designed as a five-year program from 2008-2013, but it was later extended on a yearly basis. By 2015, the program had successfully achieved its transformational objectives, having catalyzed the donor funds.

Success Despite Outside Pressures

Pakistan's Financial Inclusion Program is a story of transformation and accountability. The success of this independent program can be attributed to a strategic vision, intellectual integrity, unwavering commitment, professionalism, accountability, and an unrelenting desire to produce tangible results. The FIP team pursued "value for money" in every decision between 2008 to 2015.

We remembered that the FIP funds came from the generosity of UK citizens who intended to uplift Pakistan's poor and low-income people. We regarded this money as a sacred trust.

However, we encountered individuals and organizations who saw this money as an opportunity to advance their own ambitions. This created tension between us (the FIP team) and those who wanted the money. Early on, we encountered a request from DFID to allocate £2 million from the technical assistance component to the International Finance Corporation (IFC) for the purpose of enhancing financing for small and medium enterprises. This request was based on the premise that the IFC possessed expertise in these enterprises. To us, this request was surprising and seemingly at odds with the FIP's framework. It would have diverted grant funds from the FIP to an international public organization designed to finance technical and commercial assistance.

The FIP team, including me, firmly declined the request. I communicated our stance to the head of economic growth at the DFID, emphasizing that the request was not consistent with the FIP framework. Thankfully, he understood our concerns and the idea was dropped. Unfortunately, the issue resurfaced about two years later. The DFID staff and the IFC once again vigorously campaigned for the diversion of those funds. Ultimately, despite our strong dissent, they successfully obtained £2 million from the FIP grant for the IFC, which then provided technical assistance to a rich UAE-based bank to build capacity in banking for small and medium enterprises.

Within the dynamics of donor community work, expenditures often take precedence over prudent financial management, even if it means dispersing funds haphazardly. To exert pressure on the FIP team, even junior DFID staff would visit the State Bank of Pakistan's governor and deputy governor to express their concerns about the "under-utilization" of the FIP funds. Our response was consistent: The FIP initiatives were specifically intended for the microfinance sector and small and medium enterprises. We added that the UK had designated the £20 million to provide two credit guarantees aimed at reducing banks' risk perceptions. Unless there were calls on those guarantees, which was theoretically unlikely, the agreement was to *not spend* these funds. As stated earlier, we prudently invested this money in treasury bills to generate profits. Furthermore, DFID staff, who were not supposed to act independently, also networked extensively with microfinance industry players, government officials, and senior banking professionals across Pakistan, creating the impression that they held the FIP purse strings.

Despite these challenges, the FIP team and I steadfastly maintained financial discipline and minimized fiduciary risks by adhering to the FIP goals and targets, ensuring value for money, and adhering to the established governance structure. To use donor funds for other purposes would have perpetuated inefficiencies and contradicted our mission.

These types of problems occur because the donor community creates perverse incentives that run counter to the Paris Declaration on Aid Effectiveness. This declaration calls donor countries and organizations to collaborate, streamline procedures, and share information. Nevertheless, the USAID in Pakistan competed with other donors, including the UK Aid-sponsored Financial Inclusion Program (FIP). For example, as the FIP gained recognition for its impactful interventions, the USAID initially sought to establish its own credit guarantee fund for small and medium enterprises. Not much happened, despite more than a year of discussions. But, to capitalize on the FIP's success, the USAID in Pakistan provided a grant of $170,000 to Telenor, a Norwegian corporate sponsor of Tameer Microfinance Bank, which had already received financing through the FIP for its first branchless banking product, Easypaisa.[59]

If international donor agencies are competing to provide funds to wealthy and profitable corporations, then taxpayers in donor countries should reconsider whether they should keep funding the system. The system enables donors to gain influence, and sometimes outright control, over nearly every sphere of life in developing countries. And that influence rarely helps in any meaningful way. The donors must accept responsibility for their role in these affairs.

By contrast, consider the financial effectiveness of Pakistan's local teams who worked for the State Bank of Pakistan and the FIP. The SBP, as an institution, was not the direct beneficiary of the program. Of the £50 million in the FIP funds, only 1 percent of the total was earmarked to build the SBP's capacity. As such, the FIP was meant to benefit only the microfinance sector and small and medium enterprises, with the goal of improving the lives of people in need. The FIP agreement with the UK government made these objectives very clear, stipulating that the £50 million was a "grant" that *could not be reclaimed.* The agreement included a provision to allocate any unutilized funds at the program's conclusion toward similar objectives.

Overall, the SBP governors and the FIP team brought about innovations in international development that saved millions of dollars in UK taxpayers' money. Despite these achievements, the DFID staff finally managed to hijack the FIP funding. The staff dispersed the money without adequately addressing market failures and without properly assessing the financial health of each recipient institution. Some funding went to *unregulated* microfinance institutions, even though the recently regulated microfinance sector had achieved financial and social sustainability. These types of decisions diluted efforts to expand the number of self-sufficient microfinance organizations. More importantly, the DFID used the FIP grant to create new institutions that did not contribute to poverty alleviation or inclusive growth—a classic example of "mission drift" in the UK government's international development strategy.

This story demonstrates that dedicated and qualified workers in developing countries can do a better job of creating and managing context-relevant aid programs—and a better job of deploying donor funding—than international aid organizations or their consultants. It also shows that donor agencies are hesitant to admit those successes.

CHAPTER 6

The Hijacking of Pakistan's Self-Sustaining Development Program

As our next step, we at the SBP developed Pakistan's first-ever National Financial Inclusion Strategy (NFIS) to push forward the reforms described in the previous chapter. The aim was to leverage technological solutions designed to increase the access, usage, and quality of financial services across the country. The primary objective of the NFIS was to set the national vision for achieving universal financial inclusion in Pakistan.

Unlike the microfinance strategies of 2007 and 2011, we decided in 2015 to collaborate with the World Bank. We knew that the World Bank was unlikely to propose cutting-edge solutions for our challenges, but we wanted to put a World Bank "tag" on our efforts to hopefully gain broader acceptance from policymakers, donors, and other stakeholders. The NFIS was subsequently launched and officially adopted by the government of Pakistan in May 2015.[60]

As described in the previous chapter, the UK's Department of International Development (DFID)—now the Foreign, Commonwealth and Development Office or FCDO—took control of Pakistan's unutilized grant funding, which had been designated to further advance financial inclusion efforts in the country. Pakistan's Financial Inclusion Program (FIP), which had been managed by the State Bank of Pakistan, soon fell under the control of donor agencies and their consultants who typically lacked commitment, relevant expertise, and strategic vision and mission. These entities operated without the strong institutional support that the State Bank of Pakistan had provided. Thus, the FCDO began to disburse the funds independently.

Up to that point in the story, the SBP had been overseeing the Credit Guarantee Scheme (CGS) for Small and Rural Enterprises since March 2010. As a reminder, this program aimed to boost lending to new borrowers with inadequate collateral. It provided participating institutions with risk coverage of up to 60 percent for credit losses on their financing to small, micro, and rural enterprises. When the British took control of the FIP's grant funding, the SBP still needed a market-based mechanism to offer risk sharing to financial institutions in the SME sector. So, the SBP established the Pakistan Credit Guarantee Company (PCGC) to fill the gap. The Federal Cabinet approved its designation as a development finance institution on June 11, 2019, and the PCGC began operations in December of the same year.

However, on December 24, 2020, under pressure from the DFID, Pakistan's government approved the sale of its majority stakes in the PCGC to the UK government. This transpired through a UK entity called Karandaaz Pakistan. The transaction occurred by *converting the FIP grant into equity*. That move raised serious legal concerns and prompted strong objections from Pakistan's Ministry of Finance.

As mentioned earlier, the UK government initially provided

the FIP with a £50 million grant in 2008. An agreement was signed by the DFID, the Economic Affairs Division of Pakistan, and the State Bank of Pakistan. Under this agreement, the grant money was part of the federal consolidated fund, meaning that Pakistan's Finance Division held proprietary rights over the funds and earned a markup. Therefore, because PCGC was government-owned, any proper sale or transfer of the funds required adherence to a competitive bidding process. Karandaaz Pakistan, a Section 42 company, also needed SECP approval of any shareholding changes.

Those actions apparently did not occur. An amendment in January 2015 contradicted the original agreement by reverting the unspent funds back to the DFID.[61] As a result, the DFID used the FIP's grant as equity, which meant that the DFID became a shareholder of PCGC. The State Bank of Pakistan had issued Rs4 billion in guarantees for loans to small and medium enterprises against the UK grant of Rs2 billion, but the government approved a transfer of Rs4.1 billion in shares to the DFID-sponsored firm. The deal obviously raised concerns. Grants are typically non-refundable, and they cannot be converted into equity. Nevertheless, Pakistan's cabinet proceeded to convert grants into equity held by a foreign country. Converting the FIP grant into UK government equity also cast doubts about transparency. The move set a precedent for other donor agencies to demand similar conversions, potentially leading to the loss of control over assets funded by grants. In a stronger legal, democratic, and institutional context than Pakistan's, such a decision would have been countered by serious challenges. This example illustrates how donor funding in developing countries can compromise national sovereignty.

A Closer Look at Karandaaz Pakistan

Karandaaz Pakistan, a UK entity, was set up as a special purpose vehicle registered under Section 42 of the Companies Ordinance in August 2014. It became the implementation partner of two UK programs—the Enterprise and Assets Growth Programme and Sustainable Energy and Economic Development—controlled by the Foreign, Commonwealth and Development Office (FCDO). One was co-funded by grants from the Bill and Melinda Gates Foundation for digital financial services.

Karandaaz is a nonprofit organization set up to help small businesses gain access to financing through commercially directed investments, and it promotes financial inclusion by deploying digital solutions. Karandaaz invests growth capital in small and medium enterprises with the objective of generating commercial financial returns for Karandaaz and helping to create more employment opportunities in Pakistan.

At the time of this writing, Karandaaz had provided liquidity to six banks and financial institutions with the objective of improving commercial lending for small and medium enterprises in Pakistan.[62] The profile of these banks raises serious questions about the mandate of donors and their interventions. For example, despite the economic stress that occurred in 2023 and 2024 in Pakistan, all recipient banks already had impressive financial and operating performance. One recipient bank reported a pre-tax profit of Rs85 billion in the year ending December 31, 2024. The annual profit of that bank was more than double Karandaaz's total assets of Rs40 billion. One wonders why rich banks would need donor funding as a risk-sharing facility designed to support small businesses. In my view, these banks already had plenty of liquidity (up to trillions of rupees). The arrangement also raised questions about the UK government's development aid strategy for Pakistan—and for other developing countries. Credit guarantees are valuable during the initial phase of donor interventions, as they help address financial institutions' risk perceptions; however, it is difficult to justify their use for an indefinite period. As a reminder, the Credits Guarantee Scheme for small and medium enterprises was first launched by the SBP *in 2010.*

Karandaaz had also provided direct equity investments, called growth capital, to eight small and medium enterprises. These beneficiary companies included Pakistan's top pharmaceutical companies listed on the stock exchange. In addition, Karandaaz had provided growth capital to the auto industry, a poultry farm, a medical laboratory, a logistics company, an agriculture processing warehouse, and for the construction of a green building, among others.[63] These were all profitable, blue-chip companies. It is difficult to understand why these companies would need support from international donors. By investing in already-established businesses, Karandaaz appears to have shifted some resources away from the effort to improve financial inclusion for small and medium enterprises.

Karandaaz has also managed the Innovation Challenge Fund (ICF), which provides risk capital and grants to partners with the stated aim of generating innovative solutions for solving complex problems in areas of financial inclusion and entrepreneurship. The fund is especially focused on helping SMEs, women, and youth gain more access to financial services and formal participation in the economy.

What does the data show? In September 2010, there were 168,000 SME borrowers in Pakistan. That number increased to 189,507 by March 2020, before the Covid-19 pandemic. By January 2023, the number of SME borrowers had dropped to 155,000, despite the phenomenal growth of businesses that partner with banks and financial institutions. As a share of total private sector credit in Pakistan, financing for SMEs was 9.2 percent in December 2016. That percentage declined to 6.56 percent in March 2020. Since then, the percentage dropped to 5.2 percent in September 2024.

Interestingly, the data shows that Karandaaz's supply-driven wholesale financing support to a handful of select banks has not expanded the base of borrowers among small and medium enterprises. Of the 5.2 million SMEs in Pakistan, Karandaaz has supported 3,166 of them in ten years.

The Pakistan Microfinance Investment Company (PMIC)

The Pakistan Microfinance Investment Company was registered as a nonbank finance company in 2016. It is a wholesale investment finance firm established by Karandaaz along with the Pakistan Poverty Alleviation Fund (PPAF) and the German Development Bank (KFW). With a staff of thirty-five people, the PMIC's wholesale lending business serves around twenty-one microfinance institutions and five microfinance banks. The PMIC is effectively a spin-off of the PPAF's microfinance business. Mimicking the others, the PMIC has also launched a challenge fund to help owners of small farms gain access to finance and other value-added services through agricultural technology and microfinance providers. The PMIC provides wholesale lending (debt and equity) to twenty NGO microfinance institutions and rural support programs, but its publicity campaigns imply that it is the torchbearer for the country's financial inclusion achievements, including digital financial services, agricultural credit, and retail microfinance clients.

By June 2024, microfinance banks had successfully mobilized deposits totaling Rs640 billion, which is a substantial surplus compared to their gross loan portfolios of Rs376 billion. So, why do microfinance institutions still seek wholesale funding from the *donor-funded* PMIC? The FIP had previously steered the microfinance sector toward sustainable funding without ongoing reliance on donor support, at least for institutions that were willing to improve their internal operations. My view is that many donor-funded institutions cater more to the needs of the donors than to serving the interests of recipient countries.

There are plenty of financially healthy banks and nonbanking financial institutions that can provide Pakistan's small and medium enterprises with financing; however, Karandaaz has recently established yet another commercially driven and privately managed nonbank finance company called Parwaaz Financial Services Ltd (PFSL). This entity has been registered with the SECP to offer short-term and long-term loans, running finance, and cash finance. I fail to understand how this new finance company will help small and medium enterprises gain better access to funding than could be provided by the existing thirty-two banks and development finance institutions, nonbanking financial institutions, and Karandaaz itself. Karandaaz has not answered that question, at least not in its public relations statements. It has simply stated the problem without explaining why a new entity is needed.[64]

Karandaaz Digital

This Karandaaz entity offers technical assistance and services aimed at promoting financial inclusion through technological solutions. Its staff collaborates with national regulators, government entities, private corporations, and tech entrepreneurs to enhance the country's payment infrastructure, to facilitate the digitization of government-to-people payments, to streamline corporate supply chains, and to support fintech innovation within Pakistan. Thus, it operates in parallel with the central bank's efforts, capitalizing on the success of the State Bank of Pakistan's work to develop a modern and robust payment system in the country.

The SBP is the legitimate regulator of the payments and financial industry. It has played a pivotal role in promoting and developing digital financial services in the country for many years. The SBP has scaled up its policy efforts in recent years, in part by developing an interoperable payments infrastructure, issuing enabling regulations for retail payment providers and financial technology firms, ensuring the trust and security of digital payment channels, and promoting new technologies and innovations.

To improve Pakistan's digital payments landscape, the SBP—in partnership with the World Bank, national regulators, and industry players—has fostered a collaborative environment among stakeholders who share a common goal: digitizing the economy for the benefit of the Pakistani people.

In 2019, the SBP introduced the National Payment Systems Strategy (NPSS), which presented a roadmap for establishing a nationwide digital payments system aligned with international standards for safety, efficiency, and inclusiveness. The regulatory measures implemented by the SBP, as part of the NPSS, have played a crucial role in driving the adoption of digital channels throughout the country. These endeavors reached a significant milestone with the successful launch of the instant payment system, known as Raast, on January 11, 2021. Raast is a cutting-edge, interoperable, and secure payment platform designed to facilitate seamless, instant, and cost-effective fund transfers among consumers, merchants, and government entities. In 2022, the SBP launched a licensing and regulatory framework for setting up digital banks in Pakistan as a separate and distinct category in the banking business.

In this context, it should be clear that Karandaaz has been functioning like a typical donor organization. It has signed memorandums of understanding with the SBP to support the development of the national payments architecture. In March 2018, Karandaaz committed to assist the SBP in establishing a conducive environment for digital banks. Specifically, Karandaaz pledged to provide technical expertise to the SBP in formulating the legal and regulatory framework, including the criteria for licensing digital banks in Pakistan. Subsequently, on December 26, 2019, the SBP and Karandaaz forged another agreement to collaborate on the implementation of the micropayment gateway, a component of the National Financial Inclusion Strategy. The Bill and Melinda Gates Foundation provided funding to Karandaaz for this effort.

Although Karandaaz asserts its importance in these developments, the State Bank of Pakistan is the key policymaking institution. The SBP also possesses expertise in payment systems policy, regulations, and market development for digital financial inclusion. We might question why the SBP has formed agreements with Karandaaz when the SBP already has sufficient expertise in the payment systems landscape. Essentially, Karandaaz uses funds from the Gates Foundation to hire technical consultants for the central bank and other institutions. Nevertheless, Karandaaz is seen as a champion of digital financial inclusion in Pakistan.

We should also ask why the UK's Foreign, Commonwealth and Development Office created Karandaaz in the first place and then ask why Karandaaz has established even *more* affiliated organizations. These decisions substantially increase the costs paid by UK taxpayers, as evidenced in the Karandaaz financial statements. Karandaaz's consolidated expenditures for the year ending June 30, 2024 included projects costing nearly Rs1.551 billion. The statements also show expenditures of Rs371 million for operations support, Rs285 million for administration services, and write-off/impairment losses on financial assets of Rs449 million. Additionally, in the year ending December 31, 2023, the PMIC incurred administrative expenses of Rs510 million, of which Rs285 million was spent on wages, Rs37 million was spent on travel, and Rs38 million was spent on training.[65]

Here is the point: Karandaaz controls funds that were originally provided by UK taxpayers for a specific cause. It became a conduit for donor funding from the UK government and the Gates Foundation without, in my view, offering many improvements for small and medium enterprises, job creation (except for its own employees), inclusive growth, or poverty alleviation.

Infrazamin Pakistan

This institution was set up as a for-profit credit enhancement facility in November 2020 with equity capital from Karandaaz (40 percent) and InfraCo Asia Investments (60 percent).[66] Infrazamin aims to fill gaps in local credit markets to catalyze greater private sector participation in the long-term, local currency financing of Pakistan's infrastructure. It promises to provide guarantees to enhance the credit quality of local currency debt instruments for that purpose.

Pakistan spends only 2.1 percent of its GDP on infrastructure, which has led to a widening infrastructure deficit. Therefore, Infrazamin, in theory, has significant potential to "crowd in" the underutilized pockets of liquidity in Pakistan's financial markets. However, it is fair to ask how its mandate aligns with donor objectives; after all, it operates as a commercially driven organization that makes investments in large infrastructure projects in partnership with Asian investment funds. Meanwhile, its website highlights a flurry of typical activities that donor agencies undertake to showcase their activities without revealing their on-the-ground results. The site is full of self-congratulatory awards and highlights infrastructure gaps to justify its limited activities.[67] With Karandaaz holding a 40 percent share of this entity, we should ask whether Infrazamin truly serves the intended donor purpose.

The National Credit Guarantee Company Limited (NCGCL)

Karandaaz launched the NCGCL in partnership with Pakistan's Ministry of Finance in January 2024. This entity uses the design and architecture developed under the FIP credit guarantee for small and medium enterprises, but Karandaaz boasts about NCGCL in its publicity campaign as "the first-ever specialized SME credit guarantee company in Pakistan, and an important component of the financial system architecture of the country."

It is worth mentioning that the National Credit Guarantee Company Limited was inaugurated by Dr. Shamshad Akhter, the caretaker finance minister, on January 12, 2024.[68] While highlighting the significance of the credit guarantee firm, the minister called it a revolutionary initiative.[69] It was stated at the event that NCGCL would prepare financial products for 1.5 million small and medium enterprises. The establishment of the NCGCL was heralded as a landmark institutional reform designed to boost small and medium enterprises and thus pave the way for sustainable economic growth and development in Pakistan.[70]

Dr. Akhter previously served as the State Bank of Pakistan governor. She approved and inaugurated the Credit Guarantee Scheme for small and medium enterprises under the FIP back in 2010. NCGCL has simply given a company structure to the design and architecture of the FIP plan. It was certainly not an innovation introduced by Karandaaz, as they claim. In fact, considering the potential administrative costs of running the company, this new program was perhaps a bad idea. It will certainly benefit the highly paid NCGCL staff and further increase the already growing influence of the FCDO.

The Imitation Game

Unlike the FIP interventions and initiatives that were focused on market development, the activities after 2015 have revolved around supply-driven investments that rely on networking and relationships. This in turn has promised lucrative careers to those working with Karandaaz and its subsidiary institutions. These supply-driven efforts, however, lack original ideas or innovations. Instead, they frequently mimic existing concepts. Donor agencies involved in the financial sector have duplicated many strategies, such as risk-sharing credit enhancement facilities; wholesale capital provided to banks for financing small and medium enterprises; financial innovation challenge funds; capacity building funds; support for digital financial services; and initiatives in agricultural finance. Karandaaz even rebranded the FIP's Access to Finance surveys, which were conducted in 2008 and 2015. In 2023, Karandaaz called the replicated survey the Karandaaz Financial Inclusion Survey (K-FIS). Furthermore, the data portal and dashboards on the Karandaaz website look like a State Bank of Pakistan website, seemingly to take credit for both past and present SBP efforts.

The Erosion of Pakistan's National Sovereignty

In a significant and unexpected move, Karandaaz Pakistan began using funds from the Gates Foundation ($4 million) to support the digitalization of Pakistan's tax system and to overhaul the Federal Board of Revenue (FBR). Karandaaz hired a consulting firm to assess the existing IT infrastructure, systems, and business processes to establish the context and scope of digitalizing the country's tax system.[71] This move received extensive press coverage.[72]

An agreement between the FBR, the Gates Foundation, and Karandaaz Pakistan—an entity sponsored by the UK's Foreign, Commonwealth and Development Office—was signed on March 15, 2024. The agreement aimed to address the FBR's inefficiencies related to broadening the tax base and improving collection rates. The agreement is valid for at least two years. Karandaaz will enlist a consulting firm known for crafting comprehensive digital strategies and implementing programs tailored for large public sector organizations, with a focus on tax regulatory authorities. In collaboration with the Gates Foundation, Karandaaz will work closely with the FBR, providing financial and technical assistance, as well as necessary support and services essential for the digitalization of the tax system.

It is regrettable that Karandaaz has been tasked with modernizing the tax system. Prior to the agreement described above, the finance minister had pledged to digitize the FBR while eradicating corruption and revenue leakages. The involvement of Karandaaz and all its subsidiaries indicates that donors have penetrated various strategic areas, possibly taking control over policymaking and management processes.

The failure of successive foreign-funded projects is startling. These failures include the World Bank's $149 million Tax Administration Reform Project (TARP), the $400 million Pakistan Raises Revenue (PRR) project, and the Asian Development Bank's $300 million Domestic Resource Mobilization program. These projects included the FBR's IT upgrade effort. More worrying is the ongoing reliance on contractors. Does anyone really believe that Karandaaz-hired consultants could possibly make meaningful contributions toward improving Pakistan's taxation systems after seeing two decades of failures by World Bank and ADB consultants?

Moreover, it is alarming that Pakistan's Federal Board of Revenue (FBR) will provide Karandaaz with potentially confidential information, such as existing assessment reports, tax reform agendas, vision documents, and data supposedly to facilitate the provision of technical assistance. Pakistan appears to be allowing blatant encroachment on its state functions by organizations that have provided only minor financial contributions. Why does Pakistan's tax authority, the FBR, which collects over Rs9 trillion in revenue annually, need to surrender its institutional independence and national pride in exchange for a mere $4 million, money that will quickly be paid to a consulting firm? Tax collection is a primary function of *the state*. Karandaaz and its consultants are now tasked with "revolutionizing" Pakistan's tax system. It's incredulous!

These endeavors compromise the sovereignty and national dignity of Pakistan. I wonder whether the FCDO would dare to consider establishing a similar arrangement in the UK or India. Is there any precedent in the world where a national tax authority has sought assistance from a foreign foundation to digitalize its tax administration? This intrusion has occurred because weak policymakers and insincere political leaders want to prioritize their positions over national pride and sovereignty.

It is not a stretch to conclude that Karandaaz now operates in Pakistan like the nineteenth-century East India Company. It attempts to infiltrate all sectors by using the FIP grant (UK taxpayers' money) and Gates Foundation funds. Consequently, the country sees almost no tangible benefits while allowing donors to dictate policies and effectively control the recipient organizations. Pakistan seems to have become a colony of donors, where the donors have established a state above the state, essentially paralyzing the government's role in formulating policy. Due to the extraordinary control exerted by these donors, the country seems to have lost its direction.

The erosion of national sovereignty is evident in the unique way that Karandaaz was established in Pakistan. In the 2016-2017 annual report, the first chairman of the Karandaaz board of directors, Dr. Ishrat Husain, made the following statement.

> Karandaaz is a unique organizational structure of its kind and a business model that has not yet been tested and established elsewhere in the developing world. . . . The main objective of the organization, which is not for profit but is a corporate entity, is to reach out to micro, small, and medium enterprises through an integrated approach that brings together capital, knowledge transfer and use of technology by promoting an enabling ecosystem.[73]

In essence, Husain said that the donors created their own organization, parallel to national institutions, to increase their presence and influence in the country while controlling their own funds. The misguided and misleading impact assessments, posted on Karandaaz and PMIC websites, attempted to take credit for all financial inclusion efforts (including digital banking) without providing any evidence for the effectiveness of their interventions.

So, who reaps the benefits from the FCDO-owned institutions? The staff of supply-driven institutions, retirees serving on organization boards, and a small number of rich organizations that receive donor money. The system is funded by UK taxpayers, the people who originally provided capital to the poor people of Pakistan . . . *through the State Bank of Pakistan's own program, the FIP.*

CHAPTER 7

The Failure of Foreign-Funded Tax Reforms

Governments generally undertake tax reform to improve the efficiency of tax administration and to maximize the economic and social benefits that can be achieved through the system. Taxes can include direct levies on income and wealth (e.g., personal, corporate, property), and indirect taxes on consumption (e.g., value added and excise duties). Reforms can reduce tax evasion and avoidance, and they can allow for more efficient and fairer tax collection designed to better finance public goods and services. Proper policies can make revenue levels more sustainable, and they can promote future independence from foreign aid. Good tax reforms can improve economic growth and reduce inequality through redistribution and behavior change.

International aid donors have shown increased interest in the domestic revenue mobilization efforts of developing countries, specifically related to taxation. These donors recognize the role of taxation in state-building and state-society relations. Increased interest in taxation was fueled in part by the 2008 global financial crisis, which brought about a temporary fall in aid levels. That caused donors to renew their interest in aid effectiveness, which in turn led donors to support the revenue-raising efforts of developing countries.

This chapter critically evaluates the donor-funded tax reforms in Pakistan as a part of the broader development agenda.

Well-Meaning but Failed Tax Reforms

Pakistan has a history of turning to international financial institutions for solving its persistent tax issues. For years, the World Bank, the International Monetary Fund, the Asian Development Bank, and the UK's Foreign, Commonwealth and Development Office have all supported tax revenue mobilization reforms at the federal and provincial levels.

The 2019-2023 Extended Fund Facility (EFF) program supported by the IMF had envisaged an increase in tax revenue mobilization of 4 to 5 percent of GDP. (In 2019, Pakistan's tax revenue was 10.2 percent of GDP.) The EFF pursued reforms of personal and corporate income taxes, and goods and services taxes. Since fiscal year 2020, the IMF has provided technical assistance to the Federal Board of Revenue. This assistance has helped with medium-term tax policy and revenue administration, and with diagnostic, compliance, and risk management for the Inland Revenue Service. However, at the end of the EFF program in 2023, the tax-to-GDP ratio had declined.

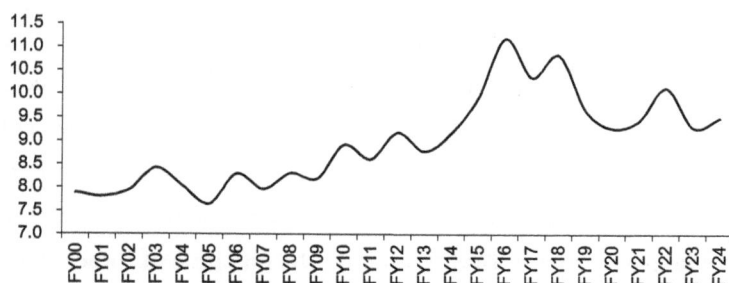

Figure 7.1: Tax-to-GDP ratios in Pakistan. Source: State Bank of Pakistan

In August 2022, the Asian Development Bank announced that it would loan $300 million to Pakistan for a domestic resource mobilization program. Pakistan's government approved this loan in September 2023, paving the way for the ADB's board to give final approval. The plan included hiring several local and international consultants who would utilize a technical assistance grant of $950,000 to improve tax administration, the pension system, and institutional capacity. Policy reforms would promote an evidence-based institutional framework for tax policy and administration; improve taxpayer integrity and compliance; promote digital transformation and automation; and improve climate-responsive taxation. In addition, the FCDO supported *inter alia* Pakistan's government through the Revenue Mobilization, Investment and Trade (REMIT) program, which was set to function from 2021 to 2025. The goal of REMIT was to strengthen the country's tax revenue mobilization reforms and initiatives.

Concurrently, in 2019, the government sought a $400 million loan from the World Bank for its five-year Pakistan Raises Revenue (PRR) project. The objective of this project was to sustainably increase domestic revenue by broadening the tax base and facilitating compliance. The project aimed to simplify the tax regime, strengthen tax and customs administration, and support the FBR with digital infrastructure and technical skills. The project's goal was to raise the tax-to-GDP ratio from a baseline of 13 percent (scaled back to 11 percent in fiscal year 2020) to 17 percent by fiscal year 2024. Another goal was to widen the tax net from 1.2 million active taxpayers to at least 3.5 million. The outcome of these efforts has been dismal. At the end of June 2024, the tax-to-GDP ratio was 10.6 percent, of which FBR taxes constitute merely 8.8 percent.

The above tax reform projects seem conceptually tenable. The timing of the projects is also hardly a surprise; the government is struggling to increase tax collections. Given the critical role of revenue mobilization in the country's fiscal sustainability, one could perhaps empathize with the government's inclination to rely on foreign funding to implement tax reforms. However, previous foreign-funded reforms were not successful, and the proposals offered by the international financial institutions could have been designed and implemented by *domestic* tax experts.

To veteran policymakers, these recent rounds of foreign-funded reform efforts feel like an ominous déjà vu. Back in 2005, Pakistan signed up for a World Bank project called the Tax Administration Reforms for Pakistan (TARP). This five-year project, with an initial cost of $149 million, had an ambitious reform agenda: to raise tax revenue by encouraging compliance with existing tax laws and to broaden the tax base; to improve the effectiveness of tax administration through institutional and procedural reforms; and to strengthen audit and enforcement procedures. The expectation was that the TARP's success would be measured with indicators such as the tax-to-GDP ratio.

The TARP project was an abject failure. First, the tax-to-GDP ratio worsened and failed to recover meaningfully during the subsequent five years. Second, the efficiency of the tax system declined, as indicated by buoyancy and elasticity estimates. Finally, in terms of tax compliance, the share of people who did not file taxes (as a proportion of registered persons) rose considerably during and after the TARP reforms. That deterioration was more prominent among those who filed income taxes, but it was also significant in the case of sales tax returns. The World Bank admitted the project's failure in its evaluation report. "The project was not able to substantially contribute to strengthening the revenue mobilization capability of the Government of Pakistan, the primary development challenge that the project aimed to address. . . . The overall outcome is rated moderately unsatisfactory."[74]

Despite the disappointing performance of the TARP, the World Bank's consultants tried to persuade domestic policymakers to take another loan ($300 million) in 2013. Thankfully, this initiative was shelved. But in 2014, the World Bank took another swing at tax issues with a four-year program called the Multi-Donor Trust Fund for Accelerating Growth and Reforms (TAGR). Among its pillars, the TAGR program attempted to support the Federal Board of Revenue with tax policy and tax administration reforms, with an emphasis on modernizing IT systems.

Successive tax reforms led by international financial institutions have failed because external technical consultants did not consider the big picture; they typically rely on one-size-fits-all solutions, which in most cases do not work. For instance, it was delusional for them to expect Pakistan's system of voluntary tax compliance, on which the entire TARP was based, to deliver in a country where it is extremely difficult to implement reliable and effective procedures for tax audits, enforcement, and legal actions against tax evaders. Similarly, TARP consultants tried to address corruption in the tax system by offering a small salary increase to Federal Board of Review officers, a big miscalculation.

In this critique, I am not implying that Pakistan's tax woes should be blamed entirely on foreign-funded reform programs and their consultants. Lack of political will, loopholes in tax policy (rooted in fiscal federalism), institutional lethargy, and corrupt practices within the tax system are major factors behind Pakistan's consistently poor performance in tax collection. My point is that Pakistan's local tax experts know what would work best in our unique socioeconomic, cultural, and political context. The country does not need technical expertise from international financial institutions. Everything about our existing tax system is imperfect, but those problems cannot be fixed using cookie-cutter approaches proposed by foreign development agencies. Instead, we need out-of-the-box thinking and strategic insights generated by Pakistanis who have a thorough knowledge of the national context and culture. Throwing loads of borrowed money at the problem, without an appreciation of deep-rooted, indigenous conditions, is not a panacea. We need home-grown solutions backed by strong political will to implement reforms.

Home-Grown Solutions

Pakistan needs tailored, strategic solutions for its tax woes— solutions that address the underlying issues and that are supported by domestic efforts, strong political determination, and equitable policies. Here I propose a five-point agenda as the foundation of those reforms.

First, there is a need to define and clearly communicate our tax policy vision, and then to act with strict adherence to it. The principle of equity, both horizontal and vertical, should supersede all the other objectives that governments typically try to achieve through tax collection. Horizontal equity means that all people who are in equal income segments should be taxed equally. Vertical equity means that all people who are in unequal income segments should be taxed unequally. In Pakistan, all tax reform efforts have consistently compromised this principle; the tax burden has fallen disproportionately across the economy's segments. Ironically, the rich pay the least, whereas the salaried class, along with a few industrial sectors and businesses, carry the bulk of the tax burden.

Second, Pakistan needs to improve *provincial* tax collection. Currently, weak provincial tax collection places the federal government under moral and developmental pressure to spend on matters that should be covered by provincial domains. This adds to the federal fiscal burden. Meager provincial taxation adds to the problem of equity, and it leaves many transactions and assets undocumented. As things stand, provinces enjoy the constitutional authority to levy and collect agriculture income tax, sales tax on services, and provincial property tax. However, the slack in their efforts is evident. Provincial authorities (collectively) cannot mobilize taxes even up to 1 percent of GDP. Despite a consistently deplorable performance, provincial tax authorities do not need to endure complaints; rather, all the flak is lobbed at the Federal Board of Revenue. The agriculture sector is not pulling its weight, at least in terms of revenue mobilization relative to its share of GDP. One possible solution is to shift the agriculture sector's responsibility for collecting income tax to the FBR, as is the case with other sectors. These revenues could then be transferred directly to provinces, minus the administrative cost incurred by the FBR, in accordance with the Constitution. This would ensure that there is no procedural distinction between sectors for the assessment and collection of income tax.

Third, Pakistan should banish the ad hoc approach to taxation. In its desperate attempts to meet revenue targets, the government often uses stopgap measures to improve tax numbers at the beginning of and during the year. The easiest ad hoc tools are tax and duty rate increases, or the imposition of withholding taxes, or the withdrawal of tax exemptions. But the frequent use of these measures has made Pakistan's tax system highly inelastic, and ad hoc approaches often conflict with enduring economic policy objectives. The government needs to design a lasting tax policy that is consistent with its long-term macroeconomic vision and strategic goals.

Fourth, the country needs a strong and effective audit mechanism. Voluntary compliance is important, but Pakistan's government has relied on half-hearted administrative measures to minimize tax evasion. It is time to make it harder and riskier to evade taxes. A heightened risk of being caught and the application of appropriate penalties serve as strong deterrents. Voluntary compliance must be backed by strong and effective audits along with competent and independent tax collecting machinery that can enforce stern actions against proven tax dodgers and delinquents.

Fifth, the Federal Board of Revenue needs serious institutional reform. It should become a professional, autonomous organization with an independent board consisting of people who are qualified in the fields of economics, public policy, law, chartered accountancy, finance, business administration, and IT. The board should drive the vision and strategic direction of tax policy while exercising oversight over the management of tax administration. The board members, having no conflict of interest, should be appointed for a fixed term with legal protections against undue pressure. Concurrently, the agency must get rid of infamously corrupt and inefficient officials. The country cannot expect serious and honest efforts from tax officers who collude with wealthy individuals and corporations to facilitate kickbacks and non-monetary favors. I believe that this type of restructuring would end half of our tax woes.

Reforming the FBR, without completely disbanding it, should occur as early as possible. The key would be to recruit professional and competent people drawn from the market and pay them competitive compensation, based on merit and without any political interference. The reform program should eliminate the practice of allowing only the Inland Revenue Service (IRS) and Pakistan Customs Service (PCS) to work at senior posts in the FBR. Similar transformations are needed in provincial tax authorities, who have yet to exhibit any serious revenue mobilization efforts.

A silver lining in the Federal Board of Revenue is its professionally competent and well-trained officers. With the right incentives in place, they could bring about the required cultural change in the organization. Additional merit-based recruitment could build on this advantage.

However, the FBR has a corrupt system run by rich tax dodgers. These people will do what they can to persuade fresh inductees to fall in line. So, what do we do? Tax officials should receive fair compensation so that they can maintain a decent lifestyle. Loyalty and conscientiousness do not come cheap, but those outcomes are worth the cost. A change in the FBR's incentive structure will promote a culture of transparency and integrity. Petty salary increases, as occurred with TARP, are destined to fail.

At a time when limited tax collection prevents Pakistan from carrying out its macroeconomic and development policy, the government needs to take bold steps to reform the tax system. All we need is a strong political will and commitment to do the work *with our own highly qualified people.* Donor-funded reforms have completely failed to improve tax administration. It is time to take charge of our own destiny.

CHAPTER 8

International Aid, Energy Reforms, and Debt

Since the 1990s, Pakistan's energy sector has undergone a significant transformation, largely due to the adoption of a 1994 policy framework that aimed to separate the responsibilities for energy policy, regulation, and operations. Before the promulgation of the 1994 framework, Pakistan's power sector was dominated by two integrated public utilities: the Water and Power Development Authority (WAPDA) and the Karachi Electric Supply Corporation (KESC). WAPDA, a government-owned statutory body, supplied power to the entire country, while KESC, a public limited liability company with government controlling interest, was responsible for providing electricity to the city of Karachi. With the adoption of the 1994 policy, WAPDA's distribution network was restructured to create eight electricity distribution companies, along with three power generation companies and the National Transmission and Dispatch Company (NTDC), which is responsible for transmitting electricity to the distribution companies. All these entities were managed under the umbrella of the Pakistan Electric Power Company.

Much more could be said about the unbundling process, but it was designed to enhance efficiency, promote competition, and create a more sustainable and consumer-centric power and energy sector in Pakistan. The results have been mixed. Instead of passing the total electricity costs to customers, the government provided subsidies to distribution companies to cover the difference between end-user and cost-recovery tariffs. Costs that could not be recovered from consumers *or* subsidies accumulated as deficits on the books of distribution companies. Those companies could not fully pay for the electricity and subsequently accumulated circular debts. This problem was exacerbated by legislative constraints that basically locked in higher losses and lower collections. In 2012, the losses reached 23 percent compared to the government's target of 16 percent. Collections were 86 percent of total billing compared to the 100 percent target. The public sector electricity companies functioned, but with low operational efficiency, poor service quality, and weak financial positions. A lack of transparency made it difficult to hold the companies accountable.

To address these issues, the government did not look for internal solutions; rather, it approached the World Bank, the Asian Development Bank, and other donors for financing and technical assistance. The ADB implemented 145 projects worth $10.32 billion. The World Bank came in with twenty-two projects and financial commitments worth $4.6 billion. Pakistan received more contributions from bilateral donors.

Despite foreign financing, the energy sector continues to suffer from chronic problems that have now devolved into a major power crisis. The public sector companies' circular debt ballooned to more than Rs2.383 trillion in June 2024 and may increase to Rs2.8 trillion by the end of fiscal year 2025 (equivalent to $10 billion) without budgetary subsidies.[75]

In other words, even after the World Bank and the ADB

implemented 167 projects, with cofinancing from bilateral donors, the project cost of $15 billion is more than the volume of the circular debt of $10 billion.

World Bank Projects

The World Bank has implemented numerous projects in Pakistan to achieve power sector reforms since the 1980s. For example, the bank implemented the Electricity Distribution and Transmission Improvement Project from June 2008 to February 2014, with a total project cost of $309.9 million. That amount included World Bank financing of $256.7 million. The actual cost upon completion was $159.03 million—lower than the estimated cost but only because the bank reduced the project's scope. This amount was financed through an IBRD loan and an IDA grant. The borrower contribution was estimated at $53.16 million, which was 36 percent of the appraised amount of $18.98 million at closure. The official ratings for this project were disappointing in relation to criteria established by an independent review. Specifically, the project needed better social and environmental safeguards. This World Bank project should have had a better upfront assessment of the population's desire for energy sector reform, which could have helped the bank tailor a system to be more aligned to local needs and perceptions.

The World Bank also provided financing of $1.2 million to Pakistan for the Tarbela Fourth Extension Hydropower project (2012-2023), and another $350 million for Ghazi Brotha Hydropower Project (1996-2013) to facilitate the expansion of Pakistan 's electricity generation capacity.

Another World Bank project was launched on June 10, 2014. The bank approved financing of nearly $1.3 million for the Dasu Hydropower Project, which was budgeted at $4.7 million and scheduled to be completed by May 31, 2024. In addition to expanding hydropower in Pakistan, the project was designed to improve community access to socioeconomic services in the project area (on the Indus River), and to build WAPDA's capacity to prepare future hydropower projects. The effort was seen as a high-risk and high-reward operation to provide low-cost noncarbon renewable energy. The World Bank approved additional IBRD financing of $700 million in fiscal year 2020 to construct a transmission line between the Dasu hydropower plant to Islamabad.

In 2021-2022, the World Bank provided a $400 million loan to Pakistan, which was designed to reduce circular debt by lowering power generation costs, decarbonizing the energy mix, improving efficiency in distribution, and retargeting electricity subsidies.

At the time of this writing, the World Bank is implementing a National Transmission Modernization Project, which was approved in December 2017 for a total project cost of $536 million, including the World Bank commitment of $425 million. The development objective of this project is to increase the capacity and reliability of Pakistan's transmission system and to modernize crucial business processes.

Finally, the World Bank is now implementing a $209 million Electricity Distribution Efficiency Improvement project, which was approved in December 2021. The development objectives of this project are to improve the operational efficiency of distribution companies, reduce transformer damage, and achieve progress on the power sector reform agenda.

Asian Development Bank Projects

The ADB, as Pakistan's anchor development partner in the energy sector, leads development coordination. The bank has helped with energy generation, transmission, distribution, energy efficiency, renewable energy development, regional gas interconnections, and analytical and advisory assistance.

For example, the ADB approved a loan for the Sustainable Energy Sector Reform Program in 2014. The program was intended to help the government with short-term stabilization measures and to start a long-term restructuring effort to create a sustainable power sector through better management of tariffs and subsidies. The program also aimed to improve sector performance and market access for private sector participation, and to improve accountability and transparency in the power sector. Fully coordinated with the International Monetary Fund under its Extended Fund Facility, the effort was implemented in phases over multiple years, with three subprograms matching the government's budget cycle. The World Bank and the Japan International Cooperation Agency (JICA) cofinanced two subprograms, and the Agence Française de Développement cofinanced the third subprogram.

The first subprogram was approved and disbursed as a single-tranche loan, with $400 million from ADB, $600 million from the World Bank, and $49 million from JICA. The second subprogram received two loans from the ADB, one for $300 million and another for $100 million. The World Bank provided $500 million while the JICA's contribution was $49 million. As for the third subprogram, the ADB provided a $150 million loan that was increased to $300 million because the program scope was expanded. The third subprogram also received cofinancing of €100 million from Agence Française de Développement. All loan proceeds were for general budget support based on the government's financing needs.

Overall, the program was expected to build on the lessons from ADB's previous interventions in Pakistan's energy sector since 2000, such as providing extensive long-term support for difficult reforms, privatizing rather than unbundling state-owned enterprises, and reducing subsidies. Some of the program's reforms and policy actions were originally proposed under the Accelerating Economic Transformation Program in 2008 and 2009, which had energy sector reforms as an integral component.

However, the Independent Evaluation Department of the ADB, in its validation report, noted that the policy actions of the program could have been more stringent to achieve the intended results.[76] The circular debt management plan of the program could not attain the required results because it did not fully anticipate a 153 percent surge in generation capacity costs. This dramatic cost increase was caused by the entry of new independent power producers between fiscal years 2017 and 2021. The program relied excessively on the distribution companies' efficiency improvements and on strategic sales proceeds from outright privatization, which were more challenging than planned. The program design did not include innovative elements or transformative effects.

To emphasize my point, the primary goal of the program was to resolve the accumulating circular debt and improve the financial sustainability of the power subsector, which was an urgent and critical task. However, the program was not able to effectively address the underlying liquidity issues in the subsector. The circular debt increased alarmingly after the program ended, from Rs729 billion in June 2017 to Rs1.6 trillion in June 2019, indicating a worsening financial situation. Thus, the ADB itself assessed the program to be less than effective. The project completion report also rated the program as subpar, specifying that the program did not adequately address the underlying causes of circular debt and did not significantly improve the sector's financial sustainability. To a large degree, this outcome occurred because the process for implementing policy actions was less than optimal and occurred more slowly than anticipated. The program lacked proper coordination among the public sector companies, which were not held accountable for their performance because of weak corporate governance, lack of transparency, and dysfunctional payment mechanisms.

An IED evaluation also found the program's results to be disappointing, especially considering the costs. It concluded that some policy actions did not require substantial funding; a push from the government and legislators would have been sufficient. This evaluation also found a lack of timely tariff adjustments and the persistence of system inefficiencies. The resurgence of circular debt required the ADB and other development partners to continue financing reforms, thereby indicating the program's less-than-satisfactory use of loan proceeds. Persistent circular debt continued to jeopardize the energy sector's sustainability.

The program did achieve some positive results, such as the amendment to the NEPRA Act, the creation of the unified Ministry of Energy, and the finalization of the guidelines for a multiyear tariff mechanism. However, it remained unclear whether long-term effects would be generated by these changes. Alarming levels of circular debt, and the high risks and uncertainties associated with the sector's commercialization all cast a shadow over the program.

Despite these shortfalls, the influx of foreign aid continues. In November 2023, the ADB approved loans worth $250 million to help expand and improve the power transmission network in the Punjab and Khyber Pakhtunkhwa provinces. The goal is still to support Pakistan's agenda to ensure grid stability, energy security, climate resilience, and increased transmission capacity to sustain economic growth in clean and efficient ways.

Who Is Accountable for Failures?

If the World Bank and the ADB claim to be Pakistan's anchor development partners in the energy sector, as they have for the past four decades, then these multilateral banks and their bilateral funders should also accept responsibility for the failure to make progress in their energy sector reforms. The staff who designed and coordinated the program's implementation were not held accountable for falling short of the goals. The failure to achieve desired outcomes did not affect their career progression. It is crucial to remember that the programs described above left Pakistan *heavily indebted.* The donors did not learn from previous experiences. As is often the case, the World Bank, the ADB, and bilateral donors did almost nothing to harmonize their programs. In fact, the donors seemed to compete to offer loans to Pakistan.

This case study of donor aid for Pakistan's energy sector demonstrates what often occurs around the world. These projects often fail miserably to achieve financial sustainability and operational viability. The recipient country is left with higher debt, and the donor agencies are never held accountable for the dismal outcomes.

CHAPTER 9

Addiction to IMF Programs

Pakistan's engagement with the International Monetary Fund dates to December 1958, soon after General Ayub Khan imposed the first martial law. Since then, the country's association with the IMF has resembled a tumultuous but enduring marriage. As of early 2025, Pakistan had entered into twenty-four agreements with the IMF, including the thirty-seven-month, $7 billion Extended Fund Facility (EFF) that began in September 2024.

Can Pakistan's economy thrive independently without IMF support? Or perhaps, more aptly stated, can the *country* survive without the IMF? Addressing this question necessitates a thorough historical examination of the IMF's financial commitments to Pakistan.

Of the twenty-four programs mentioned above, there were fourteen cases in which Pakistan did not receive the full amount pledged by the IMF. These situations occurred because Pakistani authorities deviated from the policy measures to which they had agreed. As for the other ten programs, in which Pakistan received the full amount, many were short-term programs, such as the 2023 Stand-By Arrangement. Regardless of whether Pakistan completed these programs successfully, the country found itself in a recurring cycle of financial crises, necessitating yet another IMF program. Consequently, Pakistan's reliance on the IMF has been like an addiction—an unsustainable reliance on a false hope.

This brief historical overview underscores a persistent problem: Pakistan has consistently lost its grip on fiscal responsibility, either during or after an IMF program. These failures have strained the country's fiscal accounts and expanded its deficit, leading to the rapid depletion of foreign exchange reserves. This depletion started gradually but accelerated as fiscal and monetary imprudence continued unabated.

Any economist knows the narrative of accumulating and depleting reserves, coupled with cycles of economic growth that are punctuated by periods of high inflation. The looming question is whether Pakistan will deviate from this pattern in the future. Can the country eventually wean itself from IMF programs and transition toward self-sustained domestic resource mobilization through increased tax revenues, prudent fiscal management, and the promotion of exports? I will attempt to answer this question later in this chapter, but first I will explain what occurred between 2019 and 2023 with the IMF's Extended Fund Facility (EFF), which remained incomplete and could have been avoided. This history will put things in context before I recommend urgent policy actions designed to help Pakistan stand on its own feet as a dignified sovereign nation.

Politics and the 2019-2023 Extended Fund Facility

The International Monetary Fund approved the $3 billion nine-month Stand-By Arrangement (SBA) for Pakistan in July 2023. It was designed to help Pakistan meet its urgent external financing needs. This SBA was built on extensive negotiations between Pakistani authorities and the IMF. It was part of the broader forty-eight-month Extended Fund Facility program, which remained incomplete and expired at the end of June 2023. By the end of August 2022, the overall program had passed through eight reviews. The ninth review was expected to start in October of the same year, with the IMF board meeting being set for November 2022. The program ended with $2.5 billion of undisbursed funds.

The program's incompletion was caused mostly by the Covid-19 pandemic and the country's devastating floods. However, intense domestic political developments also caused policy reversals and slow progress. Political upheaval led to colossal economic losses and caused IMF staff to deeply mistrust the country's credibility. The difficult situation was resolved after interactions between Pakistan's prime minister and the IMF's managing director, but only after Pakistani authorities agreed to IMF measures. Despite some improvements, the incomplete program left a long-term confidence crisis between the IMF and Pakistani authorities.

It is important to discern what Pakistan did wrong and to prevent those mistakes from happening in the future. Pakistan's new government, elected in 2024, negotiated a successor EFF program to address its medium-term balance-of-payments problems. During the 2019 to 2023 EFF program implementation, Pakistani officials (at times) backed away from policy commitments. Soon after four combined reviews in March 2021, the authorities reversed course. The IMF saw these actions as Pakistan's lack of ownership and hesitancy to commit to the program's economic targets. Thus, despite their support during the pandemic, the IMF staff was not as flexible during the 2022 floods.

In the wake of those cataclysmic floods, the government made repeated assurances to complete the ongoing program, but amid increasing political noise, the IMF adopted a wait-and-see approach. Therefore, the IMF did not dispatch its mission to Pakistan to undertake discussions about the ninth review until February 2023, a four-month delay. Relational tensions were high in October 2022 as public and private spats ensued between Pakistani authorities and the IMF's upper-level directors.

In addition, the finance minister's views about several economic policies irked the IMF's management. His perspectives pertained to the flexible exchange rate regime in the context of Pakistan's shallow foreign exchange market, an overly independent central bank that barred deficit financing, and a flawed monetary policy framework that created a spread between the policy rate and Treasury bills rates. The IMF staff's frustration with the finance minister's views further delayed the ninth review mission.

Some reforms were implemented during the start of the program when Pakistani authorities had better relations with IMF staff. Later in the process, subsequent Pakistani leaders began to criticize the IMF program for its harsh macro-adjustment policies. These criticisms essentially called into question Pakistan's previous negotiations with the IMF. Although some Pakistani leaders backtracked on their negative views of the IMF, the disputes caused significant delays in the program reviews and sowed seeds of mistrust among IMF staff.

In mid-April 2022, after a change in political government, a top Pakistani leader rushed to Washington, DC to repair the damage and convince the IMF management and executive board that he intended to *immediately* reverse the unfunded fuel and power subsidies and bring the program back on track. He also requested to extend the program for another nine months to show the government's commitment to reforms and policies under the EFF program. As it turned out, it took him more than two months to convince his political bosses in Pakistan to reverse the subsidies announced by the previous government. This too delayed the reviews. Discussions held in Doha in May 2022 were marred by uncertainty and decision-making paralysis. Political disruptions repeatedly interrupted the program's implementation.

In the wake of the 2022 floods, the IMF staff often acted unreasonably, at least in my view. Some would say the staff abused its power. Pakistan's difficult macroeconomic situation after the floods warranted urgent IMF support and flexibility, just as it had offered to Ukraine after Russia invaded. In the case of Ukraine, the IMF hurriedly approved a second round of emergency financing in October 2022, even without an assessment of Ukraine's debt sustainability, which is usually a precondition for all IMF financing arrangements. Such consideration was not offered to Pakistan, even though the nation was grappling with the havoc caused by floods that affected thirty-three million people.

In response to the IMF team's apprehensions about Pakistan's commitment, the government repeatedly expressed its intent to complete the ongoing program. Those entreaties did not help. The IMF delayed its review mission to Pakistan, despite the floods, on the pretext that they needed to see evidence of the authorities' changed policy priorities and fiscal position. Eventually, the difficult situation was resolved, but only after Pakistani authorities complied with the IMF's prescribed measures.

The cost of these errors and delayed policy actions was colossal for Pakistan's economy. Political disruptions devalued the currency, squeezed official inflows, and reduced foreign exchange reserves. As Pakistan's liquidity and external position became increasingly vulnerable, the ratings agencies downgraded the country's credit ratings. Concerns about a possible default created enormous uncertainty in the markets, making macroeconomic management an arduous task for policymakers.

Pakistani authorities eventually met all the IMF conditions, even beyond what was originally expected for the completion of the ninth review. However, the IMF untenably asked Pakistan to arrange for additional financing assurances as a condition for receiving help with the country's external financing needs of $6 billion. The IMF's stringency, even in a situation accentuated by a natural disaster, showed the extent of the confidence crisis.

Multilateral and bilateral development partners, and commercial lenders, waited for the IMF nod to provide support to Pakistan, but the IMF kept asking the government to meet additional requirements. Thus, the IMF defied its role as the lender of last resort in the international monetary system, which could be seen as an abuse of power. All in all, the situation elevated market uncertainties. It raised questions about the IMF's credibility, because the agency was hesitant to support a member country during a severe balance-of-payments crisis accentuated by natural disasters.

I want to emphasize that the IMF was not solely responsible for these problems. The IMF is occasionally criticized for not being even-handed, but the staff, management, and board tend to show flexibility in response to rational arguments and to support nations that do not always meet program performance criteria. As Pakistan's story demonstrates, countries that receive IMF aid also bear substantial responsibility for the outcomes. When a country is facing a severe balance-of-payments crisis, the onus is on *the country* to put its house in order. Therefore, the best course of action is to implement the policies and actions to which the recipient country and the IMF have agreed. It's incorrect to say that these policies are the IMF's "dictates" or "demands." Recipient countries must also be held responsible for their economic woes.

The mistakes that occurred during the 2019-2023 EFF program must be avoided in the future. *All* parties must adhere to policy agreements and try to resolve implementation issues with research and analysis. Unforeseen problems or circumstances should be handled with a measure of flexibility. Everyone should remember that delaying the implementation of policies is economically costly for the country, and that delays erode trust.

At the same time, it is crucial for recipient countries to build the capacity of their economic policy teams so they can negotiate financing arrangements based on sound economic principles suited to each country's context. The economic team needs to be competent, well-versed in today's international financial architecture, and knowledgeable about other country programs.

These interactions between the IMF and Pakistan hopefully illustrate some of the dynamics than can occur across the high-level international aid system. In Pakistan's case, the story did have some positive outcomes. The 2023 Stand-By Arrangement with the IMF averted an imminent sovereign default threat. It catalyzed additional financing from the multilateral and bilateral development partners, and it reduced near-term vulnerabilities. As a result, Pakistan was able to meet external debt repayments. Because the SBA was a short-term bridging arrangement, Pakistan's subsequent government after elections was able to successfully negotiate with the IMF for a successor EFF program to address its serious medium-term balance-of-payments problems. This EFF extended the original program engagement and offered a longer program duration. These measures served to support comprehensive policies needed to correct structural imbalances.

Lessons We Should All Learn

One lesson from this story is this: Member countries that borrow from the IMF should have the primary responsibility for selecting, designing, and implementing policies to make their own economic programs successful. When a country is facing balance-of-payments problems and it approaches the IMF for an extended financing arrangement, it should agree to a package of economic reforms, policies, and targets that address near-term vulnerabilities *and* long-term economic growth. The arrangement should address the underlying causes of macroeconomic imbalances. Typically, the plan should adjust fiscal consolidation, consisting of revenue and expenditure measures designed to reduce fiscal deficits and ensure debt sustainability. It should provide measures to support vulnerable citizens, the people who often incur severe harm caused by adjustment policies. The IMF programs should provide exchange-rate flexibility, which is the front line of defense against external shocks, and support monetary policies that reduce inflation.

IMF programs result from a negotiation process between governments and IMF staff. The result is an "adjustment program" of economic reforms or "conditionality" that the borrowing government must undertake. Typically, the EFF is a "high conditionality" program with specific targets and policy measures. For any IMF program to be effective, it must include policies and programs that are *genuinely* owned by the borrowing country's authorities. However, my experience at the IMF showed that these economic reform programs and policies are prepared by the IMF staff and presented to country authorities on a "take it or leave it" basis. Desperate country authorities, in urgent need of IMF support, usually agree to the agenda of reforms within the funding arrangement. The IMF then labels the agreement as the *country's* economic reform program. This typical pattern indicates that everyone needs to *improve the quality of the negotiations* to ensure that the agreement is authentically and sincerely owned by the borrowing country. This is the only way to ensure that IMF programs address the root causes of persistent economic problems without alienating domestic interest groups.

Any program's objectives and policies essentially depend on a country's circumstances. The overarching goal should always be to restore or maintain the viability of balance of payments and macroeconomic stability, and to set the stage for sustained, high-quality growth. Each country's policy commitments should focus on structural reforms that address institutional or economic weaknesses, in addition to maintaining macroeconomic stability.

All parties should comply with performance criteria. The IMF programs are typically monitored through quarterly reviews. Disbursements of tranches may be conditional on the observance of quantitative performance criteria, but progress toward structural reforms should be assessed in a holistic way. As such, it would be prudent to honor policy commitments and to ensure steadfast implementation of reforms to demonstrate the country's ownership of the IMF's economic program. That is exactly what Pakistani authorities did not do. Instead, they hesitated to implement their policy commitments on several occasions, which naturally created a credibility gap with the IMF that persisted for years. Thus, other countries should work to maintain trust with the IMF and quickly restore it when problems occur.

Each party—the recipient country and the IMF—might not see eye to eye on the causes of disagreement. This occurred in Pakistan's case. From the IMF's perspective, it showed flexibility by providing a $1.4 billion rapid financing instrument in April 2020, in the wake of the Covid-19 pandemic, and by completing four combined reviews in March 2021. The IMF also showed flexibility in bringing the program back on track after Pakistan's authorities paused the EFF and then reversed policies and program commitments.

All this is true, but not the whole truth. During the Covid-19 pandemic, the IMF provided emergency financing support to all member countries that requested help. The only exception was Iran. Pakistan received a paltry tranche of $350 million for four combined reviews despite Pakistan's large needs and availability under the IMF's access limits policy. The IMF maintained that Pakistan's position was comfortable; therefore, according to the IMF, the country did not need more access to its funding. This was an illogical argument. Pakistan would not have needed IMF support unless it had a balance-of-payments problem.

For an objective assessment, it is also important to understand how the IMF operates. It is a quota-based organization of 190 member countries. All are represented by twenty-five executive directors. Each director represents a group of countries to advance that constituency's agenda on the international stage. Under that governance framework, the IMF's staff, management, and executive board enjoy significant independence from each other. They do not interfere in each other's decision-making domains. For this reason, IMF reports are called "staff reports." For example, Iran's request for rapid financing support during the pandemic was not even *presented* to the board for consideration, which created resentment among Iranian authorities. By contrast, war-torn Ukraine received preferential treatment from the IMF. Despite these variances, the IMF usually operates within its integrated policy framework, and the organization usually responds to rational arguments from nations requesting support.

In this context, it is unhelpful to work through diplomatic channels or with the security establishment as a means of persuading the IMF to complete a program review. Such attempts serve no purpose; rather, they leave no room for possible concessions or waivers by IMF staff and management. The best approach is to respect the IMF's decision-making channels, its organizational policies, and its operational frameworks.

This is an important lesson from Pakistan's history. Recipient countries must demonstrate serious ownership of the reforms to economic policies established by both parties in IMF agreements. Countries should see their engagements with the IMF as a partnership. The IMF should not be seen as a monster that causes hardships. Country leaders should realize that people are suffering not because of harsh IMF treatment, but because of their own misaligned policies. For instance, Pakistan's tax policy has always focused on raising revenues through ad hoc measures while compromising the equity principles of taxation. Throughout Pakistan's history, the exchange rate policy has subsidized imports and imported disinflation, creating perverse incentives. The inefficient energy sector has accumulated circular debt financed by taxpayers. The cost of inefficient public enterprises (e.g., Pakistan Steel) is also borne by taxpayers. The oversized public sector is eating up the country's resources.

Another critical aspect of negotiations with the IMF involves agreement on key assumptions related to the forecasts of exchange rates, inflation, GDP growth, and balance of payments. Fiscal planning and monetary policy decisions crucially depend on these variables.

Interestingly, projections by economists at the State Bank of Pakistan, which are based on advanced forecasting models, have historically proven more accurate than the projections used by IMF teams. These projections play a vital role in designing the policy prescriptions of IMF agreements. During the EFF program negotiations held in April and May 2019, the State Bank of Pakistan offered excellent projections for the exchange rate between the US dollar and Pakistani currency for fiscal year 2020. The IMF disputed those projections. The conflict influenced the decisions of the governor and finance secretary to leave their positions at the SBP. It so happens that the SBP projections were correct. Sadly, there was no accountability within the IMF for its erroneous projections.

Another similar example occurred when the IMF projected that Pakistan's 2024 current account deficit would be $5.649 billion at the start of the Pakistan's 2023 SBA program. That was revised to $3 billion in the September 2024 IMF staff report. However, because *the original projection* was inflated, the IMF had leverage to put undue pressure on Pakistan during the ninth review of the 2019-2023 EFF. When the IMF's projections proved to be way off the mark, Pakistan's finance minister at the time was once again vindicated.

These disagreements elevate the importance of careful negotiations between countries and the IMF. Agreements must include domestic resource mobilization and expenditure efficiency, structural reforms to improve the business climate, solid measures to increase non-debt-creating external inflows, and solutions to address the root causes of long-standing problems within the energy sector. Additionally, there must be a commitment to implement the agreed-upon privatization agenda to eliminate loss-making state-owned enterprises.

Furthermore, tax reforms must focus on equity issues within the tax policy. To prevent social unrest, tax reforms should aim to increase revenues from untaxed and undertaxed sectors rather than by further squeezing existing taxpayers. Tax credits should encourage business investments and private expenditures on education and health by individual taxpayers. Within the energy sector, previous IMF programs have failed to resolve Pakistan's burgeoning circular debt through tariff increases and unjust fuel taxes. The circular debt has persisted because of inefficiency, theft, and losses faced by power distribution firms. The IMF programs must have realistic policies and goals instead of relying on outdated structural conditionality, which has not yielded fruitful results.

Finally, it is crucial for recipient countries to field a capable team of people who can negotiate effectively with the IMF. This team should formulate home-grown economic policies and secure the IMF's agreement to tackle longstanding structural problems.

Without high-level negotiating capacity, countries risk embarking on programs that leave the fundamental issues unaddressed.

Reducing Dependency on the IMF

The goal, of course, is to reduce dependency on the IMF, or for that matter, other external creditors. To do this Pakistan needs comprehensive policy actions and strong political will to initiate those measures. Stabilization policies, including those promoted by the IMF, are essential for a country's journey toward self-sufficiency. These policies entail belt-tightening to reduce fiscal and external deficits, ultimately improving debt-to-GDP ratios.

Stabilization is a necessary step toward economic self-reliance. Phasing out IMF financial assistance necessitates the continuation of IMF-based *policies,* but governments often resist the macroeconomic prudence advocated by the IMF. Lethargy often leads government ministries of finance, energy, and commerce to rely on the IMF rather than craft their own policies. Political parties in power find it easier to blame the previous government for entering IMF contracts, or to blame the IMF itself for strict impositions. This is the usual practice in Pakistan. We cannot absolve Pakistan's successive political leaders or its civil servants. They are typically addicted to signing IMF programs as a way of avoiding responsibility. They praise themselves for negotiating these agreements, earn promotions, and even get national awards, but then they blame the IMF when things go wrong.

There is a clear advantage to pursuing reforms without the IMF. Countries can avoid the parsimony of conditionality that we have seen in Pakistan's fund-supported EFF programs. Also, IMF programs are known for aggressive adjustments at the expense of growth, which is needed for critical social and development expenditures. Additionally, the authorities can prioritize the timing of their reforms to suit their own contexts.

However, each country must establish strong policy frameworks and ensure strict adherence to them. For example, in 2023 Pakistan's leaders should have recognized the government's unsustainable fiscal position. Expenditures that year amounted to 19.1 percent of GDP (Rs16.2 trillion), with interest payments accounting for 6.9 percent of GDP (Rs5.8 trillion). By comparison, revenues were only 11.4 percent of GDP (Rs9.6 trillion), resulting in a fiscal deficit of 7.7 percent of GDP (Rs6.5 trillion). Despite imposing heavy taxes in the last fiscal year, the government collected Rs7.819 trillion, hardly equal to 8.6 percent of GDP.

Even when excluding interest expenses, primary expenditures exceeded revenues. That resulted in a primary deficit of 0.8 percent of GDP (Rs690 billion). In other words, the government was borrowing to cover its interest payments, leading to an unsustainable increase in debt and potentially leading to a default.

In fiscal year 2024, Pakistan's federal budget deficit target was Rs7.6 trillion, or 7.2 percent of GDP. Interest payments were budgeted at Rs7.3 trillion. For the fiscal year 2023-2024, the federal government allocated Rs7.3 trillion for debt servicing, *which was 77.5 percent of the government's target for tax collection* (Rs.9.415 trillion). Alarmingly, Pakistan's interest payments, as a share of government revenue, were the highest in the world.

Despite this critical fiscal condition, the government chose to increase the salaries of government employees by 30 to 35 percent in the 2023 budget, and it further increased those salaries by 25 percent in fiscal year 2024. Furthermore, the government allocated Rs770 billion (a massive 40 percent expansion) in development expenditure in fiscal year 2023 and Rs950 billion for development spending in fiscal year 2024 to appease parliamentarians who wanted to finance projects for their constituencies. To avert a potential default, the government needed to at least cover its primary expenditures and generate a primary surplus, which would have gradually reduced the debt-to-GDP ratio. Regardless of Pakistan's IMF program status, that was the only path to achieve stabilization and move toward self-sufficiency.

Pakistan's public debt-to-GDP ratio in fiscal year 2023 was 77.3 percent, which came down to 69.2 because of a primary surplus in fiscal year 2024. To bring it below the 60 percent threshold, as prescribed by the Fiscal Responsibility and Debt Limitation Act of 2005, a gradual but firm fiscal consolidation was necessary. This looked simple on paper, but the actual process was complex. To end dependency on the IMF and reverse the debt-to-GDP trajectory, Pakistan needed to raise taxes from 9.2 percent of GDP to 15 percent and simultaneously reduce the expenditure-to-GDP ratio.

Government fiscal excesses tend to widen current account deficits. Mismanagement of the exchange rate can deplete foreign exchange reserves. Pakistan's inclination toward a fixed or overvalued exchange rate is well-known, but adopting a market-determined exchange rate is crucial for mitigating external sector problems. Achieving this without relying on IMF programs is vital for improving medium- to long-term export prospects.

A broad spectrum of reforms is necessary to reduce reliance on the IMF. These include fiscal and administrative reforms to increase the tax-to-GDP ratio and to reduce expenditures. In many countries, such as in Pakistan, it is important to privatize state-owned enterprises, which can diminish their financial burden on the government and enhance productivity. Pakistan, for example, needs to redesign the energy sector to tackle circular debt and reform the civil service to improve governance and efficiency.

Pakistan's history makes it difficult to be optimistic about reducing its IMF dependency, but many other countries have successfully accomplished this goal by implementing strong policy frameworks and sound economic fundamentals. There is no reason why similar measures will not work in Pakistan. However, addictions are hard to overcome, and the unhealthy dependency on international aid will make it difficult for Pakistan to be truly free.

The issue of governance in Pakistan's public institutions has reached a critical point. Sadly, the political leadership remains oblivious to the fact that their actions, motivated by political ambitions and vested interest, are eroding key state institutions: the parliament, the judiciary, and the executive branch. Consequently, Pakistan is trapped in a low-growth, low-investment cycle, facing insurmountable development challenges.

In summary, Pakistan's declining growth and investment trends are largely attributable to the continuous decline of its institutions. Without strong institutions, no government plans—such as the recent "Uraan Pakistan" program—will fare any better than previous failed initiatives.[77] We need statespersons, not self-serving politicians, to steer the country out of this mess. The same is true for many other developing nations around the world.

CHAPTER 10

Dismal On-the-Ground Realities

International donors have caused havoc in Pakistan and in other developing countries, but not everything is their fault. The recipient countries are equally responsible. Through interlocutors in government institutions and the private sector, recipient countries have developed formidable partnerships with donors. This chapter offers a fresh viewpoint on the origins of our current predicament around the world, what I call the "shady economics" of international aid. I want to expose the detrimental influence of donor agencies, but I also want to do more than be a critic. So, this chapter also presents a roadmap for critical reforms.

As a native of Pakistan who is personally familiar with grassroots hardships, I offer insights into the challenges faced by ordinary people. Based on my direct experience with the harmful effects of misgovernance, I have a unique perspective that unrobes the disturbing realities of foreign aid. First, I present economic data showing that international aid across decades has done little to improve on-the-ground circumstances. Second, continuing to use Pakistan as a case study, I document the root causes of dismal socioeconomic progress. A deeper understanding of these root causes reveals that *international aid has an extremely limited capacity to improve local situations*—unless developing countries put their own houses in order.

Overwhelming Debt

Despite numerous and overlapping donor interventions, the problems around the world are moving from bad to worse. The situation is mindboggling. Most sectors within developing countries, including energy, fiscal, industry, social development, and urban management are confronting chronic woes. And yet international donors are never held accountable for the misallocation and poor utilization of international funding.

As for their interlocutors, Pakistan is illustrative of what is happening in many other developing countries. Pakistan's public officials have become addicted to donor funding, policy interferences, and so-called technical assistance. In effect, the entire economy is being run and managed by the frequently incompetent staff of foreign donors who often lack a sense of direction or sincerity of purpose. Their programs and projects have repeatedly failed and yet they continue to boast about the nobility of their causes. Donors might have made some improvements in one sector or another, but the unchecked reliance on donor funding has resulted in unsustainable debt. Pakistan's interest payments, as a percentage of government revenues, are the highest in the world. Figure 10.1 below shows the 2022 situation.

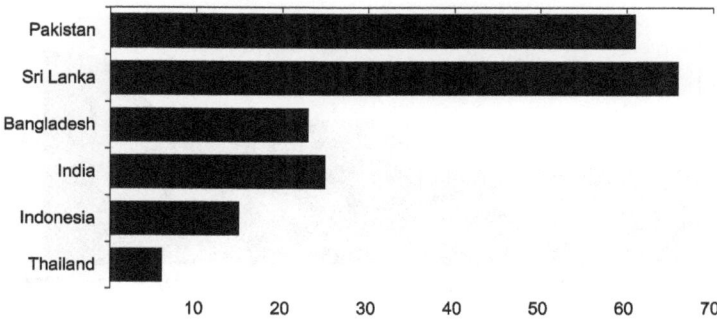

Figure 10.1: Interest payments in relation to government revenue (2022). Source: Financial Times[78]

Pakistan's debt has become so problematic that interest payments in 2024 ballooned to 65 percent of total government revenue. In absolute terms, Pakistan's interest payments in fiscal year 2024 were estimated at Rs8.5 trillion. That amount was 90 percent of the country's tax revenues for 2024 (Rs9.415 trillion). As a percentage of GDP, interest payments reached 6.8 percent of GDP in fiscal year 2023 compared to 3.79 percent in fiscal year 2017. Pakistan's tax revenue in fiscal year 2023 was 8.5 percent of the GDP. Figure 10.2 shows a worsening trend. At the same time, Pakistan's debt repayment capacity has weakened. Economic growth has declined and exports have been stagnant.

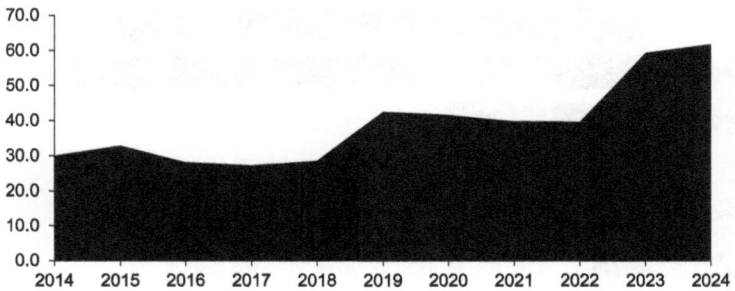

Figure 10.2: Pakistan's interest payments in relation to revenue (2014 to 2024). Source: State Bank of Pakistan Annual Reports

As discussed earlier in the book, multiple tax reform projects have failed to increase the tax-to-GDP ratio, which continues to hover at 9 percent. Other low- and middle-income countries have an average tax-to-GDP ratio of 15 to 20 percent.

Investment has come to a standstill in Pakistan, sitting at approximately 15 percent of GDP. Gross fixed capital formation, formerly known as gross domestic fixed investment, includes land improvements; plant, machinery, and equipment purchases; and the construction of roads, railways, schools, offices, hospitals, private residential dwellings, and commercial and industrial buildings.

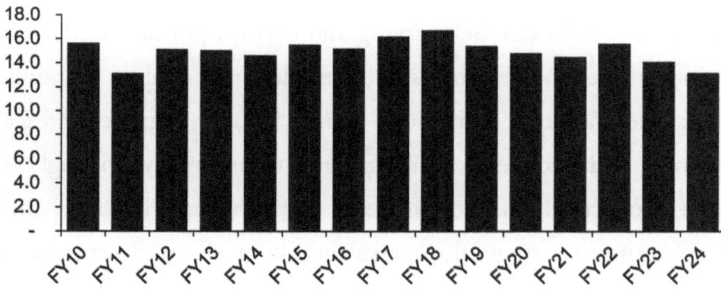

Figure 10.3: Investment as a percentage of GDP (fiscal year 2010 to 2024).
Source: State Bank of Pakistan

Sadly, Pakistan's gross fixed capital formation, which was 14 percent in 2023, is among the lowest of low- and middle-income countries. Moreover, circular debt in Pakistan's power sector continues to grow despite repeated tariff increases on a monthly, quarterly, and annual basis. This circular debt has increased because of inefficiency, theft, and the losses of power distribution firms. The debt has overburdened the energy sector and the economy.

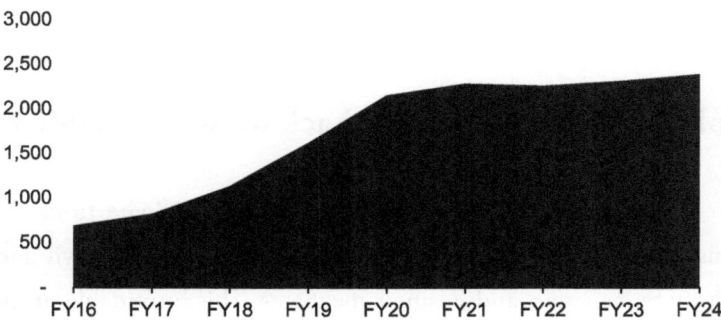

Figure 10.4: Growth of circular debt in Pakistan's power sector (Rs in billions). Source: NEPRA

In the past four decades, we have witnessed frequent political disruptions in Pakistan. Self-serving and corrupt political leadership has undermined policy consistency, eroded the quality of public services, deteriorated social and moral values, degraded ethical standards, and reduced efficiency and transparency throughout society. Collectively, these problems have pushed Pakistan into a deep economic stagnation, resulting in a sharp downturn in economic development. Average GDP growth, which had been close to 6 percent until 1980s, declined to around 4 percent between 1990 and 2023.

The multifaceted nature of these challenges can be attributed to many causes; however, the reliance on foreign donors and their technical experts has significantly contributed to Pakistan's predicament, and, as the data show, there is little evidence that international aid has improved Pakistan's situation. The solutions of foreign donors often lack a nuanced understanding of Pakistan's intricate economic issues. They usually prescribe one-size-fits-all remedies for complex challenges. A more in-depth exploration of these contributing factors is presented below.

Political Disruptions and Lack of Accountability

Pakistan faces countless challenges. Many originate from the robust alliance of influential elites, including politicians, civil and military bureaucrats, and business magnates. This formidable nexus has perpetuated the country's dire circumstances and obstructed meaningful efforts to reform Pakistan's economy. Breaking free from the shackles of this alliance necessitates comprehensive institutional and structural transformations in taxation, education, health care, exports, civil service, governance, the judicial system, and the media. Without a strong democratic system in which the will of the people is respected, the needed transformations will remain a distant dream. Frequent political disruptions prevent democracy from taking hold, which hinders reforms. It is crucial to acknowledge that self-inflicted political crises afflict the entire population and impose colossal economic costs.

Ensuring political stability is fundamental to fostering economic stability, which in turn can bolster business confidence and attract foreign investments. Market and investment behaviors respond swiftly and negatively to political instability. If the political environment is relatively stable, or if change is gradual and predictable, then investors will gain confidence. We must recognize that Pakistan's problems arise, in part, from political discontinuity.

Pakistan's recent political history, particularly during 1990s and between 2016 to the present day, has been rife with turmoil. Prime Minister Nawaz Sharif was ousted in 2017, following a prolonged period of judicial actions. Five years after Sharif's dismissal and disqualification from public office, in what many saw as a judicial intervention orchestrated by the military establishment, he managed to win the reversal of his sentence and disqualification. In 2018, Prime Minister Imran Khan assumed power with apparent support from the military establishment, which aided the government's ability to function. But in 2022, with military backing, he was deposed by a vote of no confidence in the National Assembly. This multi-year upheaval inflicted significant economic damage on the nation.

Nevertheless, Pakistan's political circus continues. At the

time of this writing, former Prime Minister Imran Khan is facing a similar fate to Sharif's. Khan, once favored by the establishment, has been removed and jailed. He faces approximately two hundred legal cases. Despite efforts to keep him sidelined from elections, widespread public support for Khan could fuel efforts to overturn court decisions, thereby allowing his return to politics.

Justice, politics, and privilege have become so intertwined that it is nearly impossible to differentiate between them. In this theatrical spectacle, the script is constantly changing, unpredictable, and absurd. Particularly distressing is the disregard for the economic toll of such disruptions on the population.

The magnitude of these losses has been colossal. Uncertainties extending from political misadventures in 2022-2023 have led to a drastic decline in GDP growth, plunging from 6.17 percent in fiscal year 2022 to a *negative* 0.17 percent in fiscal year 2023. The immediate economic losses caused by these avoidable political disruptions in fiscal year 2022 are estimated to be between $28 billion and $42 billion. Had there been no political disruption, the nation could have averted this substantial economic loss. This estimated loss was *four to six times more than the current IMF program.* Allow me to make this point again: If Pakistan had maintained political stability, the country could have been far less reliant on foreign aid.

The repercussions of political disruptions in 2022 extended beyond fiscal year 2023, impacting the potential GDP. This negative growth exacerbated fiscal challenges and necessitated additional consolidation measures. As I write, the economy is caught in a low-growth period caused by unwise decisions. The medium-term losses will far exceed the immediate economic impacts. The absence of culpability for political gamesmanship perpetuates the cycle of losses, emphasizing the imperative for a robust political and democratic system that holds nefarious actors accountable.

Failure to learn from these mistakes condemns Pakistan to a cycle of treating symptoms rather than addressing the underlying issues, such as inappropriate military and judiciary interference in politics. Without addressing the root causes of the country's problems, Pakistan will be forced to perpetually rely on financing from the IMF and supportive countries. That arrangement compromises Pakistan's sovereignty, national pride, and resilience— and it imposes ongoing suffering on citizens. Political stability, anchored in democratic norms, is the primary solution to both short-term and long-term challenges.

The 2023 IMF Stand-By Arrangement (SBA) enabled Pakistan to avert an imminent sovereign default risk. The new government then engaged with the IMF to extend the financing arrangement to meet crucial medium-term fiscal and external financing needs. It signed another thirty-seven-month extended fund facility (EFF) program worth around $7 billion. However, Pakistan's external financing risks are exceptionally high. Delays in the disbursement of planned external financing from international institutions and bilateral creditors pose major risks to a very fragile external balance. Furthermore, high food and energy prices will continue to fuel sociopolitical tensions. Pakistan, therefore, no longer has the luxury to play around with an IMF program. Any future derailment of financing from other multilateral and bilateral development partners would lead the country to default on its debt payments. That would result in junk ratings by international rating agencies and unmanageable market uncertainties.

Pakistan's Constitution has clearly defined the boundaries of the polity, which must be honored. It should not be manipulated for political expediency. The country's direction should be guided by the Constitution, not by vested interests. Failing to do so will lock the country in a prison of political and economic turmoil.

The Politicization of Civil Service

The role and conduct of Pakistan's civil servants have undergone a concerning shift. In the past, deputy commissioners, for example, held pivotal positions as patrons of their districts. They engaged with the community and contributed to social development, in addition to maintaining law and order and representing the government. They were involved in social and community activities, ensuring that government policies and services were effectively developed and delivered to the people. They played an essential role in promoting local culture and traditions. The deputy commissioners attended school events, religious celebrations, and cultural gatherings. They were responsible for ensuring that towns had sports and recreational facilities. During my high school years, I participated in speech competitions in the remote district of Sanghar, Sindh. I have fond memories of the deputy commissioners and police superintendents who graced the occasions as the chief guests and personally awarded prizes. These types of community involvement helped bridge the gap between the government and the public, fostering a sense of unity and connection.

However, as time passed, a noticeable change occurred. Deputy commissioners are rarely seen in public today, and they infrequently appear in their offices. Despite being less involved on a local level and working remotely, they enjoy opulent lifestyles financed by public funds. They are less accountable to oversight, which increases opportunities for corruption. Overall, this disturbing transformation reflects shifts in societal norms, changes in economic conditions, and evolving expectations regarding the conduct of public servants.

The politicization of civil servants has caused these changes. Today's public servants are more prone to pursue political objectives rather than actual public service. The gradual alignment of politics with civil service has negatively impacted the social fabric of society. The erosion of community engagement and moral leadership has contributed to a decline in social values and ethics.

The politicization of the police force is also evident. In 2014, police politicization influenced a tragedy in the Model Town Lahore incident, during which police killed several protestors. That was an example of the police abusing its power, but politicization also leads police forces to *avoid* involvement in combating crimes. With support from public officials, powerful mafias operate with impunity, depriving citizens of access to basic commodities, even water. To the extent that politicization causes disfunction in the civil bureaucracy and police forces, the state itself becomes less able to provide good governance for the benefit of all citizens, undermining the nation's economic potential.

The extent of Pakistan's politicized bureaucracy can be seen in the elite Pakistan Administrative Service (PAS). These officials can now easily be branded based on their loyalty to certain national political parties. They are rewarded for loyalty to the ruling elite with lucrative jobs in Pakistan or abroad. Some have been elevated to the cabinet positions of prime ministers. A rotten system of cronyism has emerged within Pakistan's civil bureaucracy, creating perverse incentives for other bureaucrats who are tempted by humongous official residences and luxurious vehicles—even though the nation is drowning in debt. Civil servants should be seen as *servants of* the public rather than *lords over* the public. Some public servants even see crises, including natural disasters, as opportunities for financial gain. The whole mess contributes to the erosion of social and moral values, ultimately leading to increased suffering among the populace.

The rise of political patronage also extends to the appointment of people to important policymaking positions based only on loyalty and personal connections. This trend has become alarmingly prevalent in Pakistan, effectively sounding the death knell for meritocracy. The practice has eroded the strength of the country's institutions, which also debases Pakistan's economic development. Appointing people based on loyalty rather than merit is highly correlated with conflicts of interest within the government. In Pakistan, top government positions have been awarded to business leaders with widespread financial interests in the industries they regulate. Without citing names, this has occurred in the sectors of taxation, energy, banking, and industry, among others.

Unfortunately, people from international donor agencies have also been appointed to high-level positions within Pakistan. These appointments are not based on qualifications and experience, but because the appointees could be trusted to push the agency's agenda. Some economic managers were appointed to promote a "Washington consensus" in Pakistan; that is, to implement efforts like neocolonialism. These individuals were not seriously knowledgeable about Pakistan's on-the-ground realties and they failed to connect local people. They were fixated on serving the agendas of the international financial institutions that appointed them. Suitcase economists have perpetuated Pakistan's economic imbalances, worsened equity in taxation, and fueled dysfunctional public policies.

These problems have persisted despite a 2013 Supreme Court ruling that called for transparent, inclusive, and fair processes for selecting people to serve in senior government positions. The ruling pushed the federal government to establish independent selection mechanisms and implement open, fair, and transparent hiring procedures while eliminating the culture of arbitrariness, favoritism, and nepotism. However, positive changes will take more than a court ruling. Public servants must search their hearts and question whether they want to serve the people or serve themselves. They need to remember that they bear significant responsibility for fostering moral integrity and public trust.

Corruption: A Societal Cancer

The first victim of Pakistan's pervasive corruption is economic development. Without development, inequality worsens. Corruption, once entrenched, extends beyond isolated sectors, permeating the entire societal fabric.

Corruption in Pakistan, like cancer, spreads wide and deep. It proliferates relentlessly within infrastructure projects, tax offices, law enforcement agencies, and virtually every government department, including education, healthcare, and social welfare. In provincial government departments, powerful officials land lucrative jobs and have no fear of accountability. Parliament is populated by individuals elected through corrupt means. To become a member of the National Assembly, a person needs to spend approximately Rs10 million. Consequently, development funds allocated to members of national and provincial assemblies essentially function as a reimbursement for the substantial sums these politicians spend during their election campaigns. This firmly entrenches corruption in the system.

Pakistan is trying to reduce corruption. Between 1999 and September 2021, Pakistan's National Accountability Bureau (NAB) has recovered Rs821 billion by investigating white-collar crime. Nevertheless, the NAB's performance has been publicly criticized by some National Assembly members who believe its investigations are too harsh. Historically, anti-corruption policymakers have focused on establishing laws and penal actions. Public demand has favored this enforcement approach, which is evident in the popular slogan *ehtesab* (accountability). However, the experience in Pakistan and in other developing countries reveals that to combat corruption at the root, governments must develop a comprehensive strategy. Isolated attempts to revive integrity in the system are destined to falter.

Government Ineffectiveness and Mismanagement

Many economists emphasize the central role of strong institutions in driving a country's economic development. This perspective broadens the traditional scope of economics to include social norms and laws, the institutional foundations of economic activities.

So, how does Pakistan fare in terms of governance? The

World Bank's Worldwide Governance Indicators (WGI) provide comprehensive governance assessments for 215 countries between 1996 and 2023. The assessments are based on six dimensions of governance, including political stability, government effectiveness, accountability, regulatory quality, rule of law, and control of corruption. The aggregated indicators amalgamate the perspectives of enterprises, citizens, and experts representing industrial and developing countries. The assessments draw from more than thirty data sources, including survey institutes, think tanks, non-government organizations, international bodies, and private-sector firms.

Based on 2023 results, Pakistan's rank in the world since 1996 has deteriorated in relation to all governance dimensions except for the "control of corruption" category.[79] When compared with other regional counterparts, Pakistan's governance performance appears subpar. India and Sri Lanka consistently outperform Pakistan by significant margins. Notably, in the "government effectiveness" metric, India's percentile rank is 67.92, while Pakistan lagged at a disappointing 30.66 in 2023. In the "political stability and absence of violence/terrorism" category, Pakistan has a dismal percentile rank of 6.64. Likewise, in regulatory quality, Pakistan's percentile rank of 19.81 is much lower than India's rank of 47.17.

The decline of governance in Pakistan's public institutions has reached a critical point, causing substantial financial losses. State-owned enterprises (SOEs) are bleeding billions of rupees annually. The annual losses of SOEs have risen to Rs500 billion, putting a strain on public finances. The unprofitable enterprises have been on the privatization list for an extended period without success. Now the problems have become much more complex, in part because these entities are financially unviable.

A glaring example is Pakistan Steel Mills (PSM). It has been non-operational since 2015, yet the government continues to pay salaries to its employees. Politically appointed employees of some SOEs reap huge benefits without contributing to the economy. This is a blatant example of bad governance, mismanagement, and politicization.

The privatization of Pakistan Steel Mills restarted in 2019 with the appointment of a financial adviser. In the last four years, the process dragged on so long that three of the four companies that prequalified for bidding backed out. There is now only one bidder. The steel company is no longer viable. It may not be able to repay its debt to the National Bank of Pakistan or to the Sui Southern Gas Company (SSGC), which would put lenders in hot water. It is important to know that PSM was built in 1973 with 1949 Russian technology. The total capacity of the mill is 1.1 million tons. To refurbish the mill so that it can increase capacity to a maximum of three million tons, the mill would need $1.4 billion.

It is not hard to see why the privatization process has been annulled. The management and staff are still on the government payroll even though operations closed in 2015. Astonishingly, gas is still supplied to the mill, costing Rs125 billion (paid by the government). Various government-appointed boards during the last fifteen years have leased thirty-six hundred acres of land to individuals and companies. Landgrabbers have illegally occupied about two thousand acres of land. It is imperative to impose accountability measures on those who are responsible for mismanagement and wasteful expenditures.

Another example is Pakistan International Airlines (PIA), which has been on the government's privatization list for over a decade. It too has become operationally and financially unsustainable. The airline is incurring monthly losses of almost Rs13 billion. Its accumulated liabilities have reached Rs713 billion, far exceeding its assets of Rs110 billion. The losses have grown to a staggering $7.1 billion since 2012, and projections for 2023 indicated a further loss of Rs112 billion ($389 million), surpassing the previous year's loss of Rs97 billion. Its flight operations are shrinking, and the fleet has been reduced to nineteen operational but aging aircraft. It cannot fly to many international destinations due to safety concerns, and it is facing stiff competition on domestic routes from new, more efficient private airlines that offer better services at cheaper prices. Previously, the airline had more than twenty-thousand employees and forty planes. The corporation now has nine thousand employees and seventeen planes. Huge debts and liabilities mean that PIA's viability is in doubt, prompting the government to expedite privatization plans, but Pakistan's fiscal deficit prevents the government from financing the airline's losses.

Mismanagement is also a negative factor in Pakistan's energy sector. Misgovernance occurs in four key areas. First, there are *losses within the system,* such as theft, nonpayment of bills, and circular debt, which reached Rs2.383 trillion by the end of June 2024. Second, there is the *expensive cost of energy production.* Most electricity production in Pakistan is provided by independent power producers (IPPs), which operate under contracts that guarantee high rates of return (in dollar terms). The government also makes mandatory capacity payments regardless of electricity usage. This was meant to attract investment, but the plan has suffered from poor contract management and corruption. There has been no accountability for those who approved those contracts with the IPPs, even though they have lost billions of rupees and imposed unaffordable tariffs on consumers. Because of these agreements, that government is paying Rs150 billion in taxpayers' money to the IPPs every month (capacity charges), even to those running below 10 percent of capacity. Four plants are receiving Rs10 billion a month each for zero electricity supply.[80] This huge amount of taxpayer money is being given to forty families under the guise of capacity charges. Third, there are *higher generation costs*. The cost of generating electricity in new plants often exceeds the "least available cost" principle, leaving consumers to foot the bill. Fourth, *indirect taxes* embedded in electricity bills reflect the government's incompetence in collecting taxes from influential elites. These levies significantly burden households.

Shoddy management of the energy sector means that actual investment and operations costs (including fuel consumption) are often overstated. The net result is that the investors make far higher returns on their investments than the already generous policy intended. Instead of addressing the structural inefficiency of the policy, successive governments have instead offered ever higher returns to attract investment in the sector. As a result, the price of power is much higher than it should be. The higher costs exacerbate theft and nonpayment, which in turn feeds circular debt, which then increases risk for investors.

Pakistan's Power Division projected that the circular debt would reach Rs2.7 trillion by the end of December 2024. In essence, circular debt is a *public* debt that arises from the cascade of unpaid government subsidies. In Pakistan, this is an acute problem in the power sector that leads to a relentless spiral of unpaid bills among distribution companies. When the distribution companies cannot pay the independent power producers, they cannot pay fuel suppliers. The energy sector thus creates a chain reaction of debt that afflicts the entire system, and subsequently all of Pakistan.

In a nutshell, when consumers pay their electricity bills, they are paying government taxes that aim to cover the downstream effects of mismanagement, theft, idle capacity, and circular debt. This situation is untenable. The government should immediately find alternative revenue sources or cut spending to subsidize low-consumption tiers in the energy sector. Ultimately, the country needs deep-rooted reforms that include effective governance, transparency, and evidence-based decision making. Foreign aid or donor-provided technical assistance is hardly a solution to these problems. To fix these chronic issues, we need strong political will to remain committed to reforms in the face of special-interest pressures.

Weak Resource Mobilization
and Limited Fiscal Space

Pakistan's economy has witnessed repeated boom and bust cycles. When the latter occurs, the country seeks assistance from the International Monetary Fund. Reliance on the IMF is driven, in part, by Pakistan's persistently high and unsustainable budget deficit. Between 2013 and 2023, Pakistan's average fiscal deficit was 6.3 percent. The Fiscal Responsibility and Debt Limitation Act of 2005 required the government to reduce the budget deficit to 3.5 percent of GDP for fiscal year 2017–2018 and then maintain that level. However, this fiscal rule was breached. High budget deficits persisted. The public debt-to-GDP ratio increased to 77.3 percent of GDP by June 2023, a level that endangers the country's fiscal sustainability.

Low revenues make it difficult to reduce the budget deficit. Between 2013 and 2023, Pakistan's total revenue (excluding grants) was 12.6 percent of GDP, the lowest in the region. Pakistan's tax-to-GDP ratio during this period was about 9.8 percent, which is significantly lower than the average tax-to-GDP ratio of 15 to 20 percent in other low- and middle-income countries.

With the passage of the Seventh National Finance Commission Award in 2010, an increased share—about 10 percent more than the previous award—of government taxes began to be transferred to the provinces. As a result, the average net revenue retained by the federal government decreased from about 9 percent of GDP to about 7 percent of GDP. This level of revenue is inadequate to finance large and inelastic public expenditures, such as debt servicing and defense, and the wages and pensions of government employees. The situation leaves little room for economic development and social expenditure. During fiscal year 2023, the net revenue retained by the federal government was lower than the debt service it incurred on domestic and foreign loans, which highlights the extremely limited fiscal space at the federal level.

The current tax structure undercuts the government's ability to raise revenue, leading to wide fiscal deficits. The burden of taxation is also highly skewed and regressive, affecting the overall business environment, discouraging investment in industry and the export sector, and widening inequalities. Unfortunately, tax compliance is weak. The system relies on presumptive and regressive tax withholdings. Since the 1990s, the scope of withholding tax has expanded considerably, covering a wide range of transactions.

Presently, withholding taxes apply to fifteen broad categories of income, with contributions from these taxes accounting for 62 percent of income tax collection in fiscal year 2023.

Weak tax compliance is starkly evident in the low number of taxpayers who file tax returns. As of June 2023, the total number of registered income taxpayers was nearly 9.9 million, with only about 4.4 million deemed to be active income taxpayers. This glaringly implies that about 5.4 million individuals and companies who are registered with the Federal Board of Revenue failed to submit annual tax statements. The FBR's ability to track the 55 percent of registered taxpayers who do not file is flimsy. The Reforms and Revenue Mobilization Commission (RRMC), in its 2023 interim report, characterized the FBR's performance as "lackluster."

In the tax year 2021-2022, the FBR collected Rs1.6 trillion in income taxes. However, the RRMC report revealed that an incredibly small fraction of taxpayers, precisely 13,958 individuals, contributed 75 percent (Rs1.194 trillion) of the total collection. That group accounted for only 0.39 percent of return filers and a minuscule 0.005 percent of the total population. The commission cited the urgent need for enhanced tax compliance and a broader tax base to achieve sustainable revenue generation for the government.

Ensuring revenue stability is crucial for effective planning, particularly from the government's perspective. Revenue stability is measured by the coefficient of variation, calculated as the standard deviation of tax revenue (usually as a fraction of GDP) divided by its mean. A lower coefficient of variation indicates greater stability. In the 1990s, tax revenues exhibited greater stability. Subsequently, increased volatility hindered accurate tax revenue forecasts, undermining budget planning efforts.

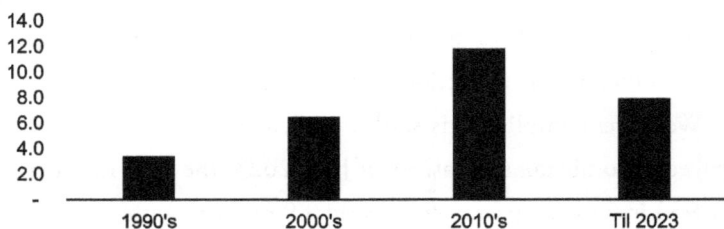

Figure 10.5: Tax stability in Pakistan. Source: State Bank of Pakistan

The convoluted and costly tax filing process contributes significantly to low tax compliance. According to the World Bank's "Ease of Doing Business in Pakistan 2020" report, the process of paying taxes takes about 270 hours. Furthermore, the "Paying Taxes 2020" report ranked Pakistan 161 out of 189 countries in terms of the hardship citizens endure to remain compliant.

These problems can be resolved. By raising the tax-to-GDP ratio to at least 15 percent, the country could raise sufficient resources to provide essential public services, address development challenges, and meet the government's fiscal needs—all without relying on external financing.

Stagnant Exports

Pakistani exports have remained stagnant for years. Paradoxically, the powerful lobbies of exporters have continuously enjoyed direct subsidies and access to subsidized credit for many years. Pakistan's exports in fiscal year 2023 amounted to $36 billion compared to India's $770 billion. For a fair comparison, Pakistan's per-capita exports were $150, compared to India's $539.

A former deputy governor of the State Bank of Pakistan, Riaz Riazuddin, analyzed the factors responsible for Pakistan's anemic exports.[81] The performance of exports is essentially a function of manufacturing capabilities. Few manufacturing entities become export firms because that requires a shift in perspective and strategy. For instance, a domestic manufacturing unit producing low-quality bath towels is less likely to venture into exports. Such a firm usually lacks entrepreneurial vision and neglects the significance of producing towels that meet international quality standards. Conversely, a more perceptive and dynamic entrepreneur will identify the potential for increased profits by catering to foreign markets. This shift requires investments to enhance productivity, improve towel quality, and train the workforce. As the firm gains traction in the export market, it continually refines its efficiency.

Exporting and non-exporting entities rely on inputs for their production processes. If these inputs are expensive due to import restrictions like duties or quotas, the costs of manufacturing and exporting will increase. That will put exporters at a disadvantage in the global market; therefore, reducing import duties on intermediate inputs is crucial. Pakistan's import duties are relatively higher than what its competitors pay. Lowering these duties can encourage more manufacturers to begin exporting their products for the first time, while existing exporters could augment their exports.

The manufacturing sector involves complex dynamics. High import duties on inputs might initially seem beneficial for promoting the reduction of a nation's imports. However, Pakistan's history demonstrates that prolonged use of high tariffs to protect national industries engenders a dependency among domestic manufacturers. Consequently, the environment becomes hostile to promoting exports, leading to a *decline* in overall manufacturing productivity.

Pakistan's exports primarily include textiles, leather goods, and rice. These products all rely on agriculture production and are therefore susceptible to fluctuations in crop and livestock outputs. The absence of technology-driven products limits diversification and growth. One primary reason for this lack of technological exports is that Pakistan receives little foreign direct investment (FDI), and not much of that is directed to the export-oriented manufacturing sector. If more FDI funding went to manufacturing, the country could introduce new technologies and management practices. However, when FDI predominantly funnels into nonmanufacturing sectors like fast food and entertainment, it does little to bolster manufacturing productivity, and it strains foreign exchange reserves through profit repatriation.

Pakistan's export market diversification lags behind competing exporters, such as Germany, Japan, Hong Kong, Russia, and Brazil. This deficiency reflects the country's weak international marketing skills and insufficient research among exporters. Pakistan's investment in research and development within our manufacturing sector is minimal.

The availability and cost of energy directly affect manufacturing and export outputs. Frequent electricity and gas outages, coupled with high costs, detrimentally impact production. Pakistan struggles with higher electricity costs compared to competitor nations due to structural issues like substantial transmission losses. Unfortunately, due to a low revenue-to-GDP ratio and a high fiscal deficit, the government struggles to subsidize electricity for manufacturers. The high cost of doing business in Pakistan also stems from high inflation, high interest rates, and security risks.

The overarching issue is macroeconomic instability, which leads to recurrent fiscal and balance-of-payment crises that cause foreign exchange shortages, substantial currency devaluations, and decreased imports and exports. Crisis-driven policies, compared to consistently sound macroeconomic governance, lead to painful medium-term adjustments. Establishing a conducive environment for doing business requires low inflation, low interest rates, prudent government borrowing, adequate revenues, and a genuinely market-based exchange rate. Achieving this necessitates short- to medium-term adjustments for consistent long-term gain.

Lazy Banking

Finance plays a crucial role in fostering investment and facilitating economic growth. However, Pakistan's financial sector has consistently fallen short of fulfilling its role as a catalyst for growth and as an intermediary for channeling capital to the private sector. The sector has seen growth in recent times, along with notable structural shifts leading to increased innovation and efficiency. Banks have remained profitable, well-capitalized, and liquid. Furthermore, the emergence of innovative financing mechanisms and institutions—real estate investment trusts, private equity funds, housing finance companies, and digital banks—have significantly reshaped the financial sector.

Nonetheless, Pakistan's financial sector remains relatively small, and it has a limited role in financing private sector activities. An important indicator of this situation is the proportion of credit or loans extended to the private sector as a percentage of GDP. The absolute volume of credit to the private sector has increased, but its relative share of GDP has declined from 29 percent in 2008 to 12 percent in 2023. In this regard, Pakistan trails behind comparable economies such as India, Bangladesh, Malaysia, and Egypt.

Financial markets connect firms to lenders and investors. This allows businesses to grow. Credit-worthy firms can obtain credit from financial intermediaries at competitive prices. Unfortunately, firm-level data from the World Bank Enterprise Surveys paints a dismal picture of financial intermediation in Pakistan. Only 5.5 percent of firms use banks to finance investments. This is low compared with Bangladesh (18.8 percent), India (56.1 percent), and the South Asian average of 22 percent. More troubling is that Pakistan's ratio has dropped significantly since 2013. This suggests that prevalent market imperfections and government-induced distortions are limiting access to credit and thus restraining growth. Excessive reliance on internal funds is a sign of potentially inefficient financial intermediation and ineffective bank supervision.

Regrettably, the banking sector in Pakistan has long been disconnected from the broader economy, which makes it difficult for banks to effectively serve the people. Commendable progress has been achieved through the State Bank of Pakistan's financial inclusion initiatives, but the banks' contributions to development finance amount to only a fraction of GDP, falling far short of what is needed to spur economic growth. A glaring example of this discrepancy is observed in the agriculture sector, which contributes a substantial 23 percent of the GDP and 37 percent of the country's employment but receives a disproportionately low share of credit (5.6 percent of the GDP). This low level of credit serves fewer than

25 percent of agricultural households. Similarly, housing finance lags significantly behind international standards, with less than 1 percent of GDP allocated to housing. Sadly, Pakistan's mortgage-finance-to-GDP ratio is one of the lowest in South Asia where the regional average is 3.4 percent.

Most of the credit allocated to the private sector goes to a highly concentrated network of corporations. Approximately 70 percent of bank loans goes to the corporate sector, leaving critical segments, such as small and medium enterprises and the agriculture sector, underserved. Pakistan's small and medium enterprises receive a mere 5.2 percent of total private sector financing. That money reaches only 155,000 small and medium enterprises, which is fewer than a decade ago. This financing, at less than 1 percent of GDP, pales in comparison to Pakistan's peers.

Many impediments prevent the financial sector from adequately financing the private sector in Pakistan. On the supply side, the single biggest hindrance is surging government borrowing, which crowds out credit to the private sector. Credit provided to the government represents around 60 percent of the banking sector's assets. On the demand side, a large informal economy poses a significant barrier. The prevalence of the informal sector means that a significant portion of households, individuals, and firms lack the documentation required to access formal financial services, compelling them to resort to informal financing, often at exorbitant interest rates.

Addressing these structural challenges necessitates coordinated efforts by the government, the State Bank of Pakistan, and stakeholders. We need holistic solutions. Reducing the government's reliance on borrowing from the financial sector, for instance, demands fiscal deficit reduction, which in turn necessitates enhanced resource mobilization and measures to consolidate expenditures. Achieving greater formality and financial inclusion also requires a reduction in regulatory burdens. The solutions to these structural impediments require medium- to long-term commitments—and political will to do the right thing.

Paradoxically, the people responsible for disconnecting the banking sector from the needs of the economy and of the population often champion financial inclusion efforts. These same people often seek high-level government positions.

Elite Capture, Inequality, and Lackluster Investment in Human Development

In 1990, Pakistani economist Mahbub ul Haq said, "People are the real wealth of a nation." With these words, he drastically shifted global development discourse. His Human Development Index (HDI) does not measure the success of a nation's economic growth; instead, the index looks at a nation's social justice conditions and its ability to promote human well-being. His work is extremely relevant to conversations about inequality.

What is Pakistan's inequality situation? The UNDP's National Human Development Report (NHDR) of 2020 estimates that the richest 1 percent of Pakistanis have access to 9 percent of the country's income.[82] The report also says that this inequality goes far beyond income and wealth.[83] The poorest and richest Pakistanis effectively live in completely different countries. Literacy levels, health outcomes, and living standards are poles apart.

The NHDR identifies three primary drivers of inequality in Pakistan: power, people, and policy. The author argues that *power* relates to groups who take advantage of loopholes, networks, and policies. The report encourages us to recognize that some people in society have privileges that others lack, and these privileges create imbalances of power.

People, the second driver of inequality, refers to the deeply embedded belief systems that foster bias against marginalized groups. For the country to be more equal, it needs a culture of empathy rather than discrimination.

Policy, the third driver of inequality, speaks to the systems and strategies that are either ineffective, or at odds with principles of social justice. The report provides a reform agenda to guide Pakistan's laws and policies toward a more equitable path. To advocate for Pakistan's vulnerable communities—to unravel the Gordian knot of power, people, and policy to alleviate inequality—demands a well-rounded, evidence-based, and contextual analysis of inequality. The report provides an excellent start. Research estimates show that the corporate sector, including industry and banking, benefits most (Rs528 billion). The feudal class (Rs370 billion) is next, followed by wealthy individuals (Rs368 billion). The next groups include large traders (Rs348 billion), state-owned enterprises (Rs345 billion), the military establishment (Rs257 billion), and exporters (Rs248 billion). Overall, the total privileges enjoyed by Pakistan's most powerful groups amounted to nearly Rs2.7 billion in 2017–2018. That is equivalent to 7 percent of the country's GDP. These privileges can be broken down into favorable pricing, lower taxation, and preferential access to public services. Some economists estimate that diverting just 24 percent of these privileges to the poor could double the benefits available to them. Redistribution along these lines is a crucial first step toward alleviating inequality.

Perhaps most importantly, the NHDR 2020 reveals that Pakistan's people do not benefit equally from public expenditures. The poorest income quintile receives 14.2 percent of public expenditures, compared to 37.2 percent for the richest quintile. This means that Pakistan's *richest quintile benefits most from government spending.*

Pakistan's state of human development situation is profoundly disheartening. The most recent UN Human Development Report highlights a significant drop of seven places in Pakistan's Human Development Index (HDI) rankings for 2021-2022. In 2020, Pakistan's HDI had already slipped by two notches, relegating it to the "low human development" category, primarily due to inadequacies in education, healthcare, and income indicators. As stated above, Pakistan ranks 161 out of 192 countries. Life expectancy at birth in Pakistan barely surpasses sixty-six years, and the average Pakistani receives only eight years of schooling, with a gross per capita national income of just over $4,600.

While Pakistan had shown consistent improvements in relation to its HDI measures since the early 1990s, the significant decline in 2021-2022 can be attributed in part to methodological changes. In 2020, the UNDP assessed 189 countries, whereas in 2021-2022, the index included 192 countries and territories. However, a more substantial reason for Pakistan's diminished HDI ranking is its relatively modest advancements compared to other nations. Pakistan lags significantly behind neighboring countries in human development.

Consider specifically Pakistan's health care situation. The

country grapples with the highest infant mortality rate in South Asia and the lowest life expectancy in the region, apart from Afghanistan. Pakistan is experiencing a severe health crisis, yet its health care system remains underfunded and strained, with only six hospital beds for every ten thousand people. There is one doctor for every thirteen hundred people. Some policies compel new and seasoned doctors to seek employment abroad.

Education in Pakistan also suffers from inadequate and inefficient government spending. Accordingly, 39.5 percent of people above the age of ten are illiterate and 36 percent (25.4 million) of all children are out of school. Teacher absenteeism and substandard school infrastructure are common problems. A recent study by Aga Khan University revealed that more than 90 percent of students at the primary and secondary levels performed poorly in math and science. Pakistan also falls short in providing adequate technical and vocational education, resulting in an under-skilled and underpaid workforce. Additionally, the country hosts a large informal sector marked by labor exploitation, particularly of women and children.

These disheartening results should not be a surprise. Successive governments have neglected human and social development. Investments in education, health, and social protection amount to a mere 5.1 percent of GDP, lower than many regional counterparts.

Under Representation of Women in the Labor Market

Women constitute 48.51 percent of Pakistan's population. To realize the country's full potential, it is critical to increase economic participation and opportunities for women, including in education and health. The World Economic Forum ranked Pakistan 142 out of 146 on its 2023 Gender Gap Index. Pakistan is at 57.5 percent gender parity, the highest since 2006. However, at the current rate of progress, full parity will only be achieved in 149 years.

Another indicator, the Economic Participation and Opportunity subindex, shows that Pakistan's gender parity has improved by 5.1 percentage points in the last decade. The current parity is 36.2 percent. There is broad progress across all indicators on this subindex, particularly in the share of women who are technical workers. Despite relatively high disparities, parity in literacy rates and school enrollment are gradually advancing, leading to 82.5 percent parity on the educational attainment subindex. Like most other countries, Pakistan's widest gender gap is related to political empowerment (15.2 percent). Although Benazir Bhutto served as prime minister from 1988 to 1990 and again from 1993 to 1996—the only woman to lead the country—women comprise one-tenth of the ministers and one-fifth of parliamentarians.

Gender inequality often stems from the underrepresentation of women in the labor market. The Economic Participation and Opportunity subindex of the 2023 WEO Gender Gap Index shows that Pakistan and Afghanistan are the countries that lag most. Women have lower workforce participation in Pakistan—22 percent compared to 82 percent for men.[84] Professional women occupy about 5 percent of senior positions in Pakistan. By contrast, women in rural areas often perform "extremely exploitative and labor-intensive work, such as planting and plucking," which is seasonal. Their income usually goes only to the men in their families. Because women often have informal jobs, they have the least access to structural rights and protections.

Gender gaps cannot be closed with public relations events filled with diplomats and CEOs at five-star hotels. Real and lasting change requires long-term grassroots work. It requires agents of change who understand the sociocultural context, including education, religion, beliefs, values, demographics, social classes, attitudes, and the economic dynamics of society.

The often-prescribed solutions for low female participation include flexible work, provision of childcare, and paternity leave. While important, these solutions do not address the elephant in the room: *social norms* that diminish the value and importance of women. Without tackling those biases, Pakistan will not achieve gender equality. The undervaluation of women's capabilities and rights in society constrain their choices and opportunities, setting narrow boundaries around what women are expected to do and be.

Conclusion

Pakistan's story and its population's hardships are like most developing countries in the world. I have shown that, despite billions of dollars in international aid across decades, there is *no evidence* that these investments have produced significant improvements.

By many measures, the on-the-ground realities in Pakistan—and in other countries—have grown worse.

I have also shown that many intrinsic problems faced by developing nations, including by Pakistan, stem from each country's own dysfunctions, such as cronyism, mismanagement, corruption, gender biases, and political instability. These factors are not the only causes of economic disarray and persistent poverty; for example, many developing nations have suffered from hundreds of years of colonialism. However, it should be clear that pouring billions of dollars of international aid on the fires will be insufficient if the recipient countries fail to put their own houses in order.

In the next section of the book, I move away from the case study of Pakistan to look more broadly at how international aid is impacting other developing nations.

SECTION III

Is Aid All Bad?

CHAPTER 11

Economic Theory, Evidence, and International Aid

International aid has evolved on the premise that it is a vital source of capital for developing countries, helping to provide resources for investment and economic growth. Robert Solow's neoclassical growth model highlighted the role of savings in accumulating capital, which is necessary for growth.[85] However, levels of domestic savings in developing countries are often insufficient. These countries rely heavily on primary product exports, and they have weak production technology, which leads to inadequate foreign exchange earnings and government revenue to import necessary capital goods.[86]

Foreign aid is sometimes seen as a solution to these challenges, for several reasons. First, it can stimulate the accumulation of physical capital by boosting domestic savings in countries with low savings.[87] R. E. Lipsey noted that foreign aid helps close the gap between saving and investment.[88] Second, foreign aid bridges the gap between government revenue, foreign exchange earnings, and the capital needed for technology and skills through sponsored and transfer programs.[89] Third, it can drive aggregate consumption, a key component of the Keynesian model for economic growth.

Interestingly, Western European countries benefited from the Marshall Plan after World War II, and nations such as China, Japan,

Singapore, South Korea, and Taiwan also received foreign aid in the past, albeit for only a few years.[90] Today, many of these countries are foreign aid *donors.*

The relationship between foreign aid and economic growth in developing countries has been extensively investigated, leading to major controversies among economists. Some researchers have concluded that foreign aid effectively stimulates economic growth, but most believe that it is ineffective. There are also those who suggest that its effectiveness is contingent on various factors, while others assert that it is detrimental to sustained growth in recipient countries. Some researchers suggest that increased foreign aid positively impacts economic growth in African economies.[91] By contrast, other researchers find that foreign aid has not significantly enhanced economic growth.[92]

A study of the effect of foreign aid on economic growth in Cambodia from 1980 to 2014 found that foreign aid affects economic growth positively in the short run.[93] However, the study's results showed that foreign aid has negative *long-term* effects on economic growth and investment. In a related study on the relationship between foreign capital inflows and economic growth in Nigeria, which covered 1980 to 2015, researchers suggested that Nigeria should not rely on foreign aid to drive economic growth. Estimates from their models indicated that foreign aid has no significant impact on economic growth.[94] Similarly, a 2020 investigation looked at the relationship between foreign aid and economic growth in Nigeria from 1980 to 2018. This study concluded that increased foreign aid to Nigeria depressed economic growth, indicating a negative effect of foreign aid.[95] These results are corroborated by findings from similar studies that show foreign aid, on its own, has no impact on economic growth.[96]

In Southeast Asia, studies of Indonesia, Thailand, and the Philippines found that foreign aid does not promote economic growth.[97] Other research has shown that foreign aid has depressed economic growth in Pakistan.[98] Several other studies support these results.[99]

An abundant trove of scholarly research has reported on the economic effects of international aid in a wide array of developing nations. One recent study examined the relationship between the amount of aid received and economic growth in developing nations, focusing on the role of institutional quality and economic freedom. Using panel data from forty-eight developing countries from 2006 to 2019, and employing a dynamic panel threshold regression, the study found that the relationship between aid and economic growth is nonlinear. Specifically, the study revealed that aid promotes economic growth only when it exceeds 7.03 percent of a country's gross national income (GNI); below this threshold, aid is detrimental. This finding supports the "big push" theory, which suggests that developing countries need substantial resource mobilization, including aid, to transform their economies. Additionally, the study highlighted the importance of institutional quality and economic freedom in shaping the relationship between aid and economic growth.[100]

As you can see, leading researchers have criticized development aid as being ineffective or even detrimental. Despite the continuous inflow of substantial foreign aid, Sub-Saharan Africa's socioeconomic conditions have continued to deteriorate, suggesting that development aid is good for nothing. In fact, as Dambisa Moyo argues, the aid might be worse than nothing. "African people are worse off; much worse off," said Moyo, asserting that aid has exacerbated poverty and hindered growth.[101] This strong condemnation is supported by development expert William Easterly, whose study "Can Foreign Aid Buy Growth" found an inverse correlation between aid and per capita growth.[102]

Despite voluminous literature on the overall ineffectiveness of aid, controversies persist over whether it helps poor countries grow *sustainably*. In this regard, a joint study by Raghuram Rajan, a former IMF chief economist and former governor of the Reserve Bank of India, who is currently a professor of finance at Chicago Booth School of Business, and Arvind Subramaniam, a former chief economic advisor to India, have reexamined (yet again!) whether aid leads to growth. They find little evidence that international aid has a meaningful positive impact on growth in cross-sectional and panel data estimations—even after correcting for the bias that aid typically goes to poorer countries. Their study suggests that for aid to be effective, the apparatus through which aid is delivered needs to be rethought (to whom, in what form, and under what conditions). These researchers argue that understanding the hindrances to effective aid is essential before we can hope for positive outcomes.[103]

With this overview of economic research in mind, we can now look at the empirical evidence from developing countries around the world.

Africa

With nearly 1.4 billion people, or approximately one-sixth of the world's population, Africa's importance in the global economy is growing. Yet, since the turn of the century, the continent has faced several economic shocks that originated elsewhere. These shocks include the 2008 global financial crisis, the Covid-19 pandemic, and the war in Ukraine.

Each shock revealed Africa's vulnerabilities. Specifically, we see the continent's need to increase its resilience and independence from the rest of the world. The crises stifled Africa's growth potential and lowered its ability to climb the development ladder. African debt, both continentally and nationally, has been rising. Debt can provide critical help in development, but the *rate* at which debt is rising in Africa has constrained growth and has limited many African countries' ability to cope with future crises or invest in development.

In 2022, public debt in Africa reached more than $1.8 trillion. This is a fraction of the overall outstanding debt of developing countries, but Africa's debt has increased by 183 percent since 2010, a rate roughly four times higher than its GDP growth rate in dollar terms. In this context, the issue of foreign aid to Africa, which has been a subject of debate for decades, has now gained renewed importance. Despite the increase in foreign aid over the years, the economic and development expectations of African countries have remained unmet, leading to questions about the effectiveness of aid.

Since the mid-twentieth century, conventional development economists have focused heavily on aid to Africa, presenting it as the solution to bridging the economic gap between the Global North and Global South, especially African countries. However, this approach has not been as effective as claimed.

Sub-Saharan Africa has received a significant share of foreign aid, yet it has the highest number of people living in poverty. In 2006, African countries received $46.66 billion or 44.3 percent of the total bilateral and imputed multilateral aid, which increased to $53.53 billion in 2022. The proportion of aid given to African countries in 2022 (25.6 percent) is at its lowest point in over two decades.

Against this backdrop, the number of Sub-Saharan Africans living in extreme poverty (below the poverty line of $2.15 per day) increased to 411 million in 2023, up 45 percent from 283 million in 1990.[104] Additionally, in Eastern and Southern Africa, 278 million people still live below the extreme poverty line, with numbers increasing at the same rate over the last three decades. African countries are home to three-quarters of the world's people living in poverty. Why, then, has this aid not yielded satisfactory results in African countries?

Region	% Change
East Asia and Pacific	-98
Eastern and Southern Africa	45
Europe and Central Asia	-87
Latin America and the Caribbean	-69
Middle East and North Africa	32
South Asia	-67
Sub-Saharan Africa	45
Western and Central Africa	8%

Figure 11.1: Number of people living in extreme poverty, shown as a percentage of change between 1990-2023. Source: World Bank Poverty and Inequality Platform (2024)

In comparison, countries in Asia and Latin America, notably China and India, which received less aid, pulled nearly 1.5 billion people out of the poverty. They did this by pursuing sound, growth-oriented economic policies while also supporting the poor. China significantly reduced rural and urban poverty, impacting more than eight hundred million people, whereas India reduced poverty by 62 percent, helping 260 million people. Likewise, Latin American countries, which have implemented strong institutional and economic reforms, and adopted sound policy frameworks, have also shown impressive performance in reducing poverty.

International aid *per se* is neither necessary nor sufficient to eradicate poverty. Countries like Bangladesh and a few others previously received huge amounts of foreign aid for economic development, but they showed remarkable progress in reducing poverty by supporting sustained economic growth and targeting policies for the poor. Moreover, countries pursuing protracted stabilization policies under IMF programs experience slower growth and job creation, pushing more people into poverty. For example, Pakistan made significant progress in reducing poverty between 2001 and 2018 with the expansion of economic opportunities and increased external remittances, but poverty has increased recently amid recent shocks, and notably slow and volatile growth. The estimated lower-middle income poverty rate was 40.5 percent ($3.65 per day in 2017) for fiscal year 2024 with an additional 2.6 million Pakistanis falling below the poverty line from the year before.[105]

Asia

Let's first look at China. Over the past forty years, the number of people in China with incomes below $1.90 per day—the international poverty line as defined by the World Bank in 2017 (not the new 2022 line of $2.15 per day) to track global extreme poverty—has fallen by almost eight hundred million people. This improvement in China comprises nearly three-quarters of the global reduction in the number of people living in extreme poverty. In 2021, China declared that it had eradicated extreme poverty, as measured by the national poverty threshold, lifting 770 million people out of poverty since 1978, and that it had built a "moderately prosperous society in all respects."

A joint study in 2022, titled "Four Decades of Poverty Reduction in China," undertaken by the World Bank and China's Development Research Center of the State Council, explores the lessons of China's experience for other developing countries. In addition, it puts forward suggestions for China's future policies.

According to the study, China's approach to poverty reduction was based on two pillars. The first was a broad-based economic transformation aimed at opening new economic opportunities and raising average incomes. The second was to provide targeted support to alleviate persistent poverty. This support was initially provided to areas disadvantaged by geography and the lack of opportunities, and then it was provided to individual households. The success of China's economic development and poverty reduction efforts benefited from effective governance, including the coordination of multiple government agencies and nongovernment stakeholders.

China's poverty reduction story is primarily a *growth* story. China's rapid and sustained economic growth is the result of comprehensive economic transformation. Reforms began in the agricultural sector, where market incentives directly improved productivity in ways that helped poor people. The development of low-skill and labor-intensive industries provided employment for workers who were transitioning away from agriculture. Urbanization offered new opportunities for migrants and boosted the incomes of their relatives in rural areas. Public investment in infrastructure improved living conditions in rural regions and connected those areas with urban and export markets.

Incremental reforms helped businesses and the population adjust to rapid changes. China's geographic size necessitated decentralized, flexible, and experimental implementation arrangements on a region-by-region basis. Competition among local governments was encouraged. Strong monitoring and accountability ensured national coherence.

Rapid economic growth since the launch of the 1978 reforms can be partially attributed to favorable initial conditions, including a relatively well-educated and healthy population, low fertility rates, high savings rates, and equitable land distribution. These characteristics were shared with other fast-growing economies, particularly in East Asia, reflecting the pace of poverty reduction in China since 1980. The primary elements of China's reforms reflected those in other high-growth economies, which all emphasized investments in human capital and infrastructure, macroeconomic stability, and structural policies supportive of competition.

China's poverty reduction success offers valuable lessons for global efforts. At the macro level, its growth trajectory aligns with research findings on sustained high growth. China wisely prioritized the sequence of its reforms, beginning with agriculture where the largest immediate gains could be achieved. High-level commitment to growth and poverty reduction, along with performance incentives and local experimentation, facilitated effective governance and policy implementation.

At the micro level, China's experience offers insights for using agricultural extension programs to foster technological progress. For example, China leveraged e-commerce and logistics networks to integrate rural areas with urban supply chains. The country did this by financing connectivity and urban development (based on rising land values), and by using survey data to identify and target poor regions and households.

Lessons from China's Story

Poverty reduction in China was a major global development milestone in the twentieth and twenty-first centuries. There are three main lessons from China's experience that could be valuable for global development.

First, China's poverty reduction efforts are deeply rooted in its specific historical context, which includes significant political, economic, and social changes. The infrastructure built through massive labor inputs before 1978 was critical for later agricultural development, which was achieved with minimal costs compared to many African countries' reliance on aid. Self-reliance and equitable social distribution *before* economic reforms were crucial for the rapid economic growth and poverty reduction *after* the reforms.

Second, China shows us that long-term economic growth is fundamental for large-scale poverty reduction. Economic growth, however, must also promote meaningful social transformation. Effective poverty reduction mechanisms need to ensure that the benefits consistently reach the poor. Poverty reduction and the eradication of absolute poverty are prolonged processes.

Finally, countries need strong political commitment and a

robust governmental role to reduce poverty, especially in contexts of rising inequality. China's success since 2012 highlights the essential role of the government, which contrasts with the experiences of Europe and the US. Europe has implemented policies to support the poor through a welfare-based system influenced by socialist thinking and workers' movements. The US has struggled with policy breakthroughs in poverty reduction, placing more responsibility on individual efforts and market mechanisms rather than relying on comprehensive income transfers. By comparison, China's approach involved a unified political commitment *across all sectors*. This approach prevented interest groups and administrative limitations from becoming barriers to redistribute wealth and opportunities.

India

Over the last ten years, India's GDP has grown by 7 percent as a compound annual growth rate, jumping to $3.6 trillion. India moved from being the world's eighth largest economy to being its fifth largest. Over the next four years, India's GDP will likely rise to $5 trillion, making it the third largest economy by 2027, overtaking Japan and Germany. It could also become the *fastest growing* major economy because it has a large and consistent labor supply, and it has seen improved institutional strength and governance.[106] Strong reform measures initiated in the last ten years should uphold solid economic growth in coming decades.

Official data released in early 2024 confirms that India has nearly eliminated extreme poverty, as commonly defined in international comparisons.[107] This is an encouraging development with positive implications for the reduction of global poverty rates. In a March 2024 article published by the Brookings Institute, Surjit Bhalla, India's former executive director at the IMF, and Karan Bhasin stated that India should raise its official poverty line, which would provide an opportunity to redefine existing social protection programs, thereby providing greater support to the genuinely poor.[108]

The data shows that India's impressive growth has greatly reduced inequality and poverty. The country's real per capita annual consumption growth has been 2.9 percent since 2011-2012 with annual rural growth at 3.1 percent, which is significantly higher than the urban growth of 2.6 percent.

In terms of inequality, India has seen an unprecedented decline in urban and rural inequality. The urban Gini ratio, a statistical measure of wealth inequality, declined from 36.7 to 31.9, and the rural Gini ratio declined from 28.7 to 27.0. In the annals of inequality analysis, this reduction of inequality is unheard of, and especially in the context of high per capita growth.

India's high growth and large reductions in inequality have combined to eliminate poverty in relation to the $1.90 per day poverty line (the World Bank's 2017 poverty line). The headcount poverty ratio for that same poverty line has declined from 12.2 percent in 2011-2012 to 2 percent in 2022-2023, equivalent to 0.93 percentage points per year. Rural poverty stood at 2.5 percent while urban poverty was down to 1 percent. These estimates do not consider the free food (wheat and rice) supplied by the government to approximately two-thirds of the population, nor does it include the utilization of public health and education services. These efforts include a national mission for the construction of toilets and attempts to ensure universal access to electricity, modern cooking fuel, and piped water. As an example, rural access to piped water in India was 16.8 percent in August 2019. Today that number is 74.7 percent. By providing access to safe water, the country has reduced sicknesses, which in turn helped families earn more income. Similarly, the government focused on improving development in 112 districts that had the lowest development indicators.

How has this happened? These remarkable results should not come as a surprise given the strong policy thrust on redistribution through publicly funded programs. India is an interesting example of a country that *reduced its reliance on unchecked foreign aid.* India's approach to foreign aid has changed since early 2000. Previously dependent on foreign aid to mitigate the impacts of disasters, famines, and rural poverty, India in recent years has transitioned from being a recipient of foreign aid to a net donor.

In addition, India has disciplined the development sector by implementing strong accountability measures that include restrictions on NGOs from accepting certain types of foreign funding. More than twenty thousand Indian NGOs have been stripped of their foreign funding licenses since 2011.[109] In early January 2022, the government revoked permits of nearly six thousand NGOs, forcing them to stop accepting foreign funding.

Although India is now a net donor of foreign aid, OECD data shows that India was still the highest recipient of ODA in the world in 2020-2021; however, that is because so much foreign aid flowed to India during the catastrophic second wave of Covid-19. The acceptance of external assistance to fight a global public health problem cannot be characterized as a reversal of India's long-standing policy against accepting humanitarian assistance from abroad.

Catherine Davison explored the India's changing approach toward foreign aid.[110] In reality, as the OECD data shows, India never stopped accepting foreign aid. What essentially changed in the early 2000s was the terms on which aid was received, with India announcing an end to bilateral aid from all but five countries and the EU. Other donors were requested to direct money via multilateral institutions such as the World Bank. The focus also shifted away from the traditional poverty-focused aid projects, with India instead encouraging investments that would spur growth. Japan, for example, India's largest bilateral aid donor, is currently funding several infrastructure projects—including a new metro system and freight corridor—through its development assistance agency JICA, according to India's receipt budget for the current fiscal year. So, in essence, it is not the quantum that has reduced but the nature of aid that has changed.

In short, India has increasingly rejected aid that is earmarked for projects directly working on poverty alleviation; instead, the country has prioritized a policy of development cooperation to boost economic growth across the country.

Latin America

Compared to Africa, Asia, and Europe, the aid flowing to Latin America has been modest: only $11 billion, or 5.7 percent of the total (including bilateral as well as imputed multilateral) aid in 2022. Over the past two decades, the inflows received by Latin America hovered around 6 to 7 percent of total aid. Meanwhile, the number of people living in extreme poverty in Latin America and

Caribbean countries declined from seventy-six million in 1990 to twenty-four million in 2023, a decline of about 69 percent. What lessons can be drawn from the region that might benefit developing countries in other regions?

First, Latin American countries managed to navigate the 2008 global crisis reasonably well, at least in economic terms. This can be attributed to two main factors: strong economic fundamentals and sound economic policies coupled with a favorable external environment.[111] In essence, both prudence and providence played a role in their success.

Since the crises of the 1980s and 1990s, major Latin American countries have built up buffers in three key areas: more resilient balance of payments, responsive inflation-targeting regimes, and reduced public debt. The transition from a fixed exchange rate regime to an inflation targeting regime in the 1990s helped stabilize inflation expectations and minimized exchange-rate impacts on inflation.

Moreover, new fiscal rules improved the public debt profile, resulting in lower public deficits and a healthier debt cycle. Timely and appropriate policy responses, such as cutting policy rates, prudent liquidity provision, and foreign exchange stabilization measures, also contributed to the region's resilience during the 2008 crisis. Limited exposure to external demand shocks allowed larger countries to rely more on domestic demand. Local financial markets became less dependent on foreign capital and increased domestic bond issuance. Improved regulation, particularly on open forex positions, helped curb losses, although some corporate-level issues in Mexico and Brazil did not escalate into systemic risks. Interestingly, one key advantage for emerging markets during the 2008 crisis was their lower level of financial deepening.

Most Asian countries avoided currency appreciation due to their export dependence, but Latin America's emerging markets used flexible inflation-targeting exchange policies that prevented currency appreciation during the 2008 crisis. This approach helped reduce current account deficits as commodity prices increased. Thus, many emerging markets in Latin America (Brazil, Chile, Colombia, Mexico, and Peru) provide a good example of sound economic policies, prudent policy frameworks, and better regulations to address economic challenges.

Summary

Economic theory, as demonstrated by academic research on the effectiveness of international aid in developing nations, and the abundant empirical evidence from around the world, all indicate that international aid has had little impact—or even negative effects—on growth and poverty reduction in developing nations. The countries with the best records of growth and poverty reduction are those that lowered their reliance on international aid and instead implemented their own sound economic reforms. In fact, the nations that have seen the most dramatic improvements in growth, poverty reduction, and other measures of human well-being have all *reduced their reliance on international aid.*

Based on all this evidence, you would think that policymakers and international donors would reconsider whether current approaches to international aid are worthwhile. But nothing changes. Why not? I will address that question in the next chapter.

CHAPTER 12

Self-Seeking Donors

As I stated in the book's preface, my critique of international aid pertains specifically to grants and concessional loans extended directly to governments by other governments or institutions such as the IMF and World Bank. I am not referring to humanitarian or emergency aid designed to alleviate suffering caused by wars, natural disasters, pandemics, and the like.

With this clarification in mind, I do want to present readers with a forceful but constructive critique of the current international aid system. In this chapter, I will address two interrelated problems: a) the imposition of donors' own agendas on the countries they are supposed to be helping, and b) the lack of accountability for poorly designed and implemented programs, which consistently fail to meet stated objectives. The two problems are inseparable; they are two sides of the same coin.

First, when donors impose their own priorities on recipient nations, they effectively erode national sovereignty. Recipient countries should be allowed to set their own development priorities and strategies, and to find ways to improve their own institutions. This can be done in partnership with donor agencies, but when donors *define* the terms and *prioritize* their own interests, it leads to the inefficient use or outright waste of donor resources, not to mention a loss of trust. Donor programs must be seen as authentic, trusted instruments to improve the lives of vulnerable people, and the best way to do that is to ensure that recipient countries maintain national sovereignty.

As for the accountability side of the coin, all stakeholders should be able to measure the tangible impact of programs on the economy and on the ultimate beneficiaries—the people. The donors and their programs need to be held accountable in meaningful ways. To rely on anecdotal success stories as the means of public accountability, which occurs so often, glosses over the reality of poor outcomes.

I am not alone in calling for these types of changes. Nearly twenty years ago, the 2005 Paris Declaration on Aid Effectiveness, which was endorsed by more than one hundred developed and developing countries, provided strong commitments and principles for making international aid more effective. The declaration stated that developing countries should set their own development strategies, improve their own institutions, and tackle their own corruption. It called on donor countries and organizations to align their support with *national* strategies, not the other way around. It encouraged donors to coordinate their actions with each other rather than compete. It pushed donors and recipient countries to measure on-the-ground results and then find ways to implement strong systems of accountability.

Unfortunately, there is little evidence that the Paris Declaration's recommendations have been put into practice, as I have shown in previous chapters! There are exceptions, of course, such as the Financial Inclusion Program (FIP) managed by the State Bank of Pakistan, which proves how adherence to the Paris Declaration's principles can yield positive results when they are put into practice. Unfortunately, the exceptions do not reflect the norm. Generally, donors fail to implement sound principles and practices.

The disconnect between donors' promises and on-the-ground realities fosters widespread distrust and cynicism. In Pakistan, for example, there is a growing sense of frustration. Donor agencies tout their positive work in Pakistan, but data on growth, tax revenue mobilization, poverty, access to justice, gender gaps, quality of public schools and government education standards, health facilities, corruption, and quality of governance, show that donor programs have produced very few real gains in Pakistan.

The Erosion of National Sovereignty

As stated above, international donor agencies often impose their own interests, values, and agendas on recipient nations. Thus, money becomes leverage for manipulation. This erodes national sovereignty.

Here is an example. The UK's House of Common's International Development Committee (IDC) noted that British aid programs, which portend to support the development of an open society, did not always fit with the Pakistani government's policy objectives and priorities. Specifically, the committee recommended that the UK government should push Pakistan toward becoming a more open society, including the need for civic spaces, and increased religious and media freedom. The committee said that the UK's Foreign, Commonwealth and Development Office (FCDO) should increase support to Pakistan's National Commission on the Status of Women and its National Commission on Human Rights.[112] Pakistan's government certainly agreed in principle with these directions, but the government wished to give higher priority to serious economic needs.

The UK Parliament's report demonstrated that its priorities for Pakistan's development were driven first and foremost by the donor's human rights values and objectives, not Pakistan's *fundamental economic challenges.* Rather than tackling pressing issues like malnutrition, health, water scarcity, and inadequate public transport in major cities, the donor agency pushed its own emphasis on promoting an open society. The UK Parliament elevated social and cultural issues over Pakistan's priorities for the use of donor funding.

To receive the UK's funding, Pakistan had to comply with detailed requirements related to open society measures. The IDC pushed Pakistan to ensure that its funds would be used with full inclusivity, particularly in relation to religious minorities. The IDC also urged a religious diversity audit of UK aid programs in Pakistan and suggested that the FCDO explicitly focus on the impact of aid programs on marginalized and minority communities. It advocated for aid programs targeted at these groups, such as women and girls from religious minorities. Again, there was nothing wrong with the UK's open society goals, but the donor's priorities should not have outweighed *Pakistan's* economic priorities and plans.

This type of situation happens frequently around the world. Evidence strongly indicates that development programs in recipient countries are shaped by the political and diplomatic priorities of donors, and those priorities often limit the effectiveness of aid. The living standards of impoverished populations remain largely unchanged.

In April 2023, when the development assistance committee of the OECD released its preliminary data on the effectiveness of development aid in 2022, Oxfam harshly criticized rich countries for diverting an alarming 14.4 percent of aid *for their own benefit*, depriving the world's poorest of vital support during multiple crises.[113]

There are also reports of donors imposing their agendas on African nations. In a commentary featured on the Brookings Institute website on November 1, 2012, Mwangi S. Kimenyi wrote about the reservations of African nations regarding international donors' interference in local matters and their lack of transparency.[114] The article highlighted a passionate address by Rwandan President Paul Kagame during the 2012 African Economic Conference in Kigali, where he expressed deep frustration with the international donor community. Kagame, visibly irritated, vehemently criticized donors, particularly rebuking various countries' decisions to suspend aid to Rwanda because those nations believed allegations that Rwanda was supporting rebels in the Democratic Republic of Congo (DRC). Kagame criticized the international community for failing to address the longstanding issues in the DRC, insinuating that donor countries were scapegoating Rwanda rather than assuming responsibility. He suggested that donor nations were attempting to influence Rwanda's decisions as a means of serving their own interests. He added that Rwanda would not succumb to blackmail.

In the context of Pakistan, I have directly witnessed the imposition of donors' agendas in national economic policy, which furthered institutional decay in Pakistan. The underlying problem on a global level, however, is addiction to IMF programs. This dependency has resulted in lethargic policymaking because, when a government is too reliant on IMF funding, it outsources its economic policy formation. The IMF gains freedom to dictate its own policies. The policies are usually focused on stabilization, but they seldom address chronic issues, such as an inequitable tax system, weak exports, lackluster investment in human capital, water scarcity, lack of adequate public transportation in cities, malnutrition, access to tertiary healthcare, and inefficient judicial systems.

The welfare of Pakistan's citizens, which ought to be the primary objective of every economic policy, has become marginalized, thereby creating a disconnect between the people and the state. Fiscal policies, including tax policy, are mostly outsourced to IMF staff. Monetary policy is supposed to be entrusted to an independent statutory committee, but it remains subservient to IMF rules. Energy sector policy remains an integral part of the IMF conditionality in the form of increasing electricity and gas tariffs and fuel taxes. Overall, IMF interference in what should be Pakistan's domain has eroded public governance. The institutions have lost their sense of direction.

To find more evidence that donors prioritize their own interests over those of recipient countries, we only need to "follow the money." Huge sums of international aid, contributed by taxpayers in wealthy nations, flow back to the coffers of nations where it originated. Money returns to developed countries in the form of fees paid to contractors and consultants. For instance, the United States is the largest source of aid among the Development Assistance Committee (DAC) member countries. A significant amount of ODA, worth $97.6 billion, went to projects in different regions between 2012 and 2021. Overall, US-based contractors won nearly 88 percent of the total contract obligations.[115]

In total, USAID obligated $52.9 billion through contracts between 2011 and 2021. All of USAID's top ten contractors are US-based. Chemonics International received the biggest share

($11.8 billion) during the ten-year period. DAI Global ranked next, with $2.8 billion over the decade, followed by PFSCM, with $2.1 billion.[116]

The lifestyles of those working in the donor community conflict with poverty alleviation objectives. CEOs and executives travel business class and stay in five-star hotels. Donor agencies hold conferences and summits in beautiful locations in Spain, France, Bali, Cape Town, and Cancun, Sharm El Shaikh, and Russia. London and Washington, DC remain their favorite places to spend taxpayers' dollars. Despite the flow of millions of dollars to the international aid sector, poverty alleviation remains an elusive dream.

The Lack of Accountability

Donor agencies can perpetuate self-serving and ineffective tactics because no international entity holds them accountable for producing results. The reasons for this lack of accountability go to the heart of the "shady economics of international aid." Let me explain how the system works.

In many countries, aid fails to reach the intended beneficiaries. In 2014, Nobel Prize-winning economist Sir Angus Deaton and numerous other economists asserted that out of the $135 billion allocated for official aid, only a fraction of the money effectively reached those in need. Likewise, Marc Cohen, an aid expert at Oxfam, highlighted the discrepancy between donors' pledges and delivery. He stated that more than $193 billion in international aid was not delivered in 2022. Cohen also described how donors often redirect funds away from the original purpose, asserting that donors redirected nearly $30 billion intended for economic aid to things like vaccine donations, refugee hosting costs, and profiting from development aid loans. To solve these global problems, he called for a robust accountability system to ensure that economic aid reaches the poorest people in the poorest countries.[117]

The 2022 total aid figures, available on the OECD website, reveal that the thirty OECD members collectively spent $204 billion on aid. However, only five countries—Luxembourg, Norway, Germany, Sweden, and Denmark—fulfilled their promise to commit 0.7 percent of their gross national income (GNI) to development aid. Rich countries, on average, allocated only 0.36 percent of their gross national incomes. Cohen further highlights that the level of development aid for the world's poorest countries falls significantly short of the UN's goal of 0.15 percent to 0.2 percent of rich countries' GNI, which is the amount needed to end poverty in the poorest countries by 2030. In 2022, the actual amount of aid in 2022 was less than 0.1 percent. Notably, donor spending to host refugees accounted for 14.4 percent of ODA, totaling $29.3 billion. Excluding the cost of hosting refugees, the real term increase in total ODA from DAC members was 4.6 percent, significantly lower than the reported 13.6 percent. Despite a fifty-year-old agreement to spend 0.7 percent of ODA, only seven countries have ever met or exceeded that target. This failure has cost low- and middle-income countries an estimated $6.5 trillion in undelivered aid from 1970 to 2021.

During the implementation stage of aid programs, most foreign money goes to insiders. According to a June 2023 report, nearly nine out of every ten dollars that USAID spent in the 2022 fiscal year went to its international contracting partners, most of which are based in or around Washington, DC. Just one out of ten dollars (perhaps less) went to frontline, local groups. The open secret in Washington, DC is that very little of American foreign aid ever leaves America's capital city.[118] A *Foreign Policy* headline summed it up in 2022: "Biden's Foreign Aid Is Funding the Washington Bubble."[119]

Likewise, researchers at the University of Washington have called America's foreign aid "phantom aid" because the government's US-based "implementing partners" keep most of the money for themselves. International NGOs are expensive to sustain. They usually operate from headquarters in expensive cities like Washington, DC, New York, Boston, or Seattle. Taxpayers pay for the overhead and overall organizational administration, which cuts deeply into the aid that could be delivered to people in need. According to one study, it is common for up to 30 percent of a project's aid funding to pay for the contracted organization's overhead costs (sometimes more). In addition, approximately 25 percent pays for headquarters staff, and another 25 percent pays for foreign staff to live in recipient countries. This leaves between 10 and 30 percent for actual program delivery, and that amount is often divided among scores of organizations that compete for the scraps. It is common for contractors' staff salaries to exceed local salaries by a factor of ten, which distorts local economies and creates a brain drain.[120]

The evidence shows that the aid industry keeps most of the money for itself. "There's a lot we need to do to change the way our US global development system works, especially to get more resources directly to the organizations on the front lines of solving the world's hardest problems. We also need to create more accountability for results," say researchers at Unlock Aid.[121]

Why do these problems persist without being corrected? Because we lack a robust system of accountability, as Marc Cohen and others have argued.

Weak Systems of Accountability Breed Waste, Abuse, and Fraud

The lack of accountability emboldens aid organizations to spend the funds irresponsibly, leading to widespread discontent and negative public perceptions about donor agencies. In early 2025, the Trump administration froze USAID funding and launched an in-depth review of its operations. The US Secretary of State Marco Rubio publicly expressed frustration with the USAID and ordered a thorough review. White House Press Secretary Karoline Leavitt cited several USAID projects as glaring examples of waste, abuse, and fraud. Addressing the reporters on February 4, 2025, Levitt said that some USAID funds went to what she called "insane priorities." She presented a long list of projects deemed to be wasteful, which amounted to about $153 million. Subsequently, during his remarks at the Republican Governors Association on February 21, 2025, President Trump further criticized US foreign aid. The US federal court system, at the time of this writing, is addressing whether the administration's funding freeze is constitutional, but the administration says that it is attempting to "get the fraud waste and abuse out of our federal government."[122]

When considering the list of aid projects presented by Leavitt, we should notice that almost none of this funding is directed toward poverty alleviation or fostering economic development in recipient nations. Rather, it appears that USAID's powerful bureaucrats have acted without fear of accountability, which allows them to misallocate US taxpayers' funds. This lack of accountability is common among all international aid and development organizations.

To make matters worse, the lack of accountability interacts with the persistence of corruption. International aid often *funds corruption.* You would think that donors would stop giving money to recipient nations that do not implement anticorruption measures. However, donor agencies are not that concerned about local corruption.

Drawing on research from Transparency International, William Pearse, in an article published on the *Inomics* website on April 7, 2021, contended that corruption markedly diminishes a country's productivity, drives up inflation, deters foreign investors, and exacerbates poverty. The link between corruption and poverty is particularly evident in Africa. When donors implement aid programs, corruption frequently surges and egregious kleptocracies take root in governments.

Foreign aid often exacerbates corruption in nations like Nigeria, for example. The country has repeatedly sought loans from multilateral development banks. National borrowing isn't inherently negative if used for development, but Nigeria's pervasive corruption has undermined the effectiveness of those loans. Nigeria ranks 145 out of 180 in Transparency International's corruption index. Instead of benefiting the population or promoting growth, international aid often funds wasteful projects and fraudulent contracts.

Aid dependency is another issue of concern. In his article "Foreign Aid Is not 'Aiding' the Development of Nigeria," published in Zambia's *Mail Guardian* on January 24, 2022, Jerome Salami argued that the Nigerian government showed little interest in finding sustainable solutions to the nation's problems. Instead, Nigeria's leaders expected to receive continuous "free" money from the West. Meanwhile, Nigerian politicians sometimes seek medical care in European hospitals while their citizens hope for the best in dilapidated government hospitals.

So, why do donor agencies continue to provide aid for corrupt and undemocratic regimes? Dambisa Moyo argues that donor agencies are driven by their own economic incentives and political advantages. A whole industry has grown around international aid. Moyo estimates that this industry employs around five hundred thousand people worldwide. And the livelihoods of these people depend on the *constant distribution of aid.* Moreover, within many of these international organizations, success is measured by the size and quantity of loans and grants rather than how the money is spent or whether it helps. If aid is not dispersed and spent, donors risk the elimination of their programs and the loss of their jobs. In other words, there is an intrinsic, self-seeking incentive to continuously send international aid to countries, even when the governments are highly corrupt.

Corruption persists, at least in part, because of a dysfunctional, codependent relationship between donor agencies and the bureaucracies of recipient countries. If the donor agencies seriously embraced an anticorruption approach, they would soon have few friends in the host countries. A breakdown in that relationship would undermine the self-interested aims of donor agencies.

In Pakistan, for example, donor agencies have established strong connections with the civil bureaucracy. Civil servants, mostly belonging to the powerful Pakistan Administrative Service (PAS), hold key positions within the federal and provincial governments. They are also employed *de facto* by donors within opaque organizational structures. Many PAS officers simultaneously work for the UK's Foreign, Commonwealth and Development Office and other donor agencies while retaining their civil service jobs, seniority, and officially provided residences. The creation of Section 42 companies has enabled a notorious method of rewarding civil servants through attractive salaries, which are typically much larger than their government salaries. Once such companies are established, both donors and the implementing agencies have a free hand in designing and implementing policies, programs, and projects. They can do these things while bypassing the scrutiny of the auditor-general and without complying with other checks and balances. In the Punjab province, for example, fifty-six Section 42 companies came under judicial scrutiny. These companies faced allegations of bypassing Pakistan's auditor-general, leading the National Accountability Bureau (NAB) to investigate malpractices. Thus, the public servants work for the very entities they are meant to regulate.

All this shows that international aid systems often lack accountability *by design*. Without strong oversight and evaluations of actual outcomes, donors and their staff are free to sustain their self-interest. Likewise, civil servants in the host countries gain ongoing access to incomes funded by the donors. No one is held accountable for tangible outcomes or the prevention of corruption.

We should not be surprised that, despite spending billions of dollars each year, conditions in recipient countries have deteriorated, as shown in the data about tax collection, poverty rates, government effectiveness, human development, and access to justice. Most of the taxpayers' money received by the donors goes back to the West through the bank accounts of the consultants. Meanwhile, recipient countries compromise their national pride, sovereignty, self-reliance, and institutional independence.

Conclusion

Pakistan's political leaders have expressed disapproval of foreign aid, but their actions have not aligned with their rhetoric. They have made minimal practical efforts to diminish the country's reliance on aid, likely because of political expediency. Pakistan's political leaders face intense pressures to accept international aid from influential donor networks, which hinders their ability to break free from dependence on external assistance. Nevertheless, they publicly acknowledge the problem.

To mention a few examples, Pakistan's former Prime Minister Imran Khan publicly deplored the idea of aid, saying that it had been one of Pakistan's biggest curses. During his address at the United States Institute of Peace in July 2019, Khan said: "I hate the idea of asking for funds. Aid has been one of the biggest curses for my country. It has created the dependency syndrome. . . . Countries rise because of self-respect and self-esteem. No country rises because of begging and borrowing for money."[123]

Referring to the loss of national dignity due to foreign aid, Pakistan's Prime Minister Shehbaz Sharif stated that many countries had been "fatigued" by seeking aid. He presented a dismal picture of Pakistan's dwindling economy and regretted that "even friendly countries have started looking at Pakistan as one that was always begging for money." As reported in 2022 by Pakistan's *Dawn News,* Sharif said, "Today, when we go to any friendly country or make a phone call, they think that we have come [to them] to beg for money." Sharif added that "we have been wandering for the past seventy-five years carrying a begging bowl."[124]

Pakistan is not alone. All developing nations need to be more disciplined and protective of their national sovereignty. They need to restrict foreign aid to projects that directly contribute to economic growth, while staying within sustainable debt limits. One-off interventions should be rejected. The habit of accepting everything regardless of the terms and conditions must be avoided. Recipient nations should carefully choose which sectors require external assistance and then clearly communicate those priorities to the donors. The primary focus should be growth-enhancing projects for which concessional financing can be beneficial.

CHAPTER 13

Do We Really Need International Aid?

The short answer might be no. Compared to the purported aims of donors, it looks as though international aid *impedes* progress.

As Zambian economist Dambisa Moyo (2009) bluntly asserted, "African people are worse off, much worse off. . . . Aid has contributed to deepening poverty and stalling growth." Her forceful critique finds support from other development experts like William Easterly, whose research highlights a troubling inverse relationship between aid and per capita economic growth. Equally perplexing is the fact that between 1970 and 1998, poverty in Africa surged from 11 percent to 66 percent, a period coinciding with peak aid inflows. It makes no sense to keep using the same model for international aid.

Governments, not foreign entities, should administer and deliver a country's public goods and services, such as justice, defense, security, social protection, and public infrastructure. The state should also provide sound regulatory and institutional frameworks to support the effective functioning of a market economy.[125] Governments should allocate resources by enhancing competition, supporting financial sector development, and strengthening governance.[126] In some cases, governments have tried to play more direct roles in raising growth and creating jobs, the lack of which they perceive as failures of markets and the private sector. However, such state-led growth strategies have often resulted in an excessive "state footprint," hampering private sector development and innovation. When coupled with weak governance and institutions, heavy state involvement can lead to large-scale misuses of public resources. Thus, better governance improves investment efficiency and productivity, stimulates private sector investment, and increases the growth impact.[127]

In Pakistan, donors have failed to fix the critical economic issues I have described in earlier chapters. Meanwhile, government leaders remain perilously dependent on foreign aid, sidestepping fiscal responsibility. During my tenure as Pakistan's representative at the IMF, I frequently received requests for alternative avenues of aid, such as the newly established Resilience and Sustainability Trust (RST) and Rapid Financing Instrument (RFI). Others sought to secure additional funds for Pakistan under the IMF's exceptional access policy. They celebrate the approval of fresh loans from the IMF, World Bank, ADB, and other donors, label them as achievements, and post congratulatory messages. This reckless financial behavior revealed a lack of self-respect and national pride, placing even the highest-ranking officials under the sway of junior IMF staff.

Pakistan received $48 billion in foreign aid (ODA) from 2000 to 2021. This aid was intended to address the country's developmental challenges; however, it paradoxically led to an unsustainable debt burden—an existential threat. Despite substantial injections of aid, finding evidence of tangible progress has been elusive. Ironically, global lending institutions have done little to help reduce Pakistan's debt through prudent reforms or increasing export competitiveness. Multilateral organizations have been unwilling to restructure their loans.

Nevertheless, the US doubled its economic support fund for Pakistan to $82 million for fiscal year 2024 to help the country recover from devastating floods, diversify the energy supply, and build emergency preparedness capabilities. According to the US State Department, this assistance to Pakistan would expand private sector economic growth, strengthen democratic institutions, and advance gender equity and women's empowerment. The UK also said it would provide a modest £41.5 million ($53 million) in bilateral ODA to Pakistan for the year 2023-2024, with a focus on accelerated family planning, education for girls, revenue mobilization, and investment and trade.

For a country with a nominal GDP of $375 billion, these amounts seem like peanuts. However, Pakistan's successive governments have repeatedly deferred to the agendas of rich countries. This deference stems from a twofold challenge. First, the country's expenditures and imports consistently surpass its revenues and exports. Second, there is a pervasive apprehension of potential sanctions. Pakistan's vulnerability to sanctions is evident in its export-dependent economy, overseas workforce, and procurement of defense equipment. The majority of the nation's noncitizen workforce comprises people who provide unskilled labor, workers who are easily replaced by people in other low-income countries. The risk of harm from a displeased Middle Eastern regime is tangible. This vulnerability has influenced strategic decisions, such as forgoing cheap gas and electricity from Iran and cheap oil from Russia.

The hesitance to capitalize on better economic opportunities is tied to the ease with which Pakistan's meager exports can be substituted. Notably, 70 percent of the country's exports consist of cotton manufactures, leather, and rice. Pakistan heavily relies on maintaining "favored status" with Western countries, which collectively constitute its major export destinations—21 percent to the US, 11 percent to China, 7 percent to the UK, and 5 percent to Germany. The nation's economic well-being hinges on securing preferential treatment. Any displeasure from Western nations could lead them to pursue imports from other countries or to refuse visas to eager Pakistani officials with expectations for future engagements.

Foreign and domestic policies are interrelated; if there is something wrong with Pakistan's foreign relations it is largely because something is wrong with its domestic policy. Powerful groups and institutions are embedded in our body politic. They have defined Pakistan's national interest to primarily serve their own interests more than the needs of the people. The system is set up to bring them back to power with ease.

A system monopolized by the elite, without reference to the people, weakens the state. In Pakistan and other nations, elite cronyism has led to personalized and noninstitutionalized governance, degrading the integrity of the policymaking process. Excessive concern with security has diverted national resources away from economic and human development. Feudalism supported by religious institutions has created self-inflicted, long-term disparities in areas such as education, women's rights, and socioeconomic emancipation. As a result, large segments of the population have been hindered from making productive contributions to national development.

A weak state remains more dependent on outside support. As a result, the state's foreign policy ends up serving the strategic interests of foreign entities, sometimes at the expense of the national interest.

A dependent foreign policy is restrictive and addictive. It robs the country of freedom to find new allies. An entrenched dependency syndrome makes the country vulnerable to exploitation. Evidence for this can be seen in the way the US has taken advantage of Pakistan's reliance on American help, at great cost to Pakistan. A dependent foreign policy is subservient to other countries' policies. Unable to be minimally self-reliant, dependent countries resort to borrowing, often with reckless abandon. What is worse, aid and massive borrowing can be an incentive for poor governance.

Pakistan and many other developing nations need an independent foreign policy, but that will not happen without systemic changes at home, including a power-balance shift away from the elite to the people, and away from the military to civilians. Pakistan also needs to rebalance its foreign policy priorities away from security and toward development.

The diversification of aid sources is important as a means of preventing a small group of donors from controlling a country's policies; however, Pakistan's aid diversification agenda faces practical limits. For example, Western aid usually includes mechanisms and budgetary support to fund social policy and socioeconomic development programs. By contrast, China's aid usually lacks those types of support. Other sources of assistance, such as Gulf-based aid, is small relative to Pakistan's needs. Western funding for social programming is channeled through a sprawling network of foreign NGOs and local development partners, all modeled on Western "civil society organizations." The relationships between these NGOs and their foreign benefactors, including some members of Pakistan's elite, have fueled populist backlash. Average Pakistanis believe that the civil society community does not always act in the national interests. So, aid diversification can be challenging for developing countries.

Beyond aid diversification, developing countries need sound economic stewardship that addresses external debt situations, creates less reliance on foreign borrowing, and establishes a bigger reservoir of funds to finance the state's activities. In most dependent countries, domestic changes do not come without barriers and opposition. Therefore, change needs to occur by gradually reducing dependence on foreign countries and the IMF, and by easing the preoccupation with external security. Pakistan, with its strong military and nuclear capability, can deter any security challenge. In essence, the country needs to balance a longer-term national vision with immediate short-term political opportunities and temptations. Pakistan's instability and polarization in 2024 posed a monumental challenge for current and future governments.

Pakistan's leaders could reduce their reliance on loans from the IMF, the World Bank, the ADB, and bilateral donors if the nation's leaders would eliminate wasteful public expenditures, including by diminishing the size of the government. The country could become more independent by improving tax revenues, reducing energy sector losses, and privatizing failed state-owned enterprises. Local experts can resolve most of these issues if there is strong political will to implement reforms instead of supporting vested interests. This approach would also ameliorate the unsustainable debt burden.

How to Reduce (or Eliminate) Dependency on Foreign Aid

Pakistan's economic mismanagement has led to a colossal waste of resources. If we juxtapose those losses with the inflows of foreign aid, we can easily conclude that proper management would eliminate all or most of Pakistan's need for that aid. By "proper management" I refer to the following recommendations, which I believe would apply in many other developing countries.

First, Pakistan needs to ensure the stability of political regimes and avert political disruptions. This would enable the country to maintain consistent economic growth and prevent substantial economic losses. To illustrate the magnitude of these losses, the uncertainties stemming from political misadventures in 2022 to 2023 led to a drastic decline in GDP growth, plunging from 6.17 percent in fiscal year 2022 to a *decline* of 0.17 percent in fiscal year 2023. This downturn translated into a direct loss of $36 billion. The GDP contracted from $375 billion in fiscal year 2022 to $339 billion in fiscal year 2023. Concurrently, the State Bank of Pakistan's net reserves plummeted from $10.5 billion in April 2022 to $4.4 billion by the end of June 2023, contributing to a total economic loss of $42 billion. This assessment defines "economic loss" by considering the GDP decline and reduction in official foreign exchange reserves. Because these reserves signify a country's net external earnings, the situation resulted in Pakistan consuming its savings for survival. This shows that if Pakistan could *avoid political disruptions,* the country could be far less reliant on international aid.

Second, Pakistan needs to increase its tax collection rates

to at least to 15 percent of GDP, which is in the lower range of the typical tax collection observed in low- and middle-income countries. Between 2000 and 2023, the government's average tax collection rate was about 9 percent of GDP. If the government had raised 15 percent of GDP during that period, it could have generated approximately Rs35 trillion (equivalent to $322 billion) in additional resources.

Pakistan's tax issues could be addressed by domestic experts who can mobilize additional revenues without recourse to any external assistance, provided there is unwavering political commitment to reforms and willingness to resist powerful interest groups. Sadly, successive donor-funded tax reform programs over two decades have failed to bring about any improvement in tax revenues, which suggests the futility of foreign technical and financial assistance.

Third, Pakistan must urgently stop the wasteful use of public resources. A country sinking under debt cannot afford to spend lavishly on the state-sponsored luxuries of its legislators, judges, and public servants. In recent years, amid mounting economic challenges that led to yet another IMF bailout, the government has increased the salaries and benefits of civil servants, ministers, members of national and provincial assemblies, and judges of the superior courts. Following a 25 to 35 percent salary hike for government employees in 2023, the government has again raised salaries for all employees by another 25 percent in 2024. To appease judges amidst its political and constitutional struggle, the government, in November 2024, sharply increased judicial allowances, including a 415 percent rise in house rent allowances for Supreme Court judges. Moreover, their superior judicial allowance soared, increasing by 148 percent. This is in addition to a hefty monthly salary raise for Supreme Court and high court judges in 2023. In another particularly painful example of fiscal irresponsibility, the Punjab Assembly in December 2024 awarded themselves substantial increases in the form of financial perks and privileges. Ministers' salaries increased by as much as 860 percent and Provincial Assembly members won a 426 percent increase. Looking at the lackluster national economic growth rates, such increases are mind-blowing. In a country struggling with severe financial constraints and scrambling for aid to meet its debt obligations, it is reckless and callous for officials to spend taxpayers' money in such extravagant ways. It reflects a complete disregard for the hardships faced by Pakistan's most vulnerable citizens. It also highlights a lack of sincerity and competence among Pakistan's inept political leadership.

Fourth, Pakistan should reform energy to escape the problem of circular debt. Despite fifty years of projects led by the ADB and World Bank, and even after a massive increase in tariffs required by the IMF, Pakistan's circular debt in the power sector swelled to Rs2.8 trillion ($10 billion) as of September 2024. This amount is equivalent to the combined financing commitments of two IMF programs between 2019 and 2023. As early as 2019, the ADB already knew that energy sector reforms could save Pakistan's economy $8.4 billion in business losses and could increase total household incomes by at least $4.5 billion per year.[128] But the reforms did not occur, and the international aid kept flowing. The lesson here is, once again, that proper fiscal management by Pakistan's government would greatly reduce or eliminate the country's need for international aid.

Fifth, Pakistan's government needs to better manage the country's state-owned enterprises (SOEs). Estimates show that inefficient and mismanaged SOEs cost the country about Rs600 billion annually. By stopping this bleeding, substantial public resources can be saved and deployed to the sectors where money is needed most. This attainable measure would also greatly reduce dependency on foreign aid.

Pakistan is not alone in these types of problems. Each country has unique needs and struggles, but the five types of reform described above are common barriers to economic growth and self-reliance around the world. So, if developing countries carefully developed plans for putting their own houses in order, and if they garnered the political will to implement change, they would not need to obtain loans from the IMF, the World Bank, the ADB, or the bilateral donors. If these countries could fix public governance issues, stop the hemorrhage of public resources, put an end to wasteful public expenditures, and minimize corruption, they could all be more independent. Either way, reforms must occur. Otherwise, many developing countries will face impending economic collapse. If that happens, foreign aid will be of no help.

This is not to say that all international aid is negative. However, donor countries must adhere to the principles of the Paris Declaration and respect the sovereignty and priorities of recipient countries without imposing their own agendas. Failed donor-funded programs should be held accountable. International aid programs should be assessed in relation to tangible economic and social improvements, not according to anecdotal evidence and heart-felt stories. Recipient countries should lead and design aid programs (and be held to account for positive outcomes). Furthermore, aid must not exacerbate the already burdensome debt of recipient countries. Aid funding should be spent within the country instead of benefiting the donor's contractors.

Unfortunately, the history of donor-funded programs around the world confirms that the above actions are a distant dream. The reforms I have recommended in this chapter conflict with the self-interested purposes international donors based in advanced countries. As I documented earlier in the book, the international aid industry comprises five hundred thousand workers. If countries no longer need international aid, then the demand for workers in the industry declines. Programs end. People lose their jobs. Governments lose their soft influence. In short, donor agencies need developing countries to be dependent and broken so that they can exist.

In my view, developing countries should stop wasting time and resources. Instead, they should shun external financing assistance, except for concessional funding from multilateral agencies for megaprojects that are beyond the country's fiscal capacity. These projects might include constructing dams, building public transportation and railway networks between major cities, improving access to clean water, and setting up tertiary hospitals. International funding for these types of projects can greatly increase the recipient country's *own productive capacity*—a long-term win for national independence—and directly contribute to human development.

CHAPTER 14

A Six-Point Plan for Reforming International Aid

Despite my critique of international aid, I believe that donor agencies can play an important role in the world. However, the international aid system needs drastic reforms before it can contribute to meaningful improvements in developing countries, helping them to become full participants in the global economy. In this chapter, I offer an attainable, practical six-point plan for reforms.

Developing Countries Must Fix Themselves

The Quran says, "Verily, Allah will not change the condition of a people until they change what is in themselves" (13:11). All people can change their lives and make a positive impact on the world. Likewise, developing countries need to have faith in themselves and believe that they can change. They can shun their addiction to foreign aid and take control of their destinies. If they don't, then international aid will never really help.

To implement necessary reforms, developing nations must elect visionary leaders capable of implementing change from within. Without a strong desire and courage to eliminate corrupt, sluggish, and dishonest leadership, it is naïve to expect international aid to make a difference. Decades of experience have shown that foreign aid often exacerbates poor conditions in developing countries, entrenching poverty, corruption, and inefficiencies.

The path to becoming a vibrant, self-reliant state is long and arduous. It takes competent and ethical leadership to embody wisdom, integrity, and courage to transform a fragile, failing state into an economic powerhouse. And it requires a robust educational system to produce dynamic leadership. Countries like China, Singapore, South Korea, Malaysia, the UAE, Turkey, and India have become dynamic states through capable leadership focused on economic development, good governance, the rule of law, quality education, and political stability. As Dr. Henry Kissinger wrote in 2022, "Leadership is needed to help people reach from where they are to where they have never been and, sometimes, can scarcely imagine going. Without leadership, institutions drift, and nations court growing irrelevance and ultimately, disaster."[129]

Each country's leaders must prevail against corruption, which so terribly erodes economies, democracies, and social well-being. Leaders must enable the government to serve the people rather than those in power. They must bolster institutions that protect the rule of law. Relying on international aid agencies to implement meaningful reforms in these areas would be unrealistic, and endless reliance on international aid will only lead to greater indebtedness, jeopardizing the nation's viability. Growth dynamism must come from within countries.

The first step is for developing countries to fix themselves. That is the foundation for everything else.

Overhaul the Architecture of International Aid

The economic development model that relies heavily on international aid has led to unintended consequences, including chronic dependency and the exacerbation of misgovernance in developing nations. Unchecked foreign aid has created perverse incentives for developing countries and donor agencies. Countries dependent on foreign aid are drowning in unsustainable debt, making it difficult for them to escape the debt trap while caring for their vulnerable populations. Many countries have lost their sense of direction and national pride. In these countries, the role of the state has been severely compromised.

To overhaul the system, donor agencies and governments need a vision for a new design and attainable goals leading to substantive reform. The 2005 Paris Declaration on Aid Effectiveness provides the vision and goals. Unfortunately, powerful vested interests will make it difficult to implement the changes recommended in that agreement. In other words, those who control the system are those who most benefit from it, so the proverbial fish will not throw themselves in the pan. Change will never occur from within the system.

Therefore, I call on *taxpayers in advanced countries* to push for reforms. The origin of all the international aid money is taxpayers, primarily in the US and Europe. Their money is often wasted, so they have every right and reason to exert pressure on their politicians. That's what people are supposed to do in a democracy.

Specifically, taxpayers should persuade political representatives to close the country offices of bilateral donors. This would immediately empower the governments of developing nations. Bilateral aid should be restricted to humanitarian aid needed to support people during natural disasters, regional conflicts, and health emergencies. Education, health, clean drinking water, and sanitation are public goods, so national governments should provide those types of essential elements of a civilization. International development agencies should not be allowed to decide what is best for these nations.

In addition, the United Nations needs to reform, restructure, and redefine its mandate. It should focus primarily on its role to maintain international peace and security. To avoid duplicating efforts and to reduce bureaucracy, UN agencies that focus on development (e.g., UNDP, IFAD, UNIDO) should also be sidelined.

Private donors and philanthropic organizations, if they desire to help needy and vulnerable people in poor countries, should be welcome to do so. However, the activities of private donors and NGOs should also be regulated and aligned with national development strategies. Ideally, national governments would regulate and monitor their activities to ensure alignment with these strategies.

Finally, advanced countries should divert ODA funding toward the expansion of scholarship programs in developing countries to provide quality education. These programs enhance human resource capacity in developing countries, and they create significant goodwill for the host countries. Scholarship programs such as the US Fulbright, British Chevening, Australian AusAID, German DAAD, and Joint Japan-World Bank programs offer quality education at prestigious universities, and they are extremely valued in recipient countries. These scholarship programs should be expanded to benefit more people in developing countries by including vocational institutions. This approach would be consistent with an old traditional adage: "Give a man a fish and you feed him for a day. Teach a man to fish and you feed him for a lifetime."

Provide Debt Relief to Heavily Indebted Countries

Debt is an important source of financing for development, but it needs to be sustainable. Unfortunately, too many nations face serious debt crises. Africa, for example, is drowning in debt. In 2022, public debt in Africa reached $1.83 trillion. African debt has grown by 183 percent since 2010. As a result of the Covid-19 pandemic, the Russian war in Ukraine, and soaring inflation, African countries have had to take on even more debt, and now twenty low-income African countries are either at high risk of being in debt distress or already in that condition. That is also the case of some middle-income countries like Pakistan, which have accumulated unsustainable debt.

The average debt-to-GDP ratio in sub-Saharan Africa has almost doubled in just a decade—from 30 percent of GDP at the end of 2013 to almost 60 percent of GDP by the end of 2022. Repaying this debt has also become much costlier. The region's interest payments-to-revenue ratio, an important metric used to assess debt servicing capacity and to predict the risk of a fiscal crisis, has more than doubled since the early 2010s and is now close to four times the ratio in advanced economies.[130]

African countries owed \$655.6 billion to external creditors as of 2022, equivalent to 29 percent of their combined GDPs. African countries needed to pay \$89.4 billion to service external debt in 2024. This was especially problematic because external debt as a share of exports had risen from 74.5 percent to 140 percent over the same period. Since many countries rely on exports, especially from extractive industries with little added value, the imbalance between debt and exports has made it more difficult for Africa to service its external debt. Even before the pandemic, more than thirty African countries spent more on debt service than on health care.[131] These trends have sparked concerns that there is a looming debt crisis in the region.

The composition of African debt has also become more complex. Previously, most African external debt was owed to official creditors, high-income countries, and multilateral lenders like the World Bank and IMF. Now, private creditors and China make up a large proportion of debt stocks, meaning more debt is non-concessional. According to the World Bank's International Debt Statistics, about 43 percent (\$282.73 billion) of African external debt in 2023 was owed to private creditors, 23 percent (\$149.12 billion) to bilateral creditors, and 34 percent (\$223.74 billion) to multilateral creditors. This increases the cost of African debt because many private loans are made on market terms compared to traditional concessional financing.

The share of private creditors in Africa has grown faster than in other developing regions, raising several concerns. First, divergent interests among creditors complicate timely and orderly debt restructuring. Second, there is limited coordination among creditors due to the absence of a formal mechanism for collaboration. Third, the stigma associated with debt restructuring deters creditors and nations from engaging in debt-sustainability talks, potentially limiting future funding sources and reducing the likelihood of debt restructuring agreements.

These challenges are evident in Africa's high borrowing costs, with the continent's average cost of financing at 11.6 percent, which is 8.5 percent higher than the current US benchmark rate. Countries like Tunisia, Egypt, and Nigeria face particularly prohibitive financing costs, making them more vulnerable to financial shocks.

Higher borrowing costs and increasing debt hamper countries' ability to finance development, forcing them to allocate a larger share of their budget to servicing and repaying debt. This diverts critical resources from essential sectors like health, education, development, and social support, exacerbating the situation for Africa's vulnerable populations. Therefore, we need reforms that put a check on multilateral and private creditors. That will be the only way to give Africa freedom to develop sustainably and lift some of the world's most vulnerable people out of poverty. Improved debt conditions will also help the continent meet the UN's sustainable development goals. To put Africa on a more sustainable pathway, the continent needs tangible debt relief.

In 2020, the G20 nations launched the Common Framework, which was intended to deal with insolvency and protracted liquidity problems, just as the pandemic was upending many nations' finances. Nearly three years later, the G20 has yet to chalk up a meaningful success. Until a widely accepted framework is in place, indebted nations will remain stuck in uncharted waters, slogging alone through each piece of their debt contracts.

African countries need a *blanket debt forgiveness*. To do this, donor countries could use ODA funds earmarked for individual nations to provide debt relief to struggling countries. Annual bilateral aid should be directed toward debt write-offs, particularly in countries where debt sustainability is a critical issue.

Beyond the African countries, emerging economies like Pakistan and Egypt also face dire situations. Pakistan's public debt is 77 percent of GDP, which is considered excessive for an emerging market. Further debt accumulation will be dangerous. Pakistan's gross financing needs (the sum of the budget deficit and debt) coming due in 2025 is estimated to be 24 percent of GDP, which is second only to Egypt among developing countries.

According to the IMF, for each of the next five years Pakistan will owe the world an average of $19 billion in principal repayments, which is more than half of its earnings from exports. It will also need a minimum of $6 billion every year to finance even threadbare projections of current account deficits. That being true, the country's total external financing bill will be at least $25 billion a year between now and 2029. Pakistan had foreign exchange reserves of less than $12 billion in December 2024. Compared to the size of its economy, the government will need to pay an average of 6.5 percent of GDP in interest over each of the next five years. This is in addition to what it already owes to residents and foreigners. Pakistan's total tax revenue is barely 8 percent of GDP.

Despite back-to-back IMF programs, Pakistan cannot meet its external financing needs without incurring more government debt—because its foreign direct investment (FDI), which is less than $2 billion, and its private investment intakes are too low. Even the $7 billion of financial assistance that the IMF has agreed to provide over the next three years is less than what Pakistan needs to repay to the IMF over the next four years, meaning that Pakistan needs to borrow more just to repay its previous loans.

Pakistan pays 6 percent of its GDP on interest, which is more than any other country in the developing world. Its interest-payments-to-government-revenue ratio is 65 percent, which is the second highest in the world after Sri Lanka. As a result, Pakistan has no resources left to spend on its people, the citizens who already languish among the poorest in the world. As an example of the country's terribly low social spending, Pakistan spends almost three times more on interest than on education. It spends almost six times more on interest than it does on health. It is not surprising, therefore, that twenty-six million Pakistani children are out of school, or that 40 percent of children under the age of five are physically stunted due to poor nutrition.

This depressing scenario calls for debt relief. The argument for debt cancellation is strong because countries with high debt-servicing costs struggle to spend their revenue on social services. It makes more sense to provide debt relief, thus allowing countries to spend the savings on social benefits to the poor. That is better than imprisoning nations under debt burdens and then giving them even more international aid to care for those same people.

As I wrote at the start of this chapter, each country must put its own house in order. Debt cancellation alone will not be a long-term solution to countries with deep-rooted political, governance, and corruption problems. But *without* debt cancellations, no efforts to enhance stronger accountability and much-needed institutional and policy reforms can occur. Indebted countries need breathing space. To address this issue, one possible solution will be to link debt write-offs to the implementation of IMF-monitored economic reform programs in developing countries, spanning three to five years.

Articulate Vision, Policy Frameworks, and Development Strategies

Developing countries need to steer their own ships. This is a matter of national pride and national sovereignty. Therefore, they must demonstrate leadership by articulating their visions for self-reliance. They must design and implement strong economic policy frameworks to ensure fiscal and external sustainability. These countries must also map out five-year national development strategies and implementation plans. To do this, they should consult with all domestic stakeholders, including political parties, university professors, think tanks, sector specialists, industrialists, business leaders, farmers, and professional communities. These development plans must be approved by each country's parliament. The IMF and World Bank teams can participate by sharing the best global practices.

Developing countries can attain self-reliance and rebuild their economies by pursuing basic economic principles, implementing strong policy frameworks, and practicing tenets of good public governance in a democratic society. They must reduce their dependence on foreign assistance. To achieve economic prosperity and the well-being of citizens requires strong institutions and respect for local traditions. A country's direction should be guided by its own constitution, not by the vested interests of foreign aid organizations. Failing to do so will lead to an abyss of political and economic turmoil.

I recommend that each nation pursue the following elements of a economic policy framework: a) sound public finances, including a sustainable public debt position; b) a healthy external position, including a manageable current account deficit with foreign direct investment as the main source of external finance; c) a capital account position dominated by private flows (portfolio inflows, foreign direct investment, long-term loans, and short-term capital flows); d) a relatively comfortable reserve position; e) low and stable inflation in the context of a sound monetary and exchange rate policy; f) a sound financial system that supports ongoing improvements to financial inclusion.

The policy framework must build the nation's economic resilience, enabling the country to rebound from possible unforeseen economic shocks, as Princeton economist Markus Brunnermeier has emphasized. Leaders will need steadfast commitment to implement the policies they design. Pakistanis, for example, are good at drafting laws and policies but very weak when it comes to implementation. Political leaders must be determined to do the right thing for the people they serve.

Encourage the IMF to Address the Concerns of Developing Nations

Unlike development banks (e.g., the World Bank and the ADB) the IMF does not lend for specific projects. Instead, the IMF provides financial support to countries hit by crises to create breathing room as they implement policies designed to restore economic stability and growth. It also provides precautionary financing to help prevent crises. IMF lending is continuously refined to meet countries' changing needs.

Within the IMF's articles of agreement, Article IV directs the organization to hold bilateral discussions with members, usually every year. During these sessions, an IMF team discusses the country's economic developments and policies. These engagements help the IMF fulfill its role as a "lender of last resort." In my view, the IMF should remain in that important role, even though the IMF is often criticized for not being even-handed, such as in the wake of Pakistan's devastating 2022 floods. As a lender of last resort, the IMF can support the central banks of developing countries during emergency situations. This support strengthens the resilience of countries that experience severe hardship, enabling them to rebound from shocks and avoid long-term economic scarring. In other words, the IMF should provide emergency funding for developing countries without attempting to interfere with normal government functions.

Despite the need for significant reforms, the IMF has an important role to play at the center of the global safety net. I propose that IMF reforms should focus on three areas: a) policy advice during surveillance and program conditionalities; b) lending policies and practices, including the surcharges policy and funding to exceptional access countries; and c) greater transparency in the appointment of the IMF's key officials and the recruitment of experienced professionals. Next I provide more detail about each of these three reform areas.

Policy Advice and Program Conditionalities

Even in its role as lender of last resort, the IMF should be attentive to the difficult trade-offs and competing challenges that developing countries are facing. The IMF's policy advice during Article IV discussions should be extremely pragmatic and country-specific, and all stakeholders should consider the importance of sociopolitical cohesion. The IMF should avoid overstretching its mandate by attempting to fix everything within a country in three or four years.

To protect the sovereignty of each government and to promote long-term self-reliance, the fund must end its practice of imposing inappropriate conditions on funding that are designed to control governments. I am not alone in making this request. The IMF's own Independent Evaluation Office (IEO), in its 2021 report, found excessive structural conditionalities in the IMF's arrangements with, for example, Pakistan and Tunisia. The IEO assessment noted that structural conditionalities generally played a positive role in promoting reforms and growth. However, one can see the high prevalence of programs with an excessive number of structural conditionalities. For example, Pakistan's 2013 EFF program had *eighty-two* conditionalities and Tunisia's 2012 program had forty-six. As the IEO report suggested, the large majority of structural conditionalities had low depth and weak growth orientation. In other words, the IMF's conditions are often counterproductive.

Despite being prolonged users of IMF resources, some countries continue to face long-standing structural rigidities. Important structural reforms related to investment, equitable tax policy, domestic savings, and trade competitiveness were not at the heart of IMF-supported programs. Instead, these programs were overly focused on adjustment. In some countries, deep-rooted structural problems were managed through a series of short-term policy adjustments under programs that could not put the economy on a growth trajectory. Similarly, balance-of-payments problems have been a recurring feature of some economies, such as Pakistan, Egypt, and Argentina, despite successful completion of IMF programs. Also, IMF arrangements are often too short to effectively tackle a country's structural reform agenda. It takes time to build consensus and implement extensive technical assistance. For these reasons, the IMF should carefully tailor its efforts to each country's conditions and priorities.

Growth and reform strategies for program designs should pay adequate attention to social and distributional consequences. Fair distribution of the burden of adjustment is important to ensure broad-based public support for each program. The IMF should also focus more on growth-friendly policies when designing and assessing programs. As the case study on Pakistan shows, IMF programs have had little or no regard for growth. The IMF teams are usually preoccupied with "gap-filling," such as closing budgets and dealing with external financing gaps. The IEO found that Pakistan's growth record had fallen well behind its South Asian neighbors. A primary reason for this outcome is the IMF's excessive focus on front loading adjustment, with little consideration for growth. This approach creates social discontent and antagonism toward the IMF.

IMF Lending Policies and Practices

In addition to reducing conditionalities on funding, the IMF needs to reform its surcharge policy. These surcharges comprise a significant portion of interest payments. They are only paid by countries that borrow heavily, generally those that are facing severe economic crises. Five members—Argentina, Egypt, Ukraine, Ecuador, and Pakistan—pay over 90 percent of the IMF's total income from surcharges.[132]

The unprecedented global economic shocks caused by the Covid-19 pandemic and the conflicts in Ukraine and the Middle East have increased the pressure on the IMF to change its surcharge policy. Some have argued that the IMF is breaking its own articles of agreement, which state that the IMF cannot do anything to be "destructive of national or international prosperity."[133] The IMF executive board considered the issue twice in 2021, but the United States, Canada, Germany, Switzerland, Austria, the Nordic countries, and Japan opposed changes.

Despite the opposition, there are compelling reasons to review the surcharge policy. First, in fiscal year 2021, surcharges represented a significant portion of the IMF's operational income. This revenue stream grew just as IMF members confronted intense pandemic-related financial pressures. As such, the IMF created a reputational risk. Member nations saw the IMF as profiting from their crises. Surcharges aggravate this reputational risk because they punish countries with greater external financing needs (i.e., those in dire straits).

Second, some IMF leaders oppose changes to the surcharge policy because, according to them, the IMF needs the income. This argument is not convincing. The IMF's precautionary balances are very small compared with the funds raised through quotas and borrowings. There is no need to build precautionary balances with procyclical and regressive policies that negatively impact highly indebted economies. Independent research by the Centre for Economic and Policy Research (CEPR) also finds that these surcharges are regressive, counterproductive, and unfair.

The topic of IMF surcharges is a complex and multifaceted issue that needs to be reassessed in the context of an evolving global economic and financial landscape. Thankfully, in October 2024, the IMF completed a review of its framework for surcharges. The managing director, Kristalina Georgieva, issued the following statement:

> In a challenging global environment and at a time of high interest rates, our membership has reached consensus on a comprehensive package that substantially reduces the cost of borrowing, while safeguarding the IMF's financial capacity to support countries in need. The approved measures, effective November 1, 2024, will lower IMF borrowing costs for members by 36 percent, or about $1.2 billion annually. The expected number of countries subject to surcharges in fiscal year 2026 will fall from twenty to thirteen. This is achieved by reducing the margin over the SDR interest rate, raising the threshold for level-based surcharges, lowering the rate for time-based surcharges, and increasing the thresholds for commitment fees.[134]

The IMF has reformed its contentious surcharge policy, reducing borrowing costs for affected countries. But opting to maintain the policy, albeit with lower costs, will allow harmful impacts on debt-stricken and climate vulnerable economies to persist. Because the IMF decides how much a country can borrow, surcharges are not needed to promote prudent borrowing. Thus, these reforms amount to tweaks at the margin of a fundamentally broken policy. That approach is harmful, counterproductive, and illogical. The views of the IMF's influential chairs have prevailed for the time being, but with debt distress mounting throughout the Global South, these leaders will have to recognize that the only viable option is to eliminate surcharges.

The IMF has a laudable history of providing emergency financing to countries in crises (with few conditionalities), including during the Covid-19 pandemic.[135] The IMF's track record of implementing organizational and policy reforms according to changing contexts is also appreciable. That said, the IMF's own in-house watchdog, the Independent Evaluation Office, has criticized the fund for not being consistent when providing its biggest bailouts during the past two decades. The watchdog stated that "perceptions of a lack of even-handedness" were affecting the Fund's credibility.[136] Although the IMF managing director has argued that the IMF needs flexibility when making funding decisions, the IMF still faces criticism that it bows to big shareholders who make large loans to countries in trouble. In October 2024, Brent Neiman, the US Treasury assistant secretary for international finance, said the IMF needed to be firmer when assessing bailouts when China was a big creditor. The IEO report said its evaluation "confirms that pressures on staff and management, exerted directly or indirectly, were strong in high-stakes cases."

The Need for Greater Transparency When Appointing IMF Leaders

The IMF needs to address concerns about its procedures for recruiting leaders, staff, and economists. The primary need is for greater transparency. Undoubtedly, the Fund recruits the best available economists through its regular Economist Program (EP) hiring stream, but the Fund has considerable discretion when selecting qualified candidates for mid-career and experienced roles. After experienced candidates qualify, by passing tests and panel interviews, they are placed in a talent pool. The hiring departments have the discretion to select any candidate from that pool. There are valid concerns that candidates from regions such as the Middle East and North Africa (MENA) remain under-represented, whereas candidates from advanced countries are selected quickly. This creates a regional imbalance in the Fund's human resource base.

Enact Sweeping World Bank Reforms

The last element of my six-point proposal is to diminish the international aid system's reliance on *bilateral* aid programs, which are often politically motivated. Instead, we need to increase the use of stronger and more effective *multilateral* funding. This should occur while respecting the sovereignty of each country.

In this context, the World Bank should be reformed fundamentally. The bank has failed the poor for eighty years. Again, I am not alone in making that statement. There are widespread demands for more resources to help the poor grapple with major crises, often caused by climate change. Others are calling for increased transparency and accountability. But meaningful reform will remain elusive unless the World Bank does more to serve the poor.

"To create a world free from poverty on a livable planet." That vision, shared by World Bank President Ajay Banga in his 2023 welcome email to staff, was not new. Ten years ago, the World Bank had already adopted an overarching goal of "ending extreme poverty and promoting shared prosperity." Reducing poverty was first articulated as a World Bank goal *fifty years ago,* in 1973, when then-President Robert McNamara stated that the bank would work "to accelerate economic growth and to reduce poverty."

I share the candid views of Matt Kennard and Claire Provost who argue that over the last half-century, under its supposed poverty-fighting mission, the bank rolled out initiatives and built institutions that left countries with two bad choices: facilitate corporate power or be disciplined by it. In 2023, they made the following statement.

> Unbeknownst to most taxpayers whose governments fill [the World Bank's] coffers, three of the bank's five branches focus explicitly on boosting private investment, including the International Financial Corporation (IFC), which directly invests in private companies itself, as well as the International Centre for Settlement of Investment Disputes (ICSID), which oversees cases filed by foreign investors against states taking actions they don't like. These branches have sat under the bank's antipoverty mission for decades, and not so surprisingly, they have harmed development goals.[137]

In July 2023, the World Bank enthusiastically announced a new Private Sector Investment Lab to "address the barriers to private sector investment in emerging markets." Fifteen CEOs and board chairs said they were "delighted," "excited," and "grateful" to be named as founding members of the bank's new entity. Most did not even mention poverty reduction in their comments.

Bertrand Badré, a former managing director of the World Bank, stated the problem this way: "Skepticism about the bank's capacity to address the challenges facing developing countries is running high."[138] This is why calls for more resources and faster disbursements will do little to change the World Bank's record and impact. The central problem that must be addressed is a long-standing mismatch between the bank's stated priority to help the poor and the on-the-ground realities.

The World Bank's leadership needs to guide the institution toward complete transparency and accountability. A good place to start would be to acknowledge that a debt crisis is engulfing developing economies. The crisis was exacerbated by the pandemic, but these countries were on a perilous path long before that global crisis. Today's debt conundrum has occurred because borrowers and lenders, including the World Bank, have pursued low-return projects that could not cover their costs. To avert future debt crises, multilateral institutions must stop financing economically unsustainable projects.

The World Bank could improve its credibility by being more transparent about the costs and benefits of the bank's investments. Stronger trust would encourage shareholders to increase the bank's capital. However, it will not be easy to change the World Bank's culture, even though many people around the world have been hoping for such an effort.[139]

In conclusion, the World Bank needs to focus on its original mission to eliminate poverty. It also needs to improve governance and align its operational policies—including HR policies for the recruitment of experienced professionals—with international norms and standards. Countries should hold the bank's leadership accountable for disappointing outcomes and invigorate better performance. Wealthy countries that fund the bank can exert their influence by linking future capital increases to the bank's implementation of substantial reforms.

Epilogue

So where do we go from here? Expecting donors to implement drastic institutional reforms on their own will be next to impossible unless taxpayers in advanced countries exert pressure through their chosen representatives. Afterall, taxpayers fund the donor agencies. Taxpayers and politicians in advanced countries should work through lawful, constitutional processes to push multilateral and bilateral donors to overhaul the international aid architecture. The new architecture should hold international donors and recipient governments accountable for subpar outcomes and misallocations. The international aid system should be aligned with the 2005 Paris Declaration on Aid Effectiveness.

The performance and impact of the Bretton Woods institutions (the IMF and the World Bank Group) are increasingly under scrutiny. Have their policy directives genuinely served the global good? While they preach good governance, their own lack of transparency in appointing senior staff undermines their credibility. They position themselves as development partners by offering concessional foreign exchange loans, but they act like typical lenders and investment bankers. Given these shortcomings, a shift away from this outdated global system seems inevitable. Simultaneously, an alternative financial system is already gaining traction emerging in Asia, providing countries with financing options that come with fewer conditions.

As I have emphasized in this book, developing countries need to put their own houses in order before international aid can produce the best results. In developing countries, political leaders often lack visionary and sincere leadership, which hinders possible reforms. Even if a country has astute politicians, politics often trump economics. Politicians fail to understand that good economics can be good politics. Unfortunately, poor nations' policymakers benefit from the rents created by the economy's inefficiencies and rigidities. These self-interested individuals will go to great lengths to ensure that the system does not change. The challenge is to find ways to persuade, or perhaps cudgel, these policymakers to prioritize the greater good over their own interests. Most policymakers know in their hearts that reforms are badly needed, but they are usually reluctant to embrace change. As Nobel Prize-winning novelist Sinclair Lewis put it, "It is very difficult to make a man understand something if he feels that his income depends on his not understanding it."

As I write this book, Pakistan is in a deep governance crisis, marked by institutional breakdown, elite capture, and military dominance. The government of Prime Minister Shehbaz Sharif came into power with the support of the military establishment, which is alleged to have engineered the 2023 elections. The results of these elections fooled no one. As such, the government is overwhelmed with its political survival. In the process, it has manipulated the Constitution, weakened the judiciary, and expanded the role of the army in political and economic spheres. While the parliament, judiciary, and media come under pressure from those in power, the executive branch is also crumbling. Civil servants fill key positions merely because they are loyal to the ruling parties, without any regard for merit or relevant expertise. Moreover, in utter disregard of civil service rules and democratic norms, serving military officials have been appointed as heads of civil institutions. Moreover, the military and its intelligence agencies now have authority to clear the appointments of professionals and top bureaucrats to the public service, practically undermining the authority of the Cabinet.

Pakistan's current struggles illustrate a fundamental principle: political stability and integrity, and strong institutions that serve people, are necessary for economic development and growth. This principle has long been recognized, including in the writings of Adam Smith and, more recently, by MIT economist Daron Acemoglu's 2024 Nobel Prize-winning work. They have all emphasized on the importance of integrity and healthy institutions. The declining growth and investment trends in many developing nations, including in Pakistan, are largely attributable to continuous institutional erosion. Without strong institutions, no reforms to the international aid system will fare better than previous failed initiatives. Developing countries cannot progress on the basis of political whims. We need visionary leaders with integrity and competence, not self-serving politicians who merely want to hold power.

Political crises in Pakistan have caused colossal economic costs. In such an undemocratic environment, taxpayers in donor countries must decide whether their money is being used for the purposes that donors claim. They must decide whether they want to become complicit or stand for meaningful change. The choice is clear: either become a part of the problem or be part of the solution. Taxpayers should closely watch how donor agencies spend their money. Are they advancing democratic values and promoting the economic welfare of citizens in recipient countries, or are they exacerbating domestic political and economic crises in developing nations, or are they merely using funds to sustain their own financial interests?

If Pakistan could uphold political stability, the country could experience consistent economic growth. Unfortunately, the political misadventures in 2022 and 2023 contributed to economic losses of $42 billion in fiscal year 2023.[140] Had there been no political disruption, Pakistan could have averted that substantial economic loss. To provide perspective, that $42 billion loss was *six times more* than the IMF's 2024 EFF program in Pakistan.

The glaring absence of accountability for political maneuvers perpetuates a cycle of economic loss. The international aid system as a whole—donors and recipients—needs a robust and accountable democratic system for each country's prosperity. This means that institutions in each developing country need to be apolitical. Political stability, anchored in strong democratic norms, is the sole solution to both short-term and long-term challenges. Frequent disruptions to the political system prevent democracy from taking a strong hold and they hinder reforms.

Pakistan's institutional chaos and paralysis originates with the country's existing leadership. They came of age starting in the 1980s. So, my hope is in Pakistan's youth. They are a demographic force—the largest cohort of the population is less than thirty years old—and they are also a beacon of integrity, enlightenment, and innovation. I am confident that young people will shape the future of Pakistan and play a significant role in nation-building. They despise corruption and public mismanagement, they are passionate about their country, and they have the courage to deliver a stinging rebuke to those in power.

The same is true in many countries. In places like Kenya and Bangladesh, among others, young people have demonstrated courage to challenge the unjust status quo. We clearly have role models for courageous leaders, including in Western countries. Finland's former Prime Minister Sanna Marin was once the world's youngest premier. Most ministers in her cabinet, twelve out of nineteen, were women under the age of forty. I would like to see Pakistan's government led by young men and women who turn their fresh ideas into action. They can steer the country toward a self-sustaining path of development, without relying on international aid.

The other option is to maintain the dismal status quo. In that case, the country's economic management will remain aid-dependent, and the living standards of common people will continue to decline. It's time for intellectual revolution.

Acknowledgements

Writing this book has been a challenging yet fulfilling journey, and I am deeply grateful to all those who supported me along the way.

First and foremost, I would like to express my heartfelt gratitude to my editor, Glenn McMahan at Upriver Press, for his excellent work in transforming the book from the first draft to the final product.

To everyone who contributed in ways big and small—my friends and colleagues at the IMF, the State Bank of Pakistan, and Cambridge University—thank you for the stimulating discussions that inspired this book.

Last, I would like to acknowledge my family for their unwavering support and encouragement throughout my career and while writing this book. A big thank you to my daughter, Ammarah, for her invaluable assistance during the writing process.

About the Author

Dr. Saeed Ahmed, who has a PhD in economics from Cambridge University, is a leading expert in international finance and development, macroeconomic management, monetary policy formulation, financial sector development, public finance and fiscal policy, tax policy and administration, and applied economic research. His professional experience includes high-level work at the State Bank of Pakistan and the International Monetary Fund.

Born into a low-income family of Sanghar, an underdeveloped rural district in the Sindh province of Pakistan, Saeed Ahmed's early life was marked by adversity and misfortune. He lost his father at the tender age of ten, requiring his elder brother, Jawaid Latif, at age thirteen, to abandon his education and assume responsibility for his father's small shop.

Saeed's mother, who never went to school, suddenly became a widow in her late thirties. She struggled to support her large family. In the face of financial hardships, Saeed dedicated his childhood to supporting his family, working at the small shop to earn a modest livelihood. With help from merit scholarships, Saeed pursued his primary and secondary education in government schools. While assisting his brother at the shop, he borrowed newspapers from neighboring shopkeepers and read everything he could find.

With an eye on establishing his capacity to provide for his family, Saeed enrolled at the NED University of Engineering and Technology, Pakistan's top engineering institution at that time. He simultaneously pursued a bachelor's degree at the University of Sindh. Upon completing the degree with a first-class, first position he discontinued his engineering studies. In June 1986, he started his professional career as a management trainee at Bankers Equity Limited, a development finance institution. Later, in 1987, he joined the State Life Insurance Corporation of Pakistan.

Saeed's career in public service began in 1992. He worked as deputy commissioner of income tax, which involved tax audits and investigations, assessments and collections, and enforcement of tax compliance. He also pursued his master's degree in economics, securing a first-class, third position at the University of Sindh. During this time, the Foreign, Commonwealth and Development Office in England awarded him a British Chevening Scholarship, which enabled him to pursue a master's degree in economics at the University of Warwick, which he completed in 1999. After working at Pakistan's Federal Board of Revenue, Saeed enrolled in a PhD economics program at Cambridge University, a degree that he completed in two years, with a scholarship awarded by the State Bank of Pakistan.

At Cambridge, Saeed conducted doctoral research in corporate tax modeling under the supervision of Professor Paul Kattuman and contributed to the European Commission's research on the development of corporate tax policies across the EU. His PhD thesis provided microeconomic analysis of corporate tax, drawing on large datasets of up to fifteen thousand firms across three sectors of the UK economy. His work also developed econometric models of company profitability, earnings, and taxes. He also reviewed official corporate tax models of some OECD countries.

After completing his PhD in 2005, Saeed transitioned to the State Bank of Pakistan where he held positions in research, monetary policy, agricultural credit and microfinance, financial inclusion programs, and HR departments. In 2015, he became the chief economist and executive director of the bank and a member of the statutory monetary policy committee, which determined the country's interest rates. In this role, he was responsible for supervising four central bank departments: monetary policy, research, economic policy review, and statistics. He provided high-level technical economic advice to the central bank's governor, board of directors, and the monetary policy committee. During his tenure, Pakistan successfully transitioned to a market-based exchange rate regime in 2019. Additionally, Saeed participated in policy formulation with the International Monetary Fund, the World Bank, and other agencies on topics related to economic development.

Saeed played a leading role in reforming Pakistan's microfinance regulatory framework, which was ranked first in the world in 2010 and 2011, and third in the world in 2012 and 2013 by the Economist Intelligence Unit (EIU) of *The Economist* magazine. He designed, implemented and monitored multi-million dollar programs, funded by bilateral donors and multilateral development banks to increase financial access for micro, small, and medium enterprises, and marginalized segments in Pakistan. In partnership with the World Bank and other stakeholders, he spearheaded the development of Pakistan's first-ever National Financial Inclusion Strategy, which, in 2015, began to address gaps in financial access.

From January 2020 to January 2023, Saeed worked at the International Monetary Fund (IMF) as senior advisor to the executive director. As a member of the IMF's executive board, he represented the economic agenda of eight emerging markets and developing countries. He also contributed to the IMF's response to the Covid-19 pandemic through policy adjustments and emergency financial assistance to countries. This work included helping to arrange for Pakistan's $6.5 billion IMF program and $1.4 billion emergency financing to mitigate the economic fallout of the pandemic.

Throughout his career, his wife, Nusrat, steadfastly supported him and their five children. At the time of this writing, he lives with his family in Australia.

Bibliography

Abate, Chala Amante. "Is Too Much Foreign Aid a Curse or Blessing to Developing Countries?" *Heliyon* 8, no. 5 (2022).

Acemoglu, Daron and James A. Robinson. *Why Nations Fail: The Origins of Power, Prosperity, and Poverty.* Crown Business, 2012.

Adams, Samuel and Francis Atsu. "Aid Dependence and Economic Growth in Ghana." *Economic Analysis and Policy* 44, no. 2 (2014): 233–242.

Adebayo, Tomiwa Sunday and Demet Beton Kalmaz. "Ongoing Debate Between Foreign Aid and Economic Growth in Nigeria: A Wavelet Analysis." *Social Science Quarterly* 101, no. 2 (2020). https://onlinelibrary.wiley.com/doi/full/10.1111/ssqu.12841.

Ahmed, Saeed. "Five Point Agenda for Tax Reform." *Dawn,* August 4, 2023.

Ahmed, Saeed. "Economic Cost of Disruptions." *Dawn,* December 16, 2024. https://www.dawn.com/news/1879040.

Aid Leap. "Development Consultants: Over-Paid, Over-Rated, and Over-Used." March 30, 2015. https://aidleap.org/2015/03/30/development-consultants-over-paid-over-rated-and-over-used/.

Akhtar, Shamshad. "Expanding Microfinance Outreach in Pakistan." State Bank of Pakistan, February 14, 2007. https://www.findevgateway.org/sites/default/files/publications/files/mfg-en-paper-expanding-microfinance-outreach-in-pakistan-feb-2007_0.pdf.

Akhtar, Shamshad. "Launch of Microfinance Initiatives." Speech delivered on December 19, 2008. https://www.bis.org/review/r090224d.pdf.

Albulescu, Claudiu Tiberiu. "Do Foreign Direct and Portfolio Investments Affect Long-Term Economic Growth in Central and Eastern Europe?" *Procedia Economics and Finance* 23, (2015): 507–512.

American Governance Institute. "Foreign Aid: An Introduction to US Programs and Policy." Congressional Research Service, January 29, 2016. https://www.everycrsreport.com/files/20160129_R40213_1f28ef17168682fc8c4804ebb789f1c0c8e8e70e.html.

Ang, James B. "Does Foreign Aid Promote Growth? Exploring the Role of Financial Liberalization." *Review of Development Economics* 14, no. 2 (2010): 197–212.

Arauz, Andrés, Mark Weisbrot, Christina Laskaridis, and Joe Sammut. "IMF Surcharges: Counterproductive and Unfair." Center for Economic and Policy Research.

Arndt, Channing, Sam Jones, and Finn Tarp. "Assessing Foreign Aid's Long-Run Contribution to Growth and Development." *World Development* 69, (2015): 6–18.

Arshad Khan, Muhammad and Ayaz Ahmed. "Foreign Aid—Blessing or Curse: Evidence from Pakistan." *The Pakistan Development Review* 45, no. 3 (2007): 215–240.

Arts, Karin. "Inclusive Sustainable Development: A Human Rights Perspective." *Current Opinion in Environmental Sustainability* 24, (February 2017).

Asian Development Bank. "Islamic Republic of Pakistan: Preparing Sustainable Energy Projects." ADB Technical Assistance Report, June 2019.

Asian Development Bank. Independent Evaluation Department. "Validation Report, Sustainable Energy Sector Reform Program." September 2022.

Asongu, Simplice and Mohamed Jellal. "Foreign Aid Fiscal Policy: Theory and Evidence." *Comparative Economic Studies* 58, (2016): 1–36.

Badre, Bertrand and Peter Blair Henry. "Changing the Culture at the World Bank." *Project Syndicate,* July 12, 2023. https://www.project-syndicate.org/commentary/ew-world-bank-president-ajay-banga-must-lead-bold-reforms-by-bertrand-badre-and-peter-blair-henry-2023-07.

Balde, Yero. "The Impact of Remittances and Foreign Aid on Savings/Investment in Sub-Saharan Africa." *African Development Review* 23, no. 2 (2011): 247–262.

Battersby, Jane. "MDGs to SDGs: New Goals, Same Gaps: The Continued Absence of Urban Food Security in the Post-2015 Global Development Agenda." *African Geographical Review* 36, no. 1 (2017).

Bhalla, Surjit S. and Karan Bhasin. "India Eliminates Extreme Poverty." Brookings Institute, March 1, 2024. https://www.brookings.edu/articles/india-eliminates-extreme-poverty/.

Boyreau, Genevieve and Sona Varma. "2021 Development Policy Financing Retrospective: Facing Crisis, Fostering Recovery." World Bank Group, 2012. https://documents1.worldbank.org/curated/en/099623509132210285/pdf/IDU0249804670b2fc0466f083850d1aad1818915.pdf.

Burke, Paul J. and Fredoun Z. Ahmadi-Esfahani. "Aid and Growth: A Study of South East Asia." *Journal of Asian Economics* 17, no. 2 (2006): 350–362.

Burnside, Craig and David Dollar. "Aid, Policies and Growth." *American Economic Review* 90, no. 4.

Chhibber, Ajay et al. "World Development Report 1997: The State in a Changing World." World Bank Group, June 1, 1997. http://documents.worldbank.org/curated/en/518341468315316376/World-development-report-1997-the-state-in-a-changing-world.

Clist, Paul. "Foreign Aid and Domestic Taxation: Multiple Sources, One Conclusion." *Development Policy Review* 34, no. 3 (2016): 365–83.

Comelli, Fabio et al. "Navigating Fiscal Challenges in Sub-Saharan Africa: Resilient Strategies and Credible Anchors in Turbulent Waters." IMF African Department, Departmental Working Paper, no. 2023/07, September 26, 2023.

Consultative Group to Assist the Poor (CGAP). "Advancing Financial Inclusion to Improve the Lives of the Poor: Strategic Directions FY2014 to FY2018." May 15, 2013. https://www.cgap.org/sites/default/files/cgap_strategy_20141018.pdf.

Dalgaard, Carl-Johan, Henrik Hansen, and Finn Tarp. "On the Empirics of Foreign Aid and Growth," *Economic Journal* 114, no. 496 (2004): 191–216.

Davison, Catherine. "India Says It Has Turned Its Back on Aid—But Is This True?" Devex, August 25, 2023. https://www.devex.com/news/india-says-it-has-turned-its-back-on-aid-but-is-this-true-106075.

Dawn. "Aid Has Been One of the Biggest Curses for Pakistan: PM Imran." July 23, 2019. https://www.dawn.com/news/1495748.

Department for International Development. "Empowering Communities in Afghanistan." Reliefweb. https://reliefweb.int/report/afghanistan/empowering-communities-afghanistan.

Department for International Development. "Our House: Pakistan Floods One Year On." July 19, 2011. https://www.gov.uk/government/case-studies/our-house-pakistan-floods-one-year-on.

Department for International Development. "Out of Syria, Back into School." February 12, 2016. https://www.gov.uk/government/case-studies/out-of-syria-back-into-school.

Department for International Development. "Restoring
 Hope in Gaza." February 26, 2015. https://www.gov.uk/
 government/case-studies/restoring-hope-in-gaza.

Devex. "Where the United States Spends Its Development Aid."
 September 2023. https://pages.devex.com/rs/685-KBL-765/images/
 where-the-united-states-spends-its-development-aid_Sept23.pdf.

Dippel, Christian. "Foreign Aid and Voting in
 International Organizations: Evidence from the IWC."
 Journal of Public Economics 132, (2015): 1–12.

Dreher, Axel. "Do Donors Target Aid in Line with the
 Millennium Development Goals? A Sector Perspective of
 Aid Allocation." *Review of World Economics* (2007).

Drine, Imed and Sami Nabi. "Public External Debt,
 Informality and Production Efficiency in Developing
 Countries." *Economic Modelling* 27, (2010): 487-495.

Easterly, William, Ross Levine, and David Roodman.
 "Aid, Policies, and Growth: Comment." *American
 Economic Review* 94, no. 3 (2004): 774-780.

Easterly, William. "Can Foreign Aid Buy Growth?" *Journal
 of Economic Perspectives* 17, no. 3 (2005): 23–48.

Easterly, William. "Can Foreign Aid Save Africa?" *Clemens Lecture Series,*
 no. 17 (2005), Saint John's University, Collegeville, Minnesota.

Ehigiamusoe, Kizito Uyi, Hooi Hooi Lean, and Russell
 Smyth. "The Moderating Role of Energy Consumption in
 the Carbon Emissions-Income Nexus in Middle-Income
 Countries." *Applied Energy*, 261, (2020): 1-13.

Ejaz, Gohar. "I'm sharing data from NEPRA . . ." X, July 20, 2024.
 https://x.com/Gohar_Ejaz1/status/1814597980629966990.

Faye, Michael and Paul Niehaus. "Political Aid Cycles."
American Economic Review 102, no. 7 (2012): 3516–3530.

Fleck, Robert and Christopher Kilby. "Changing Aid Regimes?
US Foreign Aid from the Cold War to the War on Terror."
Journal of Development Economics 91, no. 2 (2010): 185–197.

Foreign, Commonwealth and Development Office.
"Statistics on International Development, Final
UK Aid Spend 2022." September 2023.

Freistein, Katja and Bettina Mahlert. "The Potential for
Tackling Inequality in the Sustainable Development Goals."
Third World Quarterly 37, no. 12 (2016): 2139-2155.

Fukuda-Parr, Sakiko. "From the Millennium Development Goals
to the Sustainable Development Goals: Shifts in Purpose,
Concept, and Politics of Global Goal Setting for Development."
Gender and Development 24, no. 1 (2016): 43-52.

Gilligan, Andrew. "Poverty Barons Who Make a Fortune from
Taxpayer-Funded Aid Budget." *The Telegraph,* September 15, 2012.
https://www.telegraph.co.uk/news/politics/9545584/Poverty-barons-
who-make-a-fortune-from-taxpayer-funded-aid-budget.html.

Girardet, Edward. "The United Nations: More Consultants,
Fewer Rights." *Le News,* November 20, 2014. https://lenews.
ch/2014/11/20/the-united-nations-more-consultants-fewer-rights/.

Gloyd, Steve. "Phantom Aid: Money Allocated to Countries
that Ends Up Funding INGOs." University of Washington,
Department of Global Health, January 25, 2022.

Goh, Soo Khoon, Chung Yan Sam, and Robert McNown.
"Reexamining Foreign Direct Investment, Exports, and Economic
Growth in Asian Economies Using a Bootstrap ARDL Test for
Cointegration." *Journal of Asian Economics* 51, (2017): 12–22.

Government of India. "Household Consumption Expenditure Survey 2022-2023." https://www.mospi.gov.in/sites/default/files/publication_reports/Factsheet_HCES_2022-23.pdf.

Gunby, Philip, Yinghua Jin, and W. Robert Reed. "Did FDI Really Cause Chinese Economic Growth? A Meta Analysis." *World Development* 90, (2017): 242–255.

Gupta, Sanjeev, Alvar Kangur, Chris Papageorgiou, and Abdoul Wane. "Efficiency-Adjusted Public Capital and Growth." *World Development* 57, (2014): 164-78.

Hanke, Steve. "Afghanistan: A Poster Child for Foreign-Aid Failure." Cato Institute, September 21, 2021. https://www.cato.org/commentary/afghanistan-poster-child-foreign-aid-failure.

Herrero, Alicia Garcia. "Why Are Latin American Crises Deeper Than Those in Emerging Asia, Including That of Covid-19?" ADB Institute Working Paper No. 1221, (2021).

Herzer, Dierk and Oliver Morrissey. "Foreign Aid and Domestic Output in the Long Run." *Review of World Economics* 149, no. 4 (2013): 723–748.

House of Common's International Development Committee. "UK Aid to Pakistan." Sixth Report of Session 2021-2022, April 29, 2022.

Independent Commission for Aid Impact. "UK Aid to China Is Falling Rapidly but Greater Transparency Is Needed." July 13, 2023. https://icai.independent.gov.uk/uk-aid-to-china-is-falling-rapidly-but-greater-transparency-is-needed/.

International Monetary Fund. "The IMF's Exceptional Access Policy: Evaluation Report." IMF Independent Evaluation Office, December 2024.

International Monetary Fund. "The Role of IMF Financial Support in Mitigating the Covid-19 Shock." IMF Independent Evaluation Office Background Paper, 23-01/01, 2023.

Kanbur, Ravi. "Aid, Conditionality, and Debt in Africa." In *Foreign Aid and Development: Lessons Learnt and Directions for the Future,* edited by Finn Tarp and Peter Hjertholm. Routledge, 2000.

Karandaaz. "Karandaaz Annual Report 2016-2017." https://krndevelop.wpenginepowered.com/wp-content/uploads/2024/07/annual-report-final-5.compressed.pdf.

Karandaaz. Parwaaz Financial Services Ltd. Accessed February 5, 2025. https://www.karandaaz.com.pk/capital/strategic-investments/parwaaz-financial-services-ltd.

Kennard, Matt and Claire Provost. "World Bank Reforms Will Remain Elusive Until This Is Understood." Aljazeera, October 6, 2023. https://www.aljazeera.com/opinions/2023/10/6/world-bank-reform-will-remain-elusive-until-this-is-understood.

Kenny, Charles. "Biden's Foreign Aid Is Funding the Washington Bubble." *Foreign Policy,* May 6, 2022. https://foreignpolicy.com/2022/05/06/us-foreign-aid-biden-build-back-better-world-development.

Kimenyi, Mwangi. "Donor Interference and Transparency Remain Real Concern to African Countries." Brookings Institute, November 1, 2012. https://www.brookings.edu/articles/donor-interference-and-transparency-remain-a-real-concern-to-african-countries/.

Kissinger, Henry. *Leadership: Six Studies in World Strategy.* Penguin Press, 2022.

Kumar, Surinder et al. "Millennium Development Goals (MDGs) to Sustainable Development Goals (SDGs): Addressing Unfinished Agenda and Strengthening Sustainable Development and Partnership." *Indian Journal of Community* 41, no. 1 (2016): 1, 10.

Kuziemko, Ilyana and Eric Werker. "How Much Is a Seat on the Security Council Worth? Foreign Aid and Bribery at the United Nations." *Journal of Political Economy* 114, no. 5 (2006): 905–930

Leene Coralde, Janadale and Miguel Antonio Tamonan. "Who Are FCO's Top Development Contractors?" Devex, September 15, 2020. https://www.devex.com/news/who-are-fco-s-top-development-contractors-97782.

Lim, Naomi. "USAID's 'Long List of Crap': Karoline Leavitt Cites Millions in Wasteful Spending." *Washington Examiner,* February 5, 2025. https://www.washingtonexaminer.com/news/white-house/3311863/usaid-long-list-crap-karoline-leavitt-wasteful-spending/.

Lipsey, Robert E. "The Role of FDI in International Capital Flows." In *International Capital Flows,* edited by Martin Feldstein. Chicago University Press, 1999.

Liverman, Diana. "Geographic Perspectives on Development Goals." *Dialogues in Human Geography* 8, no. 2 (2018): 168-185.

Malik, Girijasankar. "Foreign Aid and Economic Growth: A Cointegration Analysis of the Six Poorest African Countries." *Economic Analysis and Policy* 38, no. 2 (2008): 251–260.

Malik, Kenan. "As a System, Foreign Aid Is a Fraud and Does Nothing for Inequality." *The Guardian,* September 2, 2018. https://www.theguardian.com/commentisfree/2018/sep/02/as-a-system-foreign-aid-is-a-fraud-and-does-nothing-for-inequality.

Masters, Jonathan and Will Merrow. "How Much US Aid Is Going to Ukraine?" Council on Foreign Relations, September 27, 2024. https://www.cfr.org/article/how-much-us-aid-going-ukraine.

Merrick, Rob. "UK Faces Criticism for Funding Soccer in China Amid Aid Cuts." Devex, August 9, 2023. https://www.devex.com/news/uk-faces-criticism-for-funding-soccer-in-china-amid-aid-cuts-106031.

Mostrous, Alexi and Billy Kenber. "Foreign Aid Investigation: Millions Are Spent on Salaries and Pointless Briefs." *The Times,* December 8, 2016. https://www.thetimes.com/article/millions-are-spent-on-salaries-and-pointless-policy-briefs-8v89m7srg.

Moyo, Dambisa. *Dead Aid: Why Aid Is Not Working and There Is Another Way for Africa.* Penguin, 2009.

Munir, Kamal. "To Fix the Economy, Start with the Private Sector." *Dawn,* March 24, 2019.

North, Douglass. *Institutions, Institutional Change, and Economic Performance.* Cambridge University Press, 1990.

Nowak-Lehmann, Felicitas et al. "Does Foreign Aid Really Raise Per Capita Income? A Time Series Perspective." *Canadian Journal of Economics/Revue Canadienne d'Economique* 45, no. 1 (2012): 288–313.

O'Connell, Stephen A. and C. C. Soludo. "Aid Intensity in Africa." *World Development* 29, no. 9 (2001): 1527- 1552.

Organization for Economic Cooperation and Development. "Finance for Sustainable Development." Accessed January 22, 2025. https://www.oecd.org/en/topics/finance-for-sustainable-development.html.

Oxfam International. "Obscene Amount of Aid Is Going Back into the Pockets of Rich Countries." April 12, 2023. https://www.oxfam.org/en/press-releases/obscene-percent-aid-going-back-pockets-rich-countries.

Perkins, John. *Confessions of an Economic Hitman, Third Edition.* Berrett-Koehler, 2023.

Provost, Claire. "DfID's Spending on Consultants to Come under Increased Scrutiny." *The Guardian,* September 17, 2012. https://www.theguardian.com/global-development/2012/sep/17/dfid-spending-consultants-scrutiny.

Purohit, Kunal. "In India, NGOs Face Funding Bans,
Reel Under 'Strangulating' Laws." Devex, January 13,
2022. https://www.devex.com/news/in-india-ngos-face-
funding-bans-reel-under-strangulating-laws-102404.

Rajan, Raghuram G. and Arvind Subramanian. "Aid and Growth:
What Does the Cross-Country Evidence Really Show?" *The
Review of Economics and Statistics* 90, no. 4 (2008): 643–665.

Rana, Shahbaz. "Circular Debt May Swell to Rs2.8tr." *The
Express Tribune,* September 24, 2024. https://tribune.com.
pk/story/2498299/circular-debt-may-swell-to-rs28tr.

Ranis, Gustav. "Towards the Enhanced Effectiveness of Foreign Aid."
In *Foreign Aid for Development: Issues, Challenges, and the New
Agenda*, edited by George Mavrotas. Oxford University Press, 2010.

Riazuddin, Riaz. "Our Anemic Exports." *Daily Dawn,* June 3, 2023.
https://www.dawn.com/news/1757624/our-anaemic-exports.

Rommel, Tobias and Paul Schaudt. "First Impressions:
How Leader Changes Affect Bilateral Aid." *Journal
of Public Economics* 185, (2020): 104-107.

Root, Rebecca L. "What's Behind the Rise of the Development
Consultant?" Devex, October 20, 2023. https://www.devex.com/
news/what-s-behind-the-rise-of-the-development-consultant-106420.

Sabbagh, Dan. "May Begins Africa Trip with Nod to
Rightwing Tories on Overseas Aid." *The Guardian,* August
27, 2018. https://www.theguardian.com/politics/2018/
aug/27/may-africa-trip-rightwing-tories-overseas-aid.

Sachs, Jeffrey D., Guillaume LaFortune, and Grayson Fuller.
"The SDGs and the UN Summit of the Future." Sustainable
Development Report 2024. Dublin University Press,
2024. https://www.developmentaid.org/api/frontend/cms/
file/2024/06/sustainable-development-report-2024.pdf.

Schuknecht, Ludger. *Public Spending and the Role of the State*. Cambridge University Press, 2021.

Sethi, Narayan. "Foreign Aid vs. Economic Development: Exploring the Empirical Linkage for India, Sri Lanka, and Maldives." Fourth IIFT Conference on Empirical Issues in International Trade and Finance (EIITF), December 18–19, 2014.

Smith, Adam. *The Wealth of Nations*. W. Strahan and T. Cadell, 1776.

Solow, Robert. "A Contribution to the Theory of Economic Growth." *Quarterly Journal of Economics* 70, (1956): 65-94.

Sothan, Seng. "Foreign Aid and Economic Growth: Evidence from Cambodia." *The Journal of International Trade and Economic Development* 27, no. 2 (2018): 168-183.

State Bank of Pakistan, "National Financial Inclusion Strategy." Accessed February 5, 2025. https://www.sbp.org.pk/Finc/NF.asp.

State Bank of Pakistan. "Governor's Annual Report 2023-2024." October 18, 2024. https://www.sbp.org.pk/reports/annual/Gov-AR/pdf/2024/Gov-AR.pdf.

State Bank of Pakistan. "Microfinance Credit Guarantee Facility Guidelines." June 21, 2012, https://www.sbp.org.pk/acd/2012/C3-AnnexA.pdf.

State Bank of Pakistan. "Strategic Framework for Sustainable Microfinance in Pakistan." January 2011. https://www.sbp.org.pk/MFD/Strategic-Framework-SM-24-Jan-2011.pdf.

Tamonan, Miguel Antonio. "How Much Are Major Donors Spending on Local Contracts?" Devex, August 30, 2023. https://www.devex.com/news/how-much-are-major-donors-spending-on-local-contracts-106073.

Tanzi, Vito. "Changing Role of the State: A Historical Perspective," *IMF Working Paper,* 114, no. 97, (1997).

Tarp, Finn. "Aid and Development." *Swedish Economic Policy Review* 13, no. 2 (2006): 9–61.

The Economic Times. "Strong Reforms Over Last 10 Years Lays Foundation of Solid Growth Over Next Decade: Jefferies." February 22, 2024. https://m.economictimes.com/news/economy/indicators/strong-reforms-over-last-10-years-lays-foundation-of-solid-growth-over-next-decade-jefferies/amp_articleshow/107912063.cms.

The White House. (Page removed by The White House). Attempted access February 2025. https://www.whitehouse.gov/briefing-room/speeches-remarks/2021/08/16/remarks-by-president-biden-on-afghanistan/.

Thiessen, Marc. "Ukraine Aid's Best-Kept Secret: Most of the Money Stays in the USA," *The Washington Post,* November 29, 2023. https://www.washingtonpost.com/opinions/2023/11/29/ukraine-military-aid-american-economy-boost/.

Todaro, Michael and Stephen C. Smith. *Economic Development, 10th Edition.* Pearson Education Limited, 2009.

Tolzmann, Molly. "CGAP Funder Survey 2020: Trends in International Funding for Financial Inclusion." Consultative Group to Assist the Poor (CGAP), 2022. https://www.cgap.org/research/publication/2020-trendsinternational-funding-financial-inclusion.

UK House of Common's International Development Committee. "DfID's Use of Private Sector Contractors." Eighth Report of Session, 2016-2017.

United Nations Development Programme. "Pakistan National Human Development Report." April 24, 2018. https://www.undp.org/pakistan/publications/pakistan-national-human-development-report.

United Nations Development Programme. "The Three Ps of Inequality: Power, People, and Policy." Pakistan National Human Development Report 2020. https://www.undp.org/sites/g/files/zskgke326/files/migration/pk/NHDR-Inequality-2020---Overview-Low-Res.pdf.

United Nations Trade and Development. "Africa 2023." https://unctad.org/publication/world-of-debt/regional-stories.

United Nations. "Transforming Our World: The 2030 Agenda for Sustainable Development." 2015.

United Nations. "Transforming Our World: The 2030 Agenda for Sustainable Development." 2019.

Unlock Aid. "Follow the Money: US Global Development Spending." https://www.unlockaid.org/follow-the-money.

USAID. "Moving Toward a Model of Locally Led Development: FY2022 Localization Progress Report." June 12, 2023.

USAID. "Seventy Years, One Partnership." (USAID website closed by Trump administration in February 2025). https://www.usaid.gov/sites/default/files/2022-05/Final_CT_Book_low-res_3.pdf.

USAID. "USAID Country Fact Sheet Year 2024." (USAID website closed by Trump administration in February 2025). https://www.usaid.gov/pakistan/our-work.

Vasquez, Ian. "Foreign Aid and Economic Development." *Cato Handbook for Policymakers.* Cato Institute, 2017.

Wasim, Amir. "Even Friendly Countries 'Fatigued' by Our Aid Seeking: PM." *Dawn,* September 15, 2022. https://www.dawn.com/news/1710196.

Wellner, Lukas et al. "Can Aid Buy Foreign Public Support? Evidence from Chinese Development Finance." Kiel Institute for the World Economy. Kiel Working Paper, no. 2214 (2022).

World Bank and the Development Research Center of the State Council, the People's Republic of China. *Four Decades of Poverty Reduction in China: Drivers, Insights for the World, and the Way Ahead.* 2022. doi:10.1596/978-1-4648-1877-6.

World Bank Group. "Worldwide Governance Indicators." Accessed February 5, 2025. www.govindicators.org.

World Bank Group. "The World Bank In Pakistan." October 3, 2024. https://www.worldbank.org/en/country/pakistan/overview.

World Data Lab. World Poverty Clock. https://www.worldpoverty.io/map.

World Economic Forum. " Global Gender Gap Report 2023." June 20, 2023.

Endnotes

1   The OCED Development Assistance Committee is an international forum of many of the largest providers of aid, including thirty-two members with the mandate to promote development cooperation and policies that contribute to implementation of the 2030 Agenda for Sustainable Development. The work includes a focus on sustainable economic development, the advancement of equality within and among countries, poverty eradication, improvement of living standards, and to a future in which no country will depend on aid.

2   These countries report their statistics to the OECD on a voluntary basis.

3   Foreign, Commonwealth and Development Office, accessed February 4, 2025, https://www.gov.uk/government/organisations/foreign-commonwealth-development-office/about.

4   Department for International Development, "Empowering Communities in Afghanistan," Reliefweb, https://reliefweb.int/report/afghanistan/empowering-communities-afghanistan.

5   Department for International Development, "Our House: Pakistan Floods One Year On," July 19, 2011, https://www.gov.uk/government/case-studies/our-house-pakistan-floods-one-year-on.

6   Department for International Development, "Restoring Hope in Gaza," February 26, 2015, https://www.gov.uk/government/case-studies/restoring-hope-in-gaza.

7   Department for International Development, "Out of Syria, Back into School," February 12, 2016, https://www.gov.uk/government/case-studies/out-of-syria-back-into-school.

8   Lukas Wellner et al., "Can Aid Buy Foreign Public Support? Evidence from Chinese Development Finance," Kiel Institute for the World Economy, Kiel Working Paper, no. 2214 (2022); Axel Dreher, "Do Donors Target Aid in Line with the Millennium Development Goals? A Sector Perspective of Aid Allocation," *Review of World Economics* (2007).

9   Wellner, "Can Aid Buy Foreign Public Support?"

10   Ilyana Kuziemko and Eric Werker, "How Much Is a Seat on the Security Council Worth? Foreign Aid and Bribery at the United Nations," *Journal of Political Economy* 114, no. 5 (2006): 905–930; Michael Faye and Paul Niehaus, "Political Aid Cycles," *American Economic Review* 102, no. 7 (2012): 3516–3530; Robert Fleck and Christopher Kilby, "Changing Aid Regimes? US Foreign Aid from the Cold War to the War on Terror," *Journal of Development Economics* 91, no. 2 (2010): 185–197; Christian Dippel, "Foreign Aid and Voting in International Organizations: Evidence from the IWC," *Journal of Public Economics* 132, (2015): 1–12; Tobias Rommel and Paul Schaudt, "First Impressions: How Leader Changes Affect Bilateral Aid," *Journal of Public Economics* 185, (2020): 104-107.

11   Wellner, "Can Aid Buy Foreign Public Support?"

12   Kenan Malik, "As a System, Foreign Aid Is a Fraud and Does Nothing for Inequality," *The Guardian,* September 2, 2018, https://www.theguardian.com/commentisfree/2018/sep/02/as-a-system-foreign-aid-is-a-fraud-and-does-nothing-for-inequality.

13   Dan Sabbagh, "May Begins Africa Trip with Nod to Rightwing Tories on Overseas Aid," *The Guardian,* August 27, 2018, https://www.theguardian.com/politics/2018/aug/27/may-africa-trip-rightwing-tories-overseas-aid.

14   Malik, "As a System, Foreign Aid Is a Fraud."

15   Malik, "As a System, Foreign Aid Is a Fraud."

16   Jonathan Masters and Will Merrow, "How Much US Aid Is Going to Ukraine?" Council on Foreign Relations, September 27, 2024, https://www.cfr.org/article/how-much-us-aid-going-ukraine.

17   Marc Thiessen, "Ukraine Aid's Best-Kept Secret: Most of the Money Stays in the USA," *The Washington Post,* November 29, 2023, https://www.washingtonpost.com/opinions/2023/11/29/ukraine-military-aid-american-economy-boost/.

18   Ian Vasquez, "Foreign Aid and Economic Development," *Cato Handbook for Policymakers,* Cato Institute, 2017.

19   Vasquez, "Foreign Aid and Economic Development."

20   Steve Hanke, "Afghanistan: A Poster Child for Foreign-Aid Failure," Cato Institute, September 21, 2021, https://www.cato.org/commentary/afghanistan-poster-child-foreign-aid-failure.

21   Page Removed by the White House, attempted access in February 2025, https://www.whitehouse.gov/briefing-room/speeches-remarks/2021/08/16/remarks-by-president-biden-on-afghanistan/.

22   American Governance Institute, "Foreign Aid: An Introduction to US Programs and Policy," Congressional Research Service, January 29, 2016, https://www.everycrsreport.com/files/20160129_R40213_1f28ef17168682fc8c4804ebb789f1c0c8e8e70e.html.

23   Organization for Economic Cooperation and Development, "Finance for Sustainable Development," accessed January 22, 2025, https://www.oecd.org/en/topics/finance-for-sustainable-development.html.

24   Rob Merrick, "UK Faces Criticism for Funding Soccer in China Amid Aid Cuts," Devex, August 9, 2023, https://www.devex.com/news/uk-faces-criticism-for-funding-soccer-in-china-amid-aid-cuts-106031.

25   Independent Commission for Aid Impact, "UK Aid to China Is Falling Rapidly but Greater Transparency Is Needed," July 13, 2023, https://icai.independent.gov.uk/uk-aid-to-china-is-falling-rapidly-but-greater-transparency-is-needed/.

26   Malik, "As a System, Foreign Aid Is a Fraud."

27   Consultative Group to Assist the Poor (CGAP), "Advancing Financial Inclusion to Improve the Lives of the Poor: Strategic Directions FY2014 to FY2018," May 15, 2013, https://www.cgap.org/sites/default/files/cgap_strategy_20141018.pdf.

28   United Nations, "Transforming Our World: The 2030 Agenda for Sustainable Development," 2015.

29   Jeffrey D. Sachs, Guillaume LaFortune, and Grayson Fuller, "The SDGs and the UN Summit of the Future. Sustainable Development Report 2024," Dublin University Press, 2024, https://www.developmentaid.org/api/frontend/cms/file/2024/06/sustainable-development-report-2024.pdf.

30   United Nations, https://careers.un.org.

31   Rebecca L. Root, "What's Behind the Rise of the Development Consultant?" Devex, October 20, 2023, https://www.devex.com/news/what-s-behind-the-rise-of-the-development-consultant-106420.

32   Edward Girardet, "The United Nations: More Consultants, Fewer Rights," Le News, November 20, 2014, https://lenews.ch/2014/11/20/the-united-nations-more-consultants-fewer-rights/.

33   Girardiet, "United Nations: More Consultants, Fewer Rights."

34   Aid Leap, "Development Consultants: Over-Paid, Over-Rated, and Over-Used," March 30, 2015, https://aidleap.org/2015/03/30/development-consultants-over-paid-over-rated-and-over-used/.

35   According to its most recent progress report, USAID obligated $33.7 billion through A and A in the fiscal year that ended in September 2022. This was up 83.2 percent from the $18.4 billion the agency obligated in 2015, which was the earliest available progress report data. Of this amount, $28 billion was obligated through the assistance mechanism, which includes grants and cooperative agreements. Another $5.6 billion was obligated through contracts, also known as acquisition. The remaining $208.9 million was obligated through interagency agreements. USAID's total obligation through A and A jumped significantly in 2020, an increase driven primarily by funding to Ukraine and continued pandemic response. However, looking closely, the growth was limited to assistance funding. From $12.5 billion in 2015, the total obligation through grants and cooperative agreements more than doubled to $28 billion in 2022. Meanwhile, the obligation through contracts remained below $6 billion during the eight-year period, while interagency agreements accounted for only a fraction of the total.

36   Between 2012 and 2021, humanitarian aid was the USAID's priority, with $86.9 billion over the period. From $4.9 billion in 2012, its ODA grew to $15.7 billion in 2021. Population and reproductive health ranked next, with $66.4 billion in the decade. It was the top sector in 2012, 2013, and 2015, with humanitarian aid topping the rest. Other priority sectors included government and civil society, with $47.9 billion; health, with $25.1 billion; education, with $14.1 billion; agriculture, forestry, and fishing, with $12.6 billion; and energy, with $7.8 billion. Another $39 billion went to projects that do not fall under a specific sector. The

OECD labels it as "unallocated/unspecified." Meanwhile, $6.6 billion went to multi-sectoral projects.

37   The Global Fund to Fight AIDS, Tuberculosis, and Malaria ranked next, with $10.2 billion—around half of what WFP received in the same period. Next came the World Bank's International Bank for Reconstruction and Development, with $8.9 billion. Meanwhile, FHI 360 was the overall top non-profit and bilateral recipient, with $3.8 billion in the decade. Catholic Relief Services ranked next, with $3.2 billion, followed by Jhpiego, with $1.9 billion, then Save the Children USA, with $1.8 billion.

38   Janadale Leene Coralde and Miguel Antonio Tamonan, "Who Are FCO's Top Development Contractors?" Devex, September 15, 2020, https://www.devex.com/news/who-are-fco-s-top-development-contractors-97782.

39   Claire Provost, "DfID's Spending on Consultants to Come under Increased Scrutiny," *The Guardian,* September 17, 2012, https://www.theguardian.com/global-development/2012/sep/17/dfid-spending-consultants-scrutiny.

40   Andrew Gilligan, "Poverty Barons Who Make a Fortune from Taxpayer-Funded Aid Budget," *The Telegraph,* September 15, 2012, https://www.telegraph.co.uk/news/politics/9545584/Poverty-barons-who-make-a-fortune-from-taxpayer-funded-aid-budget.html.

41   Provost, "DfID's Spending."

42   Alexi Mostrous and Billy Kenber, "Foreign Aid Investigation: Millions Are Spent on Salaries and Pointless Briefs," *The Times,* December 8, 2016, https://www.thetimes.com/article/millions-are-spent-on-salaries-and-pointless-policy-briefs-8v89m7srg.

43　UK House of Common's International Development Committee, "DfID's Use of Private Sector Contractors," Eighth Report of Session 2016-2017.

44　Miguel Antonio Tamonan, "How Much Are Major Donors Spending on Local Contracts?" Devex, August 30, 2023, https://www.devex.com/news/how-much-are-major-donors-spending-on-local-contracts-106073.

45　Sovereign portfolio consists of loans, grants, equity investment, and sovereign guarantees. Regional projects with loans/grants to multiple countries are reported separately.

46　USAID, "Seventy Years, One Partnership," https://www.usaid.gov/sites/default/files/2022-05/Final_CT_Book_low-res_3.pdf, (USAID website closed by Trump administration in February 2025).

47　"USAID Country Fact Sheet Year 2024," https://www.usaid.gov/pakistan/our-work, (USAID website closed by Trump administration in February 2025).

48　Molly Tolzmann, "CGAP Funder Survey 2020: Trends in International Funding for Financial Inclusion." Consultative Group to Assist the Poor (CGAP), 2022, https://www.cgap.org/research/publication/2020-trendsinternational-funding-financial-inclusion.

49　Tolzmann, "CGAP Funder Survey 2022."

50　Genevieve Boyreau and Sona Varma, "2021 Development Policy Financing Retrospective: Facing Crisis, Fostering Recovery," World Bank Group, 2021, https://documents1.worldbank.org/curated/ en/099623509132210285/pdf/IDU0249804670b2fc0466f083850d1aad1818915.pdf.

51   Shamshad Akhtar, "Expanding Microfinance Outreach in Pakistan," State Bank of Pakistan, February 14, 2007, https://www. findevgateway.org/sites/default/files/publications/files/mfg-en-paper-expanding-microfinance-outreach-in-pakistan-feb-2007_0. pdf.

52   DFID has since closed and replaced by the UK's Foreign, Commonwealth and Development Office (FCDO).

53   The survey was funded by DFID, World Bank, and the Swiss Development Corporation at the request of Pakistan's Ministry of Finance. Neilson Pakistan, in liaison with Pakistan Microfinance Network, conducted the survey throughout Pakistan. The study's research design borrowed extensively from FinScope financial surveys, which had been conducted across Africa by the Johannesburg-based FinMark Trust.

54   Shamshad Akhtar, "Launch of Microfinance Initiatives," Speech delivered on December 19, 2008, https://www.bis.org/review/ r090224d.pdf.

55   State Bank of Pakistan, "Microfinance Credit Guarantee Facility Guidelines," June 21, 2012, https://www.sbp.org.pk/acd/2012/C3-AnnexA.pdf.

56   State Bank of Pakistan, "Strategic Framework for Sustainable Microfinance in Pakistan," January 2011, https://www.sbp.org.pk/ MFD/Strategic-Framework-SM-24-Jan-2011.pdf.

57   State Bank of Pakistan, "Governor's Annual Report 2023-2024," October 18, 2024, https://www.sbp.org.pk/reports/annual/Gov-AR/pdf/2024/Gov-AR.pdf.

58   State Bank of Pakistan, "Governor's Annual Report 2023-2024."

59   USAID. In 2025, the Trump administration removed this page, https://pdf.usaid.gov/pdf_docs/PA00K88T.pdf. For further information on Easypaisa please see the SBP newsletter at https://www.sbp.org.pk/publications/acd/2011/BranchlessBanking-Oct-Dec-2011.pdf.

60   State Bank of Pakistan, National Financial Inclusion Strategy, accessed February 5, 2025, https://www.sbp.org.pk/Finc/NF.asp.

61   The UK government had provided £50 million as grant (equivalent to Rs2 billion) in 2008 under the Financial Inclusion Program. The tripartite agreement had been signed in July 2008 between the DFID, the Economic Affairs Division of the Government of Pakistan, and the State Bank of Pakistan. However, through an amendment letter signed in January 2015, after closure of the program, all unspent funds were either to be reverted to the DFID or be provided to the DFID's enterprise. This amendment subsequently ran counter to the primary agreement and was invalid *ab initio.*

62   Karandaaz, "Investing in Businesses with Potential by Unlocking Their Access to Capital," accessed on February 19, 2025, https://www.karandaaz.com.pk/capital/wholesale-investments.

63   Karandaaz, "Investing in Businesses with Potential by Unlocking Their Access to Capital."

64   Karandaaz, Parwaaz Financial Services Ltd., accessed February 5, 2025, https://www.karandaaz.com.pk/capital/strategic-investments/parwaaz-financial-services-ltd.

65   Karandaaz Annual Report 2023-24; PMIC Annual Report 2023.

66   Infrazamin, Website, https://infrazamin.com/who-we-are/.

67   Ibid.

68   Karandaaz, "Ministry of Finance and Karandaaz Pakistan Launch Pakistan's first Specialized Credit Guarantee Company for SMEs," Janaury 16, 2024, https://www.karandaaz.com.pk/news-and-media/press-releases/ministry-of-finance-and-karandaaz-pakistan-launch-pakistans-first-specialised-credit-guarantee-company-for-smes.

69   *The Express Tribune,* "Credit Firm for SMEs Launched," January 13, 2024, https://tribune.com.pk/story/2453063/credit-firm-for-smes-launched.

70   *Profit,* "National Credit Guarantee Company Launched to Bolster Financial Accessibility for SMEs," January 12, 2024, https://profit.pakistantoday.com.pk/2024/01/12/national-credit-guarantee-company-launched-to-bolster-financial-accessibility-for-smes/.

71   Federal Board of Revenue, Government of Pakistan, "FBR Signs Agreement with Karandaaz Pakistan for Digitization of Tax System," accessed February 19, 2025, https://www.fbr.gov.pk/fbr-signs-agreement-with-karandaaz-pakistan-for-digitization-of-tax-system/174032.

72   Shahbaz Rana, "Pakistan Partners with Gates' Foundation to Overhaul FBR," *The Express Tribune,* March 16, 2024, https://tribune.com.pk/story/2459484/pakistan-partners-with-gates-foundation-to-overhaul-fbr.

73   Karandaaz, "Karandaaz Annual Report 2016-2017," p. 4, https://krndevelop.wpenginepowered.com/wp-content/uploads/2024/07/annual-report-final-5.compressed.pdf.

74   World Bank Group, "Pakistan Tax Administration Reforms Project," accessed February 19, 2025, https://projects.worldbank.org/en/projects-operations/project-detail/P077306.

75   Shahbaz Rana, "Circular Debt May Swell to Rs2.8tr," *The Express Tribune,* September 24, 2024, https://tribune.com.pk/story/2498299/circular-debt-may-swell-to-rs28tr.

76   Asian Development Bank, Independent Evaluation Department, "Validation Report, Sustainable Energy Sector Reform Program," September 2022.

77   Uraan Pakistan, https://uraanpakistan.pk/.

78   "How Pakistan's Military Is Taking Over Its Economy," https://www.ft.com/content/f3dae073-c158-43e2-a8c6-628acc46a868.

79   World Bank Group, Worldwide Governance Indicators, accessed February 5, 2025, www.govindicators.org.

80   Gohar Ejaz, "I'm sharing data from NEPRA for Jan 24 to March 24 showing a capacity payment of 150 billion PKR per month. Please note how this amount is distributed to various IPPs, with half running below 10% capacity. Four power plants are receiving 1000 crores per month each with #zero power supply," X, July 20, 2024, https://x.com/Gohar_Ejaz1/status/1814597980629966990.

81   Riaz Riazuddin, "Our Anemic Exports," *Daily Dawn,* June 3, 2023, https://www.dawn.com/news/1757624/our-anaemic-exports.

82   United Nations Development Programme, "The Three Ps of Inequality: Power, People, and Policy," Pakistan National Human Development Report 2020, https://www.undp.org/sites/g/files/zskgke326/files/migration/pk/NHDR-Inequality-2020---Overview-Low-Res.pdf.

83   United Nations Development Program, "Pakistan National Human Development Report," April 24, 2018, https://www.undp.org/pakistan/publications/pakistan-national-human-development-report.

84   World Economic Forum, " Global Gender Gap Report 2023," June 20, 2023.

85   Robert Solow, " A Contribution to the Theory of Economic Growth," *Quarterly Journal of Economics* 70, (1956): 65-94.

86   Narayan Sethi, "Foreign Aid vs. Economic Development: Exploring the Empirical Linkage for India, Sri Lanka, and Maldives," Fourth IIFT Conference on Empirical Issues in International Trade and Finance (EIITF), December 18–19, 2014; Simplice Asongu and Mohamed Jellal, "Foreign Aid Fiscal Policy: Theory and Evidence," *Comparative Economic Studies* 58, (2016): 1–36.

87   Yero Balde, "The Impact of Remittances and Foreign Aid on Savings/Investment in Sub-Saharan Africa," *African Development Review* 23, no. 2 (2011): 247–262.

88   Robert E Lipsey, "The Role of FDI in International Capital Flows." In Martin Feldstein (Ed.), *International Capital Flows,* (Chicago University Press, 1999), pp. 307–362.

89   Michael P. Todaro and Stephen C. Smith, *Economic Development, 10th Edition,* (Pearson Education Limited, 2009).

90   Stephen A. O'Connell and C. C. Soludo, "Aid Intensity in Africa," *World Development,* 29, no. 9 (2001): 1527- 1552.

91   Claudiu Tiberiu Albulescu, "Do Foreign Direct and Portfolio Investments Affect Long-Term Economic Growth in Central and Eastern Europe?" *Procedia Economics and Finance* 23, (2015): 507–512; Channing Arndt, Sam Jones, and Finn Tarp, Assessing Foreign Aid's Long-Run Contribution to Growth and Development," *World Development* 69, (2015): 6–18; Paul Clist, "Foreign Aid and Domestic Taxation: Multiple Sources, One Conclusion," *Development Policy Review* 34, no. 3 (2016): 365–83; Carl-Johan Dalgaard, Henrik Hansen, and Finn Tarp,

Dalgaard, "On the Empirics of Foreign Aid and Growth," *Economic Journal* 114, no. 496 (2004): 191–216; Finn Tarp, "Aid and Development," *Swedish Economic Policy Review* 13, no. 2 (2006): 9–61.

92   William Easterly, "Can Foreign Aid Save Africa?" *Clemens Lecture Series*, no. 17 (2005), Saint John's University, Collegeville, Minnesota; William Easterly, "Can Foreign Aid Buy Growth? *Journal of Economic Perspectives* 17, no. 3 (2005): 23–48; William Easterly et al., "Aid, Policies, and Growth," *American Economic Review* 94, no. 3 (2004): 774-780; Soo Khoon Goh, Chung Yan Sam, and Robert McNown, "Reexamining Foreign Direct Investment, Exports, and Economic Growth in Asian Economies Using a Bootstrap ARDL Test for Cointegration," *Journal of Asian Economics* 51, (2017): 12–22; Philip Gunby, Yinghua Jin, and W. Robert Reed, "Did FDI Really Cause Chinese Economic Growth? A Meta Analysis, *World Development* 90, (2017): 242–255; Ravi Kanbur, "Aid, Conditionality, and Debt in Africa," In Finn Tarp and Peter Hjertholm (Eds.), *Foreign Aid and Development: Lessons Learnt and Directions for the Future*, (Routledge, 2000), pp. 409–422; Felicitas Nowak-Lehmann et al., "Does Foreign Aid Really Raise Per Capita Income? A Time Series Perspective," *Canadian Journal of Economics/Revue Canadienne d'Economique* 45, no. 1 (2012): 288–313; Gustav Ranis, "Towards the Enhanced Effectiveness of Foreign Aid," In George Mavrotas (Ed.), *Foreign Aid for Development: Issues, Challenges, and the New Agenda*, Oxford University Press, 2010; Raghuram G. Rajan and Arvind Subramanian, "Aid and Growth: What Does the Cross-Country Evidence Really Show?" *The Review of Economics and Statistics* 90, no. 4 (2008): 643–665; Seng Sothan, Foreign Aid and Economic Growth: Evidence from Cambodia," *The Journal of International Trade and Economic Development* 27, no. 2 (2018): 168-183.

93   Seng Sothan, Foreign Aid and Economic Growth: Evidence from
      Cambodia," *The Journal of International Trade and Economic
      Development* 27, no. 2 (2018): 168-183.

94   Kizito Uyi Ehigiamusoe, Hooi Hooi Lean, and Russell Smyth,
      "The Moderating Role of Energy Consumption in the Carbon
      Emissions-Income Nexus in Middle-Income Countries," *Applied
      Energy,* 261, (2020): 1-13.

95   Tomiwa Sunday Adebayo and Demet Beton Kalmaz, "Ongoing
      Debate Between Foreign Aid and Economic Growth in Nigeria:
      A Wavelet Analysis," *Social Science Quarterly* 101, no. 2 (2020),
      https://onlinelibrary.wiley.com/doi/full/10.1111/ssqu.12841.

96   William Easterly, "Aid, Policies, and Growth."

97   Paul J. Burke and Fredoun Z. Ahmadi-Esfahani, "Aid and Growth:
      A Study of South East Asia," *Journal of Asian Economics* 17, no. 2
      (2006): 350–362.

98   Muhammad Arshad Khan and Ayaz Ahmed, "Foreign Aid—
      Blessing or Curse: Evidence from Pakistan," *The Pakistan
      Development Review* 45, no. 3 (2007): 215–240.

99   Girijasankar Mallik, "Foreign Aid and Economic Growth: A
      Cointegration Analysis of the Six Poorest African Countries,"
      Economic Analysis and Policy 38, no. 2 (2008): 251–260; Rajan,
      "Aid and Growth"; James B. Ang, "Does Foreign Aid Promote
      Growth? Exploring the Role of Financial Liberalization," *Review
      of Development Economics* 14, no. 2 (2010): 197–212; Samuel
      Olorunfemi Adams and Francis Atsu, "Aid Dependence and
      Economic Growth in Ghana," *Economic Analysis and Policy* 44, no.
      2 (2014): 233–242; Dierk Herzer and Oliver Morrissey, "Foreign
      Aid and Domestic Output in the Long Run," *Review of World
      Economics* 149, no. 4 (2013): 723–748.

100 Chala Amante Abate, "Is Too Much Foreign Aid a Curse or Blessing to Developing Countries?" *Heliyon* 8, no. 5 (2022).

101 Dambisa Moyo, *Dead Aid: Why Aid Is Not Working and There Is Another Way for Africa,* (Penguin, 2009).

102 William Easterly, "Can Foreign Aid Buy Growth?"

103 Raghuram G. Rajan and Arvind Subramaniam, "Aid and Growth: What Does the Cross-Country Evidence Really Show," *The Review of Economics and Statistics* 90, no. 4 (2008): 643–665, https://doi.org/10.1162/rest.90.4.643.

104 The World Bank updated the global poverty lines in September 2022. The new extreme poverty line of $2.15 per person per day replaces the $1.90 poverty line, which was set in 2017.

105 World Bank Group, "The World Bank In Pakistan," October 3, 2024, https://www.worldbank.org/en/country/pakistan/overview.

106 *The Economic Times,* "Strong Reforms Over Last 10 Years Lays Foundation of Solid Growth Over Next Decade: Jefferies," February 22, 2024, https://m.economictimes.com/news/economy/indicators/strong-reforms-over-last-10-years-lays-foundation-of-solid-growth-over-next-decade-jefferies/amp_articleshow/107912063.cms.

107 Government of India, "Household Consumption Expenditure Survey 2022-2023," https://www.mospi.gov.in/sites/default/files/publication_reports/Factsheet_HCES_2022-23.pdf.

108 Surjit S. Bhalla and Karan Bhasin, "India Eliminates Extreme Poverty," Brookings Institute, March 1, 2024, https://www.brookings.edu/articles/india-eliminates-extreme-poverty/.

109   Kunal Purohit, "In India, NGOs Face Funding Bans, Reel Under 'Strangulating' Laws," Devex, January 13, 2022, https://www. devex.com/news/in-india-ngos-face-funding-bans-reel-under-strangulating-laws-102404.

110   Catherine Davison, "India Says It Has Turned Its Back on Aid— But Is This True?" Devex, August 25, 2023, https://www.devex. com/news/india-says-it-has-turned-its-back-on-aid-but-is-this-true-106075.

111   Alicia Garcia Herrero, "Why Are Latin American Crises Deeper Than Those in Emerging Asia, Including that of Covid-19?" ADB Institute Working Paper No. 1221, (2021).

112   House of Common's International Development Committee, "UK Aid to Pakistan," Sixth Report of Session 2021-22, April 29, 2022.

113   Oxfam International, "Obscene Amount of Aid Is Going Back into the Pockets of Rich Countries," April 12, 2023, https://www. oxfam.org/en/press-releases/obscene-percent-aid-going-back-pockets-rich-countries.

114   Mwangi Kimenyi, "Donor Interference and Transparency Remain Real Concern to African Countries," Brookings Institute, November 1, 2012, https://www.brookings.edu/articles/donor-interference-and-transparency-remain-a-real-concern-to-african-countries/.

115   Devex, "Where the United States Spends Its Development Aid," September 2023, p. 6, https://pages.devex.com/rs/685-KBL-765/images/where-the-united-states-spends-its-development-aid_Sept23.pdf.

116   Devex, "Where the United States Spends Its Development Aid," p. 22.

117   Oxfam International, "Obscene Amount of Aid."

118   USAID, "Moving Toward a Model of Locally Led Development: FY2022 Localization Progress Report," June 12, 2023.

119   Charles Kenny, "Biden's Foreign Aid Is Funding the Washington Bubble," *Foreign Policy,* May 6, 2022, https://foreignpolicy.com/2022/05/06/us-foreign-aid-biden-build-back-better-world-development.

120   Steve Gloyd, "Phantom Aid: Money Allocated to Countries that Ends Up Funding INGOs," University of Washington, Department of Global Health, January 25, 2022.

121   Unlock Aid, "Follow the Money: US Global Development Spending," https://www.unlockaid.org/follow-the-money.

122   Naomi Lim, "USAID's 'Long List of Crap': Karoline Leavitt Cites Millions in Wasteful Spending," *Washington Examiner,* February 5, 2025, https://www.washingtonexaminer.com/news/white-house/3311863/usaid-long-list-crap-karoline-leavitt-wasteful-spending/.

123   *Dawn,* "Aid Has Been One of the Biggest Curses for Pakistan: PM Imran," July 23, 2019, https://www.dawn.com/news/1495748.

124   Amir Wasim, "Even Friendly Countries 'Fatigued' by Our Aid Seeking: PM," *Dawn,* September 15, 2022, https://www.dawn.com/news/1710196.

125   Ajay Chhibber et al., "World Development Report 1997: The State in a Changing World," World Bank Group, June 1, 1997, http://documents.worldbank.org/curated/en/518341468315316376/World-development-report-1997-the-state-in-a-changing-world; Vito Tanzi, "Changing Role of the State: A Historical Perspective," IMF Working Paper, 114, no. 97, (1997).

126   Ludger Schuknecht, *Public Spending and the Role of the State,* (Cambridge University Press, 2021).

127   Sanjeev Gupta et al., "Efficiency-Adjusted Public Capital and Growth." *World Development* 57, 2014: 164-78.

128   Asian Development Bank, "Islamic Republic of Pakistan: Preparing Sustainable Energy Projects," ADB Technical Assistance Report, June 2019.

129   Henry Kissinger, *Leadership: Six Studies in World Strategy,* (Penguin Press, 2022).

130   Fabio Comelli et al., "Navigating Fiscal Challenges in Sub-Saharan Africa: Resilient Strategies and Credible Anchors in Turbulent Waters," IMF African Department, Departmental Working Paper, No. 2023/07, September 26, 2023.

131   United Nations Trade and Development, Africa 2023, https://unctad.org/publication/world-of-debt/regional-stories.

132   In fiscal year 2021, five countries (Argentina, Egypt, Ukraine, Pakistan and Ecuador) paid 95 percent of the total surcharges. The other eleven surcharge-paying members paid 4.8 percent. There were fifty-three members with general resource account credit, and only sixteen countries were paying surcharges.

133   Mark Weisbrot, Andres Arauz, and Joe Sammut, "IMF Surcharges: Counterproductive and Unfair," *Centre for Economic and Policy Research,* September 2021.

134   International Monetary Fund, "IMF Managing Director Kristalina Georgieva's Statement on the Review of Charges and the Surcharge Policy," October 11, 2024, https://www.imf.org/en/News/Articles/2024/10/11/pr-24368-imf-md-kristalina-georgieva-statement-on-the-review-of-charges-and-surcharge-policy#:~:text=The%20approved%20package%20will%20take,benefit%20from%20support%20when%20needed.

135   International Monetary Fund, "The Role of IMF Financial Support in Mitigating the Covid-19 Shock," IMF Independent Evaluation Office Background Paper, 23-01/01, 2023.

136   International Monetary Fund, "The IMF's Exceptional Access Policy: Evaluation Report," IMF Independent Evaluation Office, December 2024.

137   Matt Kennard and Claire Provost, "World Bank Reforms Will Remain Elusive Until This Is Understood," Aljazeera, October 6, 2023, https://www.aljazeera.com/opinions/2023/10/6/world-bank-reform-will-remain-elusive-until-this-is-understood.

138   Bertrand Badré and Peter Blair Henry, "Changing the Culture at the World Bank," Project Syndicate, July 12, 2023, https://www.project-syndicate.org/commentary/ew-world-bank-president-ajay-banga-must-lead-bold-reforms-by-bertrand-badre-and-peter-blair-henry-2023-07.

139   Badre, "Changing Culture at the World Bank."

140   Saeed Ahmed, "Economic Cost of Disruptions," *Dawn,* December 16, 2024, https://www.dawn.com/news/1879040.

Index